The Illusions
of 'Post-Feminism'

Feminist Perspectives on The Past and Present Advisory Editorial Board

The Illusions of 'Post-Feminism'

New Women, Old Myths

Vicki Coppock, Deena Haydon
and Ingrid Richter

Taylor & Francis
Publishers since 1798

UK   Taylor & Francis Ltd, 4 John St., London WC1N 2ET
USA   Taylor & Francis Inc., 1900 Frost Road, Suite 101, Bristol, PA 19007

© Copyright Vicki Coppock, Deena Haydon and Ingrid Richter 1995

First published 1995

A Catalogue Record for this book is available from the British Library

ISBN 0 7484 0237 3
ISBN 0 7484 0238 1 (pbk)

Library of Congress Cataloging-in-Publication Data are available on request

Typeset in 10/12pt Times
by Solidus (Bristol) Limited

Printed in Great Britain by Burgess Science Press, Basingstoke on paper which has a specified pH value on final paper manufacture of not less than 7.5 and is therefore 'acid free'.

Contents

Preface

The research for this book is derived in three discrete but closely associated projects which were conceptualised, conducted and realised simultaneously. Each of the projects reflects a clear commitment to feminist research. Feminist research has directly, and fundamentally, challenged the way in which academic knowledge takes a consistently patriarchal form. Far from being 'neutral', established academic research has reflected gender bias by concentrating on the social world of *men* and *male* definitions of 'knowledge' and 'truth' (P. Scraton, 1991). This has been validated by *male* researchers and theorists (Smith, 1973). Feminist researchers have set out to redress the balance by focusing research *on* women, *by* women and *for* women (Stanley and Wise, 1993, 1983; Stanley, 1990; Griffin, 1985; Oakley, 1981). There is a commitment within feminist research to develop and use methods, and methodologies, which accommodate and legitimise women's personal experiences and stress the validity and relevance of their memories (Maynard and Purvis, 1994; Harding, 1987; Haug, 1987). It is acknowledged, however, that there is no definitive feminist method of research (Scott, 1985) and that men can make important contributions (Harding, 1987).

The first project examined in depth the experiences of professional women in paid work. Focusing on their education, work and interpersonal relationships, it assessed the impact of equal opportunities policy, legislation and practices on the lives of those women considered to have most benefited from such reform. Using a similar focus, the second project took one male-dominated institution with long-standing organisational traditions and work practices and analysed the gendered paid-work experiences of women throughout the institution (professional, administrative, domestic). Central to this project was the position of women in the home, the relationship between home and work and the significance of child-rearing to this relationship. Finally, the third project considered the media as the primary institution responsible for the maintenance and reproduction of gendered ideology. It focused on the representation of Liverpool women in film, theatre and

television productions using detailed content analysis and in-depth interviews with creators, producers, conveyors or authors of the representations.
Given the focus of the impact of equal opportunities initiatives and the much-
claimed advent of liberated 'post-feminist' women in both the organisations
and representations studied, the projects converged to present a collective
analysis of the claims of 'post-feminism'.

The book is divided into two parts. Part One serves as: a comprehensive
overview of the key theoretical debates within contemporary feminism; an
appraisal of the theoretical tensions between Liberal feminism, past and
present, and more critical approaches; and a theoretical grounding for the
case material developed in Part Two. Chapter 1 explores the concept of 'post-
feminism' and reveals the many contradictions in its usage. It also considers
the significance of the backlash debate in contemporary feminism. Analysis
of Liberal feminist theoretical traditions demonstrates the basis upon which
contemporary policy and legal changes have been formulated. The historical
legacy of liberalism, with its focus on reform and equal opportunities, is
established as the basis of 'post-feminist' discourses. In Chapter 2 critical
feminist perspectives – which centralise power – are overviewed. The key
concepts and themes within feminist theory and politics are examined. These
are directly relevant to, and underpin, the case studies which form Part Two
of the book.

Part Two presents in-depth research and analysis of the lived experiences
of women in the late 1980s and early 1990s at personal, institutional and
ideological levels. It draws on theoretical debates, combined with women's
personal accounts, to expose and challenge the myths implicit in the concept
of 'post-feminism'. Thus, Chapters 3, 4, 5 and 6 illustrate the ineffective
nature of Liberal reformism within education, the workplace, the media and
interpersonal relationships. The conclusion to the book exposes the illusions
of 'post-feminism' in contemporary British society. Despite the assumption
that equal opportunities legislation would make a difference to women's
lives, this research reveals how power relations lie at the heart of the
continuing oppression of women.

Vicki Coppock, Deena Haydon, Ingrid Richter
July 1994

Acknowledgements

We would like to thank the following people for helping us to realise the possibility of writing this book:

Phil Scraton and Kathryn Chadwick inspired our original research projects through their teaching and commitment to critical research and social justice. It was Phil's suggestion to combine and develop these projects. He has been a sounding board for many of our ideas and helped us unravel our thoughts, particularly when we were working through the theoretical material. He has also spent a great deal of time reading and commenting on the work. Both he and Kathryn have been a constant source of support and encouragement. Their suggestions have always been helpful and constructive.

As founders of the Centre for Studies in Crime and Social Justice, Phil and Kathryn have facilitated the development of critical research and the formation of the Advanced Research Group. Our colleagues in this group have been supportive throughout, and their enthusiasm has spurred us on, making us feel that the project was worthwhile in our moments of doubt.

Jalna Hanmer gave early feedback and has maintained an interest in the project since its inception for which we are really grateful. Thanks also to Juliet Wells for her comments on the manuscript, and to Comfort Jegede at Taylor and Francis for her continuous encouragement.

The time and effort spent by Barbara Houghton, Karen Lee and Ingrid on typing and retyping (!!) the work has been invaluable and is greatly appreciated, as is Jacqui Wright's work on the original bibliography.

Our respective families, friends and colleagues have provided an endless amount of practical and emotional support, without which the project would never have been completed.

Finally, all the women, and the few men, who gave generously of their time and thoughts were open and honest. They have contributed much to knowledge by, for and about women's lives. Our personal and political commitment to feminist work has been reinforced by our close involvement with them. It is to these people that we would like to dedicate this book.

Part One

Part One

Chapter 1

Introduction: Locating 'Post-Feminism', Exploring the Myths

The Concept of 'Post-Feminism'

'Post-feminism' happened without warning. It seemed to arrive from nowhere. One minute there were feminisms, identified by their diverse political standpoints and their contrasting campaign strategies, the next ... it was all over. The change, mysteriously, had happened: interpersonal relationships and institutional arrangements had stepped beyond feminism. Features writers, arts broadcasters, television presenters, their subjects ranging from work to play, from fashion to music, grabbed the concept as one of common-sense: 'In this post-feminist period'; 'now we are in the era of post-feminism'; 'the post-feminist woman'; 'the post-feminist man'; 'post-feminist style'; and so on. Whatever was meant by 'post-feminism', whatever was being claimed for the concept, one thing was certain – it had arrived.

It was no coincidence that 'post-feminism' emerged as initiatives in government and industry were announced promoting the 1990s as the decade of gender equality. This was premissed on the assumed fact that two decades of social policy and legal reform, informed by equal opportunities initiatives, had provided the foundations for measurable social change and institutional advancement. Comment in the media, in politics and in industry became scattered with references to the 1990s as an 'enlightened' and 'post-feminist' period. Now, it was argued, all had been achieved, in fact over-achieved, to the point that many men were left confused, their identities shattered, and many women struggled with over-expectancy. The irony is, however, that the proclamation of 'post-feminism' has occurred at precisely the same moment as acclaimed feminist studies demonstrate that not only have women's real advancements been limited, but also that there has been a backlash against feminism of international significance. Could it be that 'post-feminism' as a concept is derived somewhere within the backlash? For despite its wide-ranging currency on dust-jackets, on late night talk-shows and in 'serious' features articles, 'post-feminism' has rarely been defined. It remains the product of assumption.

Perhaps it was inevitable that once sex discrimination/equal pay legislation was in place and 'equal opportunities' policies were adopted by government agencies and influential corporations, a new 'post-feminist' dawn would be celebrated. Such baseline objectives and their achievement were not the only dynamic in the 'post-feminist' lobby. An early reference was made by Susan Bolotin in an article entitled 'Voices from the post-feminist generation' (*New York Times Magazine*, 17 October 1982). Interviewing a range of 18 to 25-year-old women, she found that 'feminism' was, in their view, a discredited politics. Despite their experiences showing that women did not receive equal pay, and endured harassment and other forms of discrimination, they condemned feminism and denounced its potential for effectively challenging inequality. Beyond this, they considered that feminism undermined heterosexual relationships. The young women were keen to reinforce institutionalised notions of heterosexuality, marriage and the family and rejected feminists as unhappy, embittered, man-hating women. Bolotin's thesis was that it was the rejection of feminist theory and politics by this new generation of women that affirmed the arrival of 'post-feminism'.

More than a decade after Bolotin's article was published, the powerful, yet contradictory, messages concerning the 'new dawn' of equality persist. If the claim to a 'post-feminist' society is underpinned by any one principle it is that women have 'made it', or they have the opportunity to 'make it'. The proposition that women can decide on their priorities and 'go for them' – career, motherhood, world traveller, etc. – is at the heart of the image-makers' construction of the 'superwoman'. Features writers continually focus on women like Laura Noel, a successful health service manager working until she went into labour and back at her desk doing a 55 hour week four months after giving birth (W. Moore, 1992). The career-mother epitomises the new era in which it is assumed that social change and political reform provides her with the non-discriminatory, open access and fully protected context in which both roles can flourish. Qualifications, access, promotion and job security are assumed to have been accepted and established principles of equality, prevailing in all organisations and their management structures.

Alongside the imagery of the 'superwoman' is the imagery of a 'new man'. The product of the late 1980s, he has learned the lessons of feminism, accepts joint responsibility for domestic labour and child-rearing, and recognises the objective of gender equality (Leston, 1990). Consequently feminist theory and politics is viewed as *passé*, its relevance surpassed by real advances. Moreover it is often proposed that the pendulum has swung the other way with women being favoured (Quest, 1992). A highly contentious consequence of this line of reasoning is that women have only themselves to blame if equality is not achieved in their personal lives. Through their relationships with their mothers and their idealisation of men it has been argued that they collude with men in reproducing and maintaining traditional roles and expectations (Coward, 1992).

A further claim is that women are desperately unhappy with their newly established status and that feminism is the culprit. It is a theme which has preoccupied social policy commentators (Quest, 1994, 1992) and popular journalists. Women fiction writers such as Maeve Haran (*Having It All*, 1992) set out to demonstrate that women cannot have success in paid work, their relationships and as mothers. The upshot of this is that independence and career success is incompatible with true happiness found within the 'natural roles' of wife and mother. Supported by 'pop psychology' this position has contributed to what Shere Hite has termed the 'psychological battering' and 'emotional terrorism' endured by women (Briscoe, 1992 p. 30).

Geneva Overholser (*New York Times*, 19 September 1986, p. 30) identified two groups of women who now denounce the 'achievements' of feminist struggle. The first are those who tried to combine work and domesticity but feel that both love and their families have suffered 'because they set too high a priority on self-satisfaction'. The second group consists of women who decided to follow the career path 'only to discover that work wasn't so great after all'. While some women called for equality at work these women rejected it. Like many others, both sets of women realised that 'No women, even "superwomen", can indefinitely do all that they have been doing at home plus all that men have been doing at work. Since women *are* at work, something has to give'. But the suggested response is that *women* should give. Overholser points out that this argument is 'distinctly *pre-feminist*'! The limited changes of the last twenty years, and the persistent demand for further change, are disliked, feared and resented by many men and women who advocate a return to 'traditional' roles and attitudes. Women, and men, calling for a resurgence of 'old values' propose rigidly defined roles for females and males in which the public and private realms are distinctly segregated. Thus, men enter the workforce to earn the 'family' wage and provide for their wives and children while women cook, clean, support and service their husbands and children in the home. As Overholser concludes, 'to call that post-feminism is only to give sexism a subtler name' (ibid.).

Similarly, criticising feminism for oppressing *men* has become positively fashionable. Camille Paglia has established an international reputation in dismissing contemporary feminists as whiners and 'namby-pamby, wishy-washy little twits' (S. Moore, 1992). She is probably most notorious for her statement that 'if civilisation had been left in female hands we would still be living in grass huts' (Heller, 1992 p. 3).

In this she has much in common with men like Robert Bly (1990), David Thomas (in Bedell, 1992) and Neil Lyndon (1992) each of whom has bemoaned their emasculation at the hands of feminism. Bly attributes this emasculation to overexposure to strong and angry women, particularly mothers. Consequently these men have taken a 'female view' of men and their own masculinity. Basically, men have gone 'soft'. Bly's remedy is a male separatist movement – New Age masculinism – where men can rediscover 'the beast within' on wilderness weekend retreats. Thomas (1992) also wants to 'open the window on the pain a lot of men are suffering' because of 'totalitarian' feminism. Lyndon argues that the claims for patriarchal dominance cannot be sustained since it is *men* who are second-class citizens. As evidence for this he cites the denial of paternity rights for unmarried men, discrimination against men in divorce courts and 'unfair' maintenance arrangements. Moreover, he challenges the validity of feminist claims regarding the nature and extent of rape and domestic violence.

These discrepant, often bewildering, themes of 'post-feminist' discourse have provoked a fierce debate in contemporary feminist theory and politics. Far from accepting that feminism has 'failed' women (and men), or that feminism is *passé*, American journalist Susan Faludi (1992, p. 14) contends that feminism has not gone far enough. In this Faludi claims that there has been an 'undeclared war against women' – a 'backlash'.

Central to the 'backlash' argument is the assertion that whenever feminism has appeared to be gaining ground a whole series of repressive political, social, economic and ideological forces are mobilised in direct response. Marilyn French's *The War Against Women* (1992, p. 11) charts the global history of patriarchal oppression and how 'in reaction to women's movements across the world' it is now 'taking on a new ferocity'. It is suggested that as well as the tangible evidence of a backlash, a more subliminal, multi-layered system of oppression is operating. This tightens once women are seen to be making gains and stepping out of place. Historically, then, the pursuit of equality by women has been responded to by a backlash against it.

Feminism, along with other liberationist movements, has been rocked by the force of the political shift to the right since the 1980s. Moreover, it could be argued that the women's movement has been ill-prepared to meet this challenge, apparently beset by internal dissent and disunity. Younger generations of women have related their feelings of alienation from feminism. Some of the young women in Bolotin's study were sympathetic to feminism, but disillusioned. They considered that their youth denied them the experience of direct involvement in the active feminist struggles characteristic of their 'older' sisters of the 'second wave'. 'Third wave' feminists have inherited institutions which profess to have adopted equal opportunities policies but which intrinsically have not changed. In real terms these women do not directly experience the successes that have been expected from the struggles and consequent reforms of the 1960s and 1970s. Many of these young women feel, and have been, castigated by older feminists for not doing enough to challenge the structures which perpetuate and reinforce inequality. At the same time they are pressurised by popular discourses which tell them the world is their oyster. The implication is that if they do not know what they want, or cannot achieve it, individual lack of purpose or ability must be the cause of failure.

Other disillusioned young women have been drawn towards the 'newer' political movements of the 1980s (Seager, 1993). New Age and environmentalist movements have occupied the space created by the lack of viable socialist, left politics. While the appeal of such alternatives lies in a seemingly more holistic and humanistic politics, existing patriarchal structures and relations are rarely challenged.

Mary Smeeth (1990, p. 31) suggests that 'second wave' feminism was 'based on the false premise that differences between women were less important than what united them: men as the common enemy'. This led to the exclusion of many women whose oppression was denied by others not oppressed in the same way. The consequence was a split in the women's movement as differences between women, involving class, 'race', mobility and sexuality, were recognised and gained importance. The impact of post-modernism and post-structuralism on feminist theory has accentuated this emphasis on 'difference' (MacCannell, 1991; Hekman, 1990). The anti-essentialist works of writers such as Lacan, Althusser, Derrida and Foucault have formed the basis of contemporary 'French' and 'post-modern' feminisms (Kristeva, 1981; Irigaray, 1981; Cixous, 1981). In these analyses notions of identity and 'the subject' have been disputed. Gender and sexual difference have, in some sense, become arbitrary. Deconstruction of the category 'woman' has had a resonance with feminist analyses which challenge the social construction of 'womanhood'. However, taken to its logical conclusion the post-structuralist position renders all feminisms meaningless because it is said to be impossible to make any generalisations about, or political claims on behalf of, a group called 'women' (Modleski, 1992; Walby, 1992).

The construction of 'post-feminism' has led to, and emphasised, differences between women. It has also directed the focus away from the real advances, such as increased appreciation of diversity and experience, and shared frustration or disillusionment leading to collective resistance. Instead women are blamed, or blame themselves and one another, for their feelings of dissatisfaction and the underlying causes remain ignored or refuted. The majority of women seek to make sense of their lives and accommodate the often conflicting desires of autonomy and alliance. If women feel they are to be judged, or placed on a hierarchy of oppression by other women, they will cease to express their views or discuss the significant and inherent contradictions in their lives.

'Post-feminist' ideology, fuelled by the political arguments of the New Right, has been given credence through the development of artificial divisions and categories of feminism. Implicitly this has placed each cohesive and identifiable strand of feminist thought in a position of competition and conflict with others in a bid to assert the primacy of a specific issue or standpoint. Ultimately, this leaves feminist positions falsely strait-jacketed and divided within the analysis. It has also contributed to the anti-feminist backlash in which feminists collectively are blamed for the dilemmas facing contemporary women. Looking beyond the rhetoric of conflict surrounding feminism, it is clear that existing divisions are rooted primarily in political action. This has both resulted from and encouraged differences in theoretical emphasis.

Central to what follows is an acknowledgement that all feminist contributions to the theoretical and political debates have validity. While the emergence of 'post-feminism' has brought into question the issues and debates fundamental to feminist analyses and critiques, the important claim to be answered is that women's subordination and oppression has been resolved through equal opportunities initiatives and sex discrimination legislation. By focusing on the lives and experiences of over fifty women, and considering in depth their perceptions of education, work, the media and interpersonal relationships, this claim can be contested. For if the claims of 'post-feminism' are to be substantiated it has to be in the lives of contemporary women and their daily personal, ideological and institutional experiences and encounters.

The Historical Context: The Legacy of Liberalism

The three projects discussed above reflect a commitment to the theoretical and analytical priorities of contemporary feminism. They reject the long-established construction of 'value-freedom' as an attainable objective, arguing that all theory and methodology is grounded within politics and motive. What this work also rejects is the idea that the deficiencies of established academic work can be corrected by simply 'adding on' research by women about women. Alongside many other feminist studies, it sets out to question the foundations of established knowledge as being in part the product of patriarchal priorities and demands. How history has been conceptualised and written forms a crucial part of such academic knowledge and discourses. It is essential here to trace the historical legacy of feminist theory, emphasising the liberal tradition of the 'first wave' and the influence of reformism as contemporary feminism advanced its agenda.

Historically, the aims of feminist analysis, writing and action have responded to those issues central to the maintenance and reproduction of women's oppression. While this work has been wide-ranging, concerning all aspects of women's lives and experiences, the dominant politics within feminism has emerged from the liberal-democratic tradition with an emphasis on marginal reform rather than fundamental change. The primary objective is 'equality of opportunity', in which personal advancement is prioritised over fundamental changes in the structural organisation of society. This classical liberal democratic position suggests that state intervention focuses on achieving a balance between individual freedom and community welfare; that it serves to mediate between competing interests. Liberal feminism, then, is committed to achieving greater gender equality through legislative and policy reform. Its concern is to construct and pursue 'implementary' strategies for change; achieving equality for women through adjustment within the political processes and social policies of liberal democracy.

In the late eighteenth century Mary Wollstonecraft (1792) argued that enforced self-indulgence and restricted physical activity damaged the health of middle-class women, while dependency, over-protection and isolation curtailed their personal liberty and limited their powers of reasoning. She considered that women had an equal right to self-determination and that education would enhance their rational and moral capacities, giving ascendency to 'reason' and 'rationality' over 'emotion'. Both Harriet Taylor Mill (1851) and John Stuart Mill (1869) pursued the concern of equality. They believed that 'gender justice' could be achieved through equality of opportunity in education, economics and civil liberties. Sexual equality would then provide the basis for a more complete form of personal happiness. J. S. Mill argued that through 'male' education and work opportunities women could achieve liberation from their dependent and secondary status, although marriage and motherhood would remain their primary concern.

For Mill, if women were to contribute to the advancement of society and gain independent citizenship, their right to vote should be recognised. By contrast, Taylor Mill wanted women to be represented at all levels of education, industry, municipal politics and central government. Such massive change would encourage women to develop identities beyond marriage and motherhood. This could only be secured through economic independence and a challenge to the division of labour within the middle-class family in which men were the sole earners and dispensers of family income.

The struggle for the vote remained the central issue in the fight for personal liberty, public recognition and equal rights (Levine, 1987; Banks, 1986; Vicinus, 1985; Hollis, 1979; Strachey, 1928; Reid, 1843). However, women differed in their campaign strategies. Some were committed solely to constitutional means for winning the vote (the suffragists of the National Union of Women's Suffrage Societies). Others, the so-called 'militant suffragettes' of the Women's Social and Political Union, founded by Mrs Pankhurst in 1903, advocated any means, lawful or otherwise, to win the vote (Atkinson and Hornsby, 1993; Garner, 1984; Raeburn, 1976). The common objective was full citizenship, with women and men working together to improve standards for everyone through social democracy.

The first decade of the twentieth century was marked by political turmoil in Britain and throughout Europe. Domestic political struggles around the right to work, the politics of trades unionism, the growth of socialism and women's suffrage were matched by a destabilised Europe and persistent uprisings in the colonies (Hobsbawm, 1969). The Great War temporarily stalled the campaigns around the vote as women became active either in pacifist movements or in the 'war effort' to protect the 'nation' (Condell and Liddiard, 1987).

With the introduction of the 1918 Representation of the People Act approximately eight-and-a-half million women over the age of 30 gained the vote and the right to stand for Parliament (Rosen, 1974). However, this did not secure equality and, in 1928, after continued campaigns, all women over the age of 21 gained the vote on equal terms with men. While many women recognised the importance of this achievement they were not complacent about the effects it would have. The *Manifesto to the Women Voters of Great Britain* (National Union of Equal Citizenship, 1929) highlighted the causes of inequality and called upon women to use their 'natural' qualities in 'comradeship' with men for 'the benefit of the community' (Taylor, 1983).

Thus the libertarian ideal was established and women were encouraged to fight for general reforms for the benefit of all people. The reforms demanded by middle-class women were radical given the historical context of the time. They were expected to be 'the angel in the house' (Gorham, 1982). Public campaigning and overt challenges to the social and political order were identified as a threat to the Victorian way of life. The consequences of provoking such confrontation involved great personal costs – financially, emotionally and physically. The ultimate price for many women was death (Leneman and Whatley, 1993; Liddington, 1984; Morrell, 1981). While middle-class women were campaigning for the vote, many working-class women, often influenced by the Owenite movement during the 1830s, formed unions and cooperative societies to further women's economic or political interests (Llewelyn-Davies, 1931; Liddington and Norris, 1979). Feminist historians have emphasised the historical tradition of a women's movement concerned with the sexual dynamics of history (Harris, 1993; Barret-Ducrocq, 1991; London Feminist History Group, 1983); women's experiences in the home and family (Dyhouse, 1989; Lewis, 1986); the construction of women's sexuality (Kingsley Kent, 1990; Mendus and Randall, 1989; Nead, 1988; Jeffreys, 1985). Such texts are a constant reminder that, 'there has always been a women's movement this century' (Spender, 1983) and that women have struggled consistently to voice their views, pursue active campaigns and resist oppression.

Despite this, the 'first wave' was dominated by an 'equal rights' feminism derived from the politics of liberalism. The expectation was that once enfranchised all people would possess, via representative politics, the means to work towards personal liberation. Bonnie Anderson and Judith Zinsser (1988) chart the development of equal rights feminism and the disillusionment that occurred when women's use of the vote made little difference to the lives of most women. Once the vote was won some equal rights feminists fought for new causes, while others, especially politically active women, became involved in socialism. Anderson and Zinsser argue that both Liberal and Socialist feminist groups turned to welfare issues. They developed ideas and campaigns for reform relating specifically to women during the inter-war years (Banks, 1993; Alberti, 1989). These included maternity protection in the form of benefits, infant and child allowances, medicine (including contraception and abortion), housing, education and other social issues. Many women involved in these struggles distanced themselves from feminism. The independent, politically active women who continued to challenge patriarchy and capitalism were caricatured as man-hating, hysterical, anarchic aberrations.

Important anti-fascist work by women extended after the Great War and the subsequent winning of the vote. On the eve of the Second World War Virginia Woolf (1938) wrote about the traditional masculine and warlike values glorified by fascism. She reflected the early radical commentaries in proclaiming that women's subjection to male violence in the 'private' world of the family was inseparably linked to the public world of emergent fascism in Europe and the USA. For Woolf, war was rooted in the socialised male character and its driving force of dominance (Liddington, 1989).

The consequences of the arrival of the Second World War were massive for the entire population and women's secondary status was brought into sharp relief. The 'war effort' in Britain and in the USA demonstrated that women could do 'men's' jobs equally well. Yet the 'woman behind the man behind the gun' soon became the 'woman behind the man behind the job' (Braybon and Summerfield, 1987).

For the sake of rebuilding the war-stricken nation, women's primary role was defined in British social policy as that of homemaker and childrearer. The Beveridge Report (1942) clearly indicated how the ideal of the welfare state relied on the reassertion of traditional sex roles. Whereas Wollstonecraft and other early pioneers of equal opportunities had argued that social inequalities could be reversed through education, post-war reformers saw equal educational opportunity solely in terms of class. Not only should gender differences be maintained, it was the role of education, particularly secondary education, to build on those differences to secure the nation's future (The Crowther Report, 1959; The Newsom Report, 1963). The impact of government policies, education reports, medical research and media pressure on women was clear. It was underpinned by influential academic writing on the negative effects of maternal deprivation (Bowlby, 1953). Feminist voices were silenced by a rising tide of patriotism, economic expansionism and new consumerism. If 'women's issues' were addressed it was only in terms of making their lives easier in the home so that chores could be completed more quickly, freeing surplus time for part-time paid work on early morning or twilight shifts. Not only did the post-war reconstruction of capitalism depend on domestic labour, it also came to utilise part-time, poorly-paid and virtually unprotected women's labour (Oldfield, 1994; Pugh, 1992).

As the giant corporations consolidated their pre-war expansion to become truly multinational, and the US industrial/military complex gained a presence on most continents, the opportunities for women outside the home remained restricted mainly to servicing work. Women's paid work was little more than the public extension of their private 'duties'. It was in this climate that Betty Friedan wrote *The Feminine Mystique* (1963) defining, analysing and challenging the effects of the limitations placed on women by patriarchal ideologies, gender stereotyping and shared assumptions about 'femininity'.

Friedan argued that through the processes of socialisation and schooling, young women were directed towards finding a man, marriage and child-rearing; their femininity, adjustment and early maturity as wives and mothers applauded by experts. With child development theories underlining the significance of the caring ever-present mother on the early years of childhood, the media promulgated the 'dream image' of the suburban housewife: freed from drudgery by labour-saving devices, from the dangers of childbirth or illness by science, and 'respected as a full and equal partner to man in his world' (Friedan, 1963 p. 16). Yet Friedan's detailed description and accounts revealed the gulf between the image of women reinforced and reproduced by social institutions and the reality of their lives. Women's dissatisfaction – defined by Friedan as 'the problem that has no name' – was explained away as the product of personal inadequacies, the over-education of women or even the result of enfranchisement. However, Friedan pointed out that it was not possible to attribute the problem to loss of femininity, since women who suffered had geared their lives to the pursuit of feminine fulfilment. Moreover, housewives from all educational backgrounds expressed common feelings of desperation.

Friedan's response to the 'feminine mystique' was to encourage women to combine motherhood, domesticity and a career. Not unlike the writings of the Mills a century earlier, Friedan maintained that combining a career and family would enable women to achieve true fulfilment and equality. Returning to the priorities of the 'first wave', Friedan saw education as holding the key for change. The education of girls towards achievable goals in settings which could boost confidence and develop personal resources would replace their preoccupation with the culture of femininity. She concluded that women would no longer require 'the regard of boys or men to feel alive' (Friedan, 1963 p. 331). Friedan's book soon became the 'classic text' of its time and its ideas have been identified as central to the development of the contemporary women's movement. With the benefit of hindsight and the emergence of more radical perspectives, however, it has been criticised, often harshly (Uszkurat, 1990; Bowlby, 1987). Shared domestic labour and responsibilities were not on Friedan's agenda and, like many of her nineteenth-century counterparts, her focus was on white, middle-class, heterosexual, educated, suburban women. However, this does not make her work irrelevant. In fact Friedan's work moved against the tide of post-war conservatism in recognising and articulating women's shared experience of a patriarchal oppression serviced by the consumerism of advanced capitalism.

The Feminine Mystique was one of several important contributions which collectively represented women's opposition to the post-war re-affirmation of women's roles and duties within the home and workplace. These public statements make it clear that women's primary responsibilities as wife, mother and carer were not being accepted passively and without resistance. The 'second wave' of Liberal feminism established public debate over equality of opportunity and equality of treatment. Renewed Liberal feminist politics demanded reforms in social policy, welfare, education and health-care, guaranteed by legislation. High on the agenda were demands for equal pay and an end to sex discrimination. In Britain the introduction of a limited right to abortion (Abortion Act, 1967) together with earlier reform of the divorce laws gave the appearance of major gains for women. As with the Equal Pay Act (1970) and Sex Discrimination Act (1975) which followed, however, they were advances with set boundaries and clear limitations. Such limitations were not simply the product of badly drafted or ill-conceived laws. Rather, they were inherent in a politics of reformism in which fundamental changes involving institutionalised power relations could not be achieved. The move towards equality of opportunity was a political commitment to access, to participation, to 'fair' treatment and to meritocratic progress. The opportunity structure of organisations and the limitations traditionally placed on women's participation and progress were targeted. Such implementary approaches suggested that if more women could gain access, become participants and 'climb the ladder of success', if equality with men could be achieved in pay and working conditions, then gender divisions within civil society could be eroded and, eventually, dismantled. However, such reforms assumed that patriarchy was no more than a gender imbalance within an otherwise fair and just democratic system. The Liberal feminists' programme of reform, while important in highlighting and moving against *social* inequalities, did not present a programme which could challenge the *structural* inequalities endemic within the fundamental power relations and knowledge base of patriarchy.

Chapter 2

Theorising Power in Women's Oppression

Introduction

Alongside the emergence of 'equality struggles' during the 1960s was a resurgence of radical politics which included a range of international issues as well as domestic concerns (e.g. the war in Vietnam; apartheid laws in South Africa; international arms trading) (see: Crawford, Rouse and Woods, 1993). Within this context, struggles around gender, sexuality and 'race' developed a radical edge, rejecting the limitations seen as inherent within reformism. Women involved in those political organisations which opposed established interests argued that such organisations only paid lip-service to equality, since women's contributions were confined to peripheral or servicing roles in deference to exclusive male leaderships (Coote and Campbell, 1987; Sargent, 1981; Evans, 1980). At the same time women began to question the terms on which the so-called era of sexual liberation had been established (Greer, 1970). This range of struggles, often disparate, represented a convergence of the 'personal and political' experienced by women as they endured subordination and oppression *as women*. A sharper, more direct, politics grew impatient with claims for advancement based solely on *access*: to education, to paid employment, to contraception and to abortion. Women's freedom, it was argued, was illusory.

In 1970 the first national Women's Liberation Conference – the 'Ruskin Conference' – was held at Ruskin College, Oxford. It provided a clear demonstration of the strength of radical politics among feminists. Proclaiming sexual contradictions, over class, as being the primary force in the organisation of society, the conference demanded substantive research into women's history and alternatives to the nuclear family and conventional childrearing practices. It established campaigns for free contraception, a full right to abortion and an end, through legislation, to all forms of sex discrimination (Coote and Campbell, 1987). The strength of the movement was reflected in the publication of a number of influential texts (Rowbotham, 1973; Mitchell, 1971; Greer, 1970; Millett, 1970; Morgan, 1970). As the debates were extended so the process of theorising and the form of political activism progressed. In 1975 three demands were added: financial and legal independence; an end to all discrimination against lesbians; a woman's right to define her own sexuality. By 1978 the political agenda included: freedom from intimidation by threat or use of violence or sexual coercion, regardless of marital status; an end to all laws, assumptions and institutions which perpetuate male dominance and men's aggression towards women. These events had a major impact on the direction of feminist theoretical debates and analysis. As women's groups were formed throughout Britain they focused on specific campaigns and challenges through direct action. 'Socialist' feminists also questioned traditional forms of political activity, particularly left-wing organisations which failed to recognise gender as a significant issue in the class struggle (Rowbotham, *et al.*, 1979).

Increasingly it became clear that women's struggles against subordination and oppression could not be reduced to a shopping list of single, self-contained issues. As feminist analyses were incorporated by a wider constituency of women (through publications, journals, magazines, television and radio, courses, groups and campaigns) it became obvious that women's experiences were not universal. Women from different class and cultural backgrounds, with contrasting sexualities, identified quite distinctive theoretical and political priorities. There was shared acceptance that women's experiences had been hidden from public view and denied any substantive reality and that 'history' had been written and legitimised from a masculinist perspective. But, the precise location and consequences of male power were fiercely debated. Such was the strength and diversity of the ensuing political debate it was inevitable that contrasting standpoints should emerge. Central here was 'equality of the sexes versus difference or otherness' with broader political strategy contextualised as 'reform versus revolution' (Haug, 1989, p. 13). The emphasis shifted away from the reformist priorities of Liberal feminist politics and redirected attention towards power centres and power relations. The need to identify the sites of oppression in women's lives became crucial to the development of feminist theoretical debates.

Attempting an understanding of how, why and where women experience oppression has revealed a complex web of interrelated strands. These pervade all areas of women's lives and are, therefore, unquestionably difficult to unravel. Contemporary feminist debates stress that care must be taken not to assume that all women's experiences of subordination and oppression are common. The impact and effect of religion, culture, class, 'race', disability, age, physicality, sexuality and geographical location (national and international) need to be recognised as significant factors in the way women experience oppression. As feminist theoretical debates have evolved, they have made use of and developed existing key concepts such as: discourse, ideology, patriarchy, gender, sexuality, physicality, class and 'race'.

Key Concepts

During the 1970s much of the academic debate around **ideology** was informed by the writings of Louis Althusser. In dealing with the significance of ideas and their relationship to the structural contradictions of advanced political economies he argued that 'ideology represents the imaginary relationship of individuals to their real conditions of existence' (Althusser, cited in McQuail, 1987 p. 66). While at first sight such a statement smacks of 'the intellectual' patronising the 'common people', Althusser's point was that dominance and oppression could be achieved through the organisation and transmission of ideas more effectively than through direct coercion. This led to the observation by Stuart Hall (1982) that the key to the success of social democracies was the 'management of conflict' (political, economic, religious, social) through the 'manufacture of consent'. It is clear that individuals live their lives through an inheritance and development of common-sense assumptions, often based on prejudices, images and reputation, but it is when those ideas and beliefs cohere and become institutionalised that they become ideologies. They outlive individuals, are passed on through a range of social institutions (religion, education, family, media, the legal system) and become part of the fabric of the state, interwoven into its institutions (Eagleton, 1991; Donald and Hall, 1986; McLellan, 1986).

Closely related to the debate around ideology, much of which was concerned with whether a single 'dominant' ideology existed, has been the rediscovery of Antonio Gramsci's conceptualisation of **hegemony**. At the core of Gramsci's (1971) argument is the proposition that over time social democracies become ordered and political stability becomes underwritten by social forces rather than by physical force. These social forces represent the embodiment of a range of ideologies, each dominant in its own sphere, which collectively assume and reproduce a nation's identity. As with ideology, hegemony is rooted in the social and cultural institutions of a society and individuals are politically socialised accordingly. Class conflict, gender divisions, 'racial' supremacy together with a range of other hierarchical relations become central to the organisation of the social order and are reinforced and reproduced through the routines, decisions and interventions of social and political institutions. The 'common-sense' assumptions of the family and the community become the collective 'common-sense' of the 'nation'. As part of 'national identity', ways of thinking about the world become naturalised (Showstack Sassoon, 1982).

A further dimension to the debate around ideology and hegemony has been the impact of **discourse analysis**, based on the work of Michel Foucault. His concern was to identify and analyse how ideas/ideologies function within the established relations of power and domination and, accordingly, become institutionalised. The importance of discourse analysis lies in the relationship between power and knowledge. Foucault (1977) argues against a simple reduction of knowledge to power proposing that the relationship is dialectical. Power relations take a range of diverse forms, both structural and interpersonal, and 'knowledge' is implicated in the maintenance of power relations as well as influencing the structures of power. Within this context, discourses become a vocabulary, language, text and expression of relations of power. Official discourses, reflecting hegemonic relations, become essential to state intervention in policy and also to professional agencies in their practice (P. Scraton, 1987, 1985; Macdonell, 1986).

Feminists have applied discourse analysis in the development of a critical theoretical model which explains the social construction of female identity. They suggest that a variety of discourses – medical, legal, political and religious – each produces forms of knowledge about women and women's sexuality. These are then reproduced in cultural forms and define 'acceptable' and 'desirable' roles and relationships for women in society. Thus, ideologies (as 'clusters' of ideas, beliefs, assumptions) reflect and reinforce the discourses constructed by dominant individuals or institutions. Within most ideologies women's experiences and meanings have been defined by men, and women's knowledge and experiences have been subordinated to those of men (Ramazanoglu, 1993; McNay, 1992).

The various debates around the concept of **patriarchy**, and its impact on *all* women's lives, are particularly significant to this book. Patriarchy defines the personal, physical and institutional power that men exert over women. Through the process of hegemony the dominance of men over women is achieved and maintained. This takes the form of social arrangements, cultural traditions and political management. Through these, personal relations are contextualised and accepted as 'normal' and 'right'. Thus, patriarchy maintains and sustains structures of male dominance through systems of ideas, beliefs and shared assumptions about gender, sexuality and reproduction, material subordination and coercion.

'Patriarchy' is a complex term since it refers to women's collective experiences of subjugation at social, institutional, political, economic and ideological levels. Although the degree of subjugation within and between any of these relations may differ, *all* women throughout the world experience the institutionalised and interpersonal dominance of men. Patriarchy, albeit diverse, is universal. While recognising cultural, social and political diversity between patriarchies, it is important to stress that women experience oppression *as* women, mediated by other structural factors, both in the public and private realms of their lives. Professional ideologies and discourses, whether in education establishments, the workplace, the media, the church, the medical or legal professions, or the welfare state, are underpinned by the language and practice of patriarchy. These discourses are formed within a framework of social relations which are distinctly genderised.

Differences between the sexes are seen to be the source of **gender** differences. Within these gender differences the **sexuality** of a female or male (i.e. appearance, presentation and behaviour) is clearly defined. Medical, moral, legal and social discourses produce and reinforce the idea that *biology* is the determinant of behaviour (Moir and Jessel, 1991). In this, sexuality is perceived to be the product of inbuilt 'sex drive' or 'sexual instinct'. The strong, vagrant and uncontrollable instinct of the man is put against the maternal, receptive and passive instinct of the woman. It is her biological destiny to quell and quieten the aggression and vagrancy of the male inheritance (Scruton, 1986; Storr, 1978). Alternative views suggest that sexuality is a *social construction* in which ideas about biological sex, gender and female/male roles are intertwined (Haug, 1992; Lorber and Farrell, 1991; Notman and Nadelson, 1991). An emphasis on anatomical differences between women and men produces a set of stereotypes in which 'femininity' and 'masculinity' are formulated and polarised. Accordingly, 'masculinity' becomes associated and defined in terms of aggression, dominance and power while 'femininity' is defined in terms of passivity, submission and self-sacrifice. Boys and men are socialised into the stereotype of competitive, adventurous, self-confident, ambitious males whereas girls and women are socialised into dependent, passive, subjective, non competitive, under-confident females (Coveney *et al.*, 1984; MacKinnon, 1982). Gender divisions are sustained through the process of genderisation and within this there is a hierarchy of sexuality. Patriarchy relies on the formation of what Bob Connell (1987) calls 'hegemonic masculinity' and 'emphasised feminin-ity' within the development of distinctive heterosexual identities. In this, women are subordinated to men and accommodate their needs and desires. Hegemonic masculinity also incorporates 'subordinate masculinities', whereby younger men are subordinated to their seniors and homosexual men are subordinated to heterosexual men.

The social relations between women and men are defined within the context of **compulsory heterosexuality**. In this, men and women are expected to live together as husband and wife with clearly defined roles

(Mort, 1987). A woman is not expected to discover or express her sexuality since this is seen to be a quality held in trust by her father to be 'given away' to her husband (Clark and Lewis, 1977). She is thus defined in relation to a male 'provider' and 'protector': initially her father, then her husband. Her destiny is not only to produce children but also to care for them, their father and the 'family' home.

A woman's **physicality** connects the process of biological reproduction to the politics of reproduction (S. Scraton, 1992). Women are subordinated through childbirth and an emphasis on the continued 'need' of a child for its mother. The significance of the politics and ideology of biological reproduction extends to patriarchal control over the organisation and administration of reproductive technologies (Pfeffer, 1993). Material subordination is directly related to physicality. Global evidence clearly shows that women are materially dependent on men (Federici *et al.*, 1993; Bryson, 1992; Delphy and Leonard, 1992; Mitter 1986) and that this subjugation is guaranteed by a combination of physical fear, systematic lack of opportunity and political marginalisation. Women's dependency is maintained by state institutions which perpetuate the images and reality of a male as provider and master in 'his' home. Welfare provision, workplace organisation, levels of pay and the legal system militate against the economic independence of women.

Neo-Marxist analyses of **class** have been developed within feminist scholarship to argue the material oppression of women through the exploitative labour processes inherent within advanced capitalist production. Links have been made between production (and reproduction) in the home and production in the workforce. Economic hierarchies also prevail in non-capitalist societies, for example, those caste and kinship systems which determine ownership and control of production. The concept of patriarchy has been harnessed to explain who controls production, whether inside or outside the family. Debates have been refined to show the interrelationship between gender and class relations, previously seen as autonomous. Feminist analyses now show how patriarchy resides in both systems (Ferguson, 1989; Jaggar, 1983; Sargent, 1981; Young, 1981; Hartmann, 1979).

Women are also subjected to personal, physical dominance by men who assert their masculinity with the threat or actual use of physical strength, and often **violence**. This subordination is reflected in the violence inflicted on women through sexual harassment, rape and portrayal in pornography and other media. The acceptable use of force or violence against women is extended beyond the private sphere of interpersonal relationships to include state, religious and cultural institutions.

A subject of fierce debate within contemporary feminism has been the invisibility of '**race**' within analyses of oppression. Both feminist theory and politics have been severely criticised, not only for their middle-class origins but also for their ethnocentrism (Frankenberg, 1993; Ware, 1992). While women from *all* cultures and societies have been engaged in struggles against the global pre-eminence of patriarchy, in its various forms, the analyses and political movements of 'second wave', 'western' feminism have reflected cultural imperialism. British women of Irish, Mediterranean, Asian, African and African-Caribbean descent not only experience directly the racism inherent in British culture but also have distinctive cultural backgrounds and different histories. Black and non-European women not resident in Britain or in any neo-colonialist society, are denied their historical and cultural experiences, including anti-imperialist struggles against the colonisers and their legacies. The tendency has been for 'white women' to become the new 'experts', speaking and writing for black women as if they are incapable of articulating and analysing their own experiences (hooks, 1984; Amos and Parmar, 1984). Key concepts and dominant ideas used by 'established' feminist theory and politics to define women's oppression – e.g. the family, patriarchy and reproduction – are clearly deficient in interpreting or understanding the experiences and lives of black women (Amos and Parmar, 1984; Carby, 1982; Joseph, 1981).

Black women who have organised and written about their histories and contemporary experiences have exposed the racism they endure: in the workplace (Bryan, Dadzie and Scafe, 1985); at the hands of state authorities (Mama, 1989; Gordon, 1981); and in their neighbourhoods (Chigwada, 1991; Dunhill, 1989). This has informed the move towards the consolidation of a 'black women's standpoint' (Hill Collins, 1991 p. 21; and see: Davis, 1984, 1981). Some consider that solidarity based on a broad feminist movement remains a worthwhile and achievable goal, provided it is also grounded in anti-racist theory and politics (Ramazanoglu, 1989).

As with 'race', 'mainstream' feminists have made assumptions concerning physical and mental capacities and age. The experiences of women with disabilities, older women and girls have been marginalised within debates and publications, and casual references to physicality and 'able-ness' often go unchallenged (Morris, 1991; Lonsdale, 1990).

While these key concepts are significant in themselves, they remain interrelated and without clearly identifiable boundaries. It is precisely the complexity of the interrelationships between the key concepts which has led feminist writers to develop detailed and diverse analyses of the structures and institutions which subordinate and oppress women. If 'key concepts' have provided the currency of sharp analytical debate within contemporary feminism, the subsequent political debate reflects a range of key themes.

Key Themes

A double standard of morality operates to divide women into historically reproduced categories of 'virgin' or 'whore'. These underpin discourses about femininity which focus on the importance of appearance and the development of appropriate behaviour and roles for women. A woman's sexuality is regulated and controlled in a number of ways: from lack of access to 'space' and economic constraints, to the threat of violence and restrictions imposed due to domestic and child care responsibilities (S. Scraton, 1987; Smart and Smart, 1978). Although differences in age, class, race and geographical location affect the extent of individual women's experiences of such restrictions, they have an impact on the lives of all women (Griffin, 1981). The politics of appearance forms one context of female sexuality, another being sexual politics. Both are constrained and restricted by patriarchal ideologies concerning women and femininity.

The **images of women** portrayed by societal institutions reinforce discourses based on notions of femininity (Bonner, *et al.*, 1992; Screen, 1992). Heather Smith (1989 p. 37) points out that 'images make a complex statement about identity. Such statements are culturally and historically specific and, while their messages are not fixed or static, in the twentieth century they are the products of capitalism, imperialism and patriarchy'. Feminist analyses have shown how successive generations of white, middle-class men have presented their views as the *only* view: in art, literature, newspapers, magazines, on television, films, radio (Coote and Campbell, 1987). Much of the feminist analysis of representations of women has focused on the media since the images presented reflect societal views about women and consumerism. Women are persistently excluded from the 'serious' coverage of political, economic or technological issues but appear with disproportionate frequency in advertising where they are portrayed as objects of desire, 'continually reduced to bland stereotypes' (Flanagan, 1985 p. 239). In this, women are defined and differentiated with reference to men, as in Simone de Beauvoir's (1949) concept of 'other'.

When they are not objects of male desire women are represented in passive, nurturing roles which focus on domesticity, motherhood and servicing others. John Berger (1972) proposes that the essential way of seeing women is based on the assumption that the spectator is male. Debate about images of women has revolved around the meanings attached to them and how these relate to other discourses. Although an image may not be directly sexist, sexism is produced because it draws on elements from other images and uses notions, concepts and myths already culturally available. It reflects these and reforms them to produce new meanings (Cowie, 1977). All institutions in society produce sexist images of women which, taken together, reinforce the discourse of femininity.

As debate over the work of Andrea Dworkin (1987) and Catherine MacKinnon (1994) has demonstrated, there is a fine line between images of women that are classified as pornographic and those which are not. To many women the pin-ups in newspapers are as degrading and oppressive as hard porn photographs. Feminists agree that pornography is undesirable and exploitative but do not agree over its regulation. The 'pro-censorship' lobby argues that pornography condones and reinforces oppressive male behaviour and violence against women (MacKinnon, 1994, 1987; Itzin, 1993; Every-woman, 1988; Dworkin, 1981). Further to this is the argument that the 'ruling group', with power and money, should not be allowed to display 'sadistic', 'dehumanising' and 'degrading' views of a 'less powerful section of society' (Rhodes and McNeill, cited in Coote and Campbell, 1987 p. 219). In contrast, those against censorship argue that legislation would extend the power of the patriarchal state. Thus the already precarious freedom of gays and lesbians would be threatened and women would be prevented from exploring and defining their own sexuality (Segal and McIntosh, 1992). They also feel that such laws would prove to be unenforceable. Banning pornography from the public arena does not challenge the attitudes or transform the power structures which find expression in pornography (Lacombe, 1988). Susan Kappeler (1986) argues that the feminist critique of pornography needs to be reclaimed from the issue of censorship. For her the political role of pornography is central, as are forms of representation of women which have 'emerged and thrived in a patriarchal culture in which man has social, political and economic supremacy' (cited in Coote and Campbell, 1987 p. 220). This has enabled men to suppress the ideas and opinions of others through 'control of access to the market and to the "ideological state apparatus" where ideas and opinions are disseminated'.

A proposed alternative to male-defined images of women are 'women centred' images, with women imagining and constructing *their* space on *their* terms. In art, for example, women are traditionally presented by male artists as passive. They engage the 'gaze' of the spectator (male) and offer a position of ownership and possession to him. Numerous women artists have produced paintings, carvings, sketches and sculptures, which present images of women free from male stereotypes. The work of women artists is often based on investigation and expression of patriarchy, racism and imperialism. Many incorporate personal experience into their work. Materials, techniques and traditional skills developed by women are often prioritised and celebrated in exhibitions, and there are examples of women working collectively to produce large-scale pieces (Chadwick, 1991). Women artists have prioritised the importance of gender, race, class, sexuality and disability by adopting and appropriating male-defined artistic modes.

Others argue that women cannot reclaim themselves in this way since there is no female equivalent to the work developed by men. They propose that such work only seems to reinforce male perspectives. In considering women's attempts to decolonise the female form/body, Griselda Pollock (1977 p. 29) expresses a fear that feminist imagery which focuses on an affirmative exposure of female sexuality through celebratory images of female genitalia 'walks a tightrope between subversion and reappropriation, and often serves to consolidate the potency of the signification rather than actually rupture it'. Within this debate, however, feminists have raised the distinction between 'women's art' and 'feminist art'. They have also questioned the possibility, or necessity, of drawing a line between 'art' and 'politics' (Coote and Campbell, 1987; see also: Nead, 1986; Ecker, 1985).

In the experiences of women, the **politics of appearance** are loaded with significance. As Rita Freedman (1988) states: 'the idealisation of female appearance camouflages the underlying belief in female inferiority'. Cosmetic, fashion, leisure and female media industries constantly recuperate and reassimilate new or previously unheeded 'facets of femininity' (Carter, 1984 p. 188). These are supposedly based on the 'needs' or 'desires' of women revealed by market researchers engaged in a vast apparatus of consumer surveillance. Yet they reflect prevailing ideas, beliefs and attitudes about femininity which are imposed on women whether they like it or not. The presentation of women, and their bodies, is promoted through an appeal to 'individuality', structurally located within the context of ascribed femininity. Conformity and competition are promoted in the interests of profit and power. Heather Smith (1989 p. 37) illustrates how concepts of superiority and inferiority are central: 'Affirmation depends on negation: white is valued at the expense of black, status is attached to youth by the devaluing of ageing'.

In the 'West' much of femininity assumes women's inadequacies. Hence, women spend their lives adapting or changing their appearance to attain 'ideal' womanhood. Wendy Chapkis (1988 p. 6) notes that by seeking legitimacy and the right of citizenship through 'acceptable' femininity, women deny their undisguised self. The underlying message implied by 'feminine' acts (e.g. applying make-up) is that 'improvements' can be made or 'problems' corrected. As Alison Jaggar (1983) notes, women are gradually alienated from their bodies as they work on themselves (plucking eyebrows, shaving, painting nails, etc.) to gain approval and compete for male attention and relationships (Wolf, 1990; Chapkis, 1988; Haug, 1987). Constant striving to overcome perceived 'inadequacy' means women cannot proclaim or accept their 'beauty' or be satisfied with their appearance. Wendy Chapkis (1988) points out that feminist claims that all women have 'natural' beauty have been rewritten and incorporated into discourses about femininity. In a commercial translation described as 'the natural look' women are directed to achieve surreptitiously what few possess naturally. The current ideal construct of 'Western' beauty remains narrow-hipped, high-breasted, flaw-less complexion but achieved without recourse to girdles, wired bras or a mask of make-up. Frigga Haug (1987 p. 264) suggests that society laments the distancing from nature that has occurred. While she admits that the emphasis on, and use of, 'natural' products is no doubt healthier, she asks: 'what have we gained if we are still hopelessly torn as to what type of lemon cream to buy?'

Puberty and adolescence are represented as a period of instability for young people. It is a time of contradiction when childhood and adulthood are not clearly separated. For young women the regulatory nature of social control is frequently heightened and much of their behaviour is linked to supposedly 'emerging sexuality'. This is a time of preparation for their specific roles in the family. Feminist studies have highlighted the importance of talking and planning around fashion, make-up and boy-friends for young women. The themes of 'romance' and the 'culture of femininity' are central in their daily lives (Lees, 1993, 1986; McRobbie, 1991, 1978; Hudson, 1983). These form the basis of a **sexual politics** for women.

Sexual 'reputation' becomes a crucial determining factor in the lives of young women. As women are objectified through their sexuality and assumed sexual actions they are judged on their perceived adherence to sexual codes of conduct. All aspects of the lives of young women come to be dominated and regulated by concern over reputation (Lees, 1987, 1986; Wood, 1987; Jones, 1985). They experience the emphasis placed by boys, other girls, parents, teachers and neighbours on their sexual reputation. Judgements about their 'respectability' relate to appearance (amount of make-up, length of skirt, jewellery, etc.) and to their contact with boys. The language used to define girls reflects a continuum of respectability from virgin to whore and is male defined. Whatever their contact with – and physical response to – boys, girls are labelled as 'slags', 'cows', 'dogs', 'sluts' or, alternatively, as 'frigid', 'tight', 'lessies'. Reputation, however, is based on *perceived* activity, rumour, or the boasts of male teenagers as they publicly define young women in their community.

Young women often retreat to the culture of the bedroom where they spend time with female friends safely discussing or reading magazines about how to become an ideal woman. As Angela McRobbie (1982) illustrates, teenage magazines are based on unrealistic common definitions of girl/womanhood in which clearly identifiable priorities include concentration on appearance, romance and fulfilment of female roles. That is, looking good, catching a man and servicing him. Powerful ideologies of femininity extend to women's magazines where appropriate sexuality, and romance, occupy a privileged position (Ballaster, 1991). Even *Cosmopolitan*, aimed at the 'liberated', 'open-minded', 'independent' career woman of the 1990s persistently publishes features concerned with sex, beauty, fashion, men and relationships, occasionally including articles which resist such ideology.

Within the culture of femininity there is a strong relationship between **beauty and body**. Although the particulars of beauty packaging may differ (minimally) over time, a woman's 'value' relates to the 'ideal' body shape and size of the moment. Being slim equates to sexual attractiveness. For many women 'slimming' becomes a health hazard as they subject themselves to stomach stapling, lipo-suction, plastic surgery or dieting through pills or pseudo-medical programmes. Pressure to achieve the 'ideal' body shape is a major factor in the contemporary upsurge of eating disorders such as anorexia nervosa (Orbach, 1993; McFarland, 1991; Garner and Garfinkel, 1980). Anorexia has been described by Sheila MacLeod (1981) as a 'political problem' through which women attempt to preserve a personal identity or autonomy and shed the burden of womanhood rather than seek it. When their bodies change at puberty, becoming heavier and rounder, many young women experience what Susie Orbach (1993) describes as a 'major psychological split' between their view of their body and their sense of self-worth. Their immature, youthful physique conforms to the stereotype of feminine beauty, and a mature body of womanhood is perceived as less attractive.

Images of 'attractive women' fall into two clearly defined categories. The first is the 'child-woman' – 'slim', 'young', 'not pregnant', 'all smooth', 'all gleaming' (Taylor, 1985 p. 68). The second is the over-forty, physically fit, mid-life (usually famous) beauty. These representations do not challenge ideas of beauty but 'raise the threshold of self-hate faster than the age span', as women 'who failed to look like Brooke Shields at 17 can now fail to look like Sophia Loren at 50' (Goodman, cited in Chapkis, 1988 p. 10). Since it is argued that it takes effort and hard work to maintain the ideal of beauty over forty years, those women who do not 'measure up' are presented as lacking in self-discipline, as failures. Entire industries based on 'health and fitness', cosmetic surgery, diet and fashion emphasise this failure and underwrite competitiveness.

Fitness and care of the body can be positive for women and a source of liberation and empowerment. The sense of achievement and control derived from fitness can encourage women to tackle other physical, mental, social or political challenges. However, the ideal body image presented as 'accept-able' remains a stereotype of a 'feminine' body, with only certain muscles, in the 'right' place and proportion, being acceptable. There is also a clear distinction between 'leisure' and 'sport'. Activities relating to health, fitness and leisure are presented as legitimate for women whereas many sports are purported to be dangerous for reproductive health and to threaten 'femininity' (S. Scraton, 1992; Lenskyji, 1986).

Through language women's bodies are depersonalised, fragmented and discussed in terms of physical 'problem' areas – 'sagging bottoms', 'flabby thighs', 'drooping breasts'. Any reference to 'fat' is negative. Heather Smith (1989) relates how fear and hatred of 'fat' pervades 'Western' cultures. Fat bodies are defined as 'disgusting' or 'diseased' and fat women are considered to be, or represented as being, asexual, maternal, or sexually desperate. The diet and body shape industries thrive on the promise of transformation which will bring love, desirability, happiness and self-esteem (Jenkins, 1988; Orbach, 1979). Most women are aware that the 'ideal' body is unattainable but feel compelled to attempt transformation and consequently develop a punishing self-hating relationship with their bodies.

Feminism has helped women to resist images of female beauty and attractiveness. Women have organised or joined sport and leisure activities suited to their own abilities as a means of achieving the positive qualities of health and fitness within supportive and non-threatening environments. Groups such as the 'Fat Women's Group' support women against negative images by redefining 'fat' and encouraging self-esteem. Women with disabilities have claimed the right to their own physicality and to challenge dominant ablist assumptions (Boylan, 1991; Morris, 1991, 1989; Lonsdale, 1990; Deegan and Brooks, 1985; Campling, 1981). Older women deny representations of the 'ageing process' and their consequent marginalisation during and beyond menopause (Greer, 1992; Franklin and Franklin, 1990; Macdonald and Rich, 1984).

Fashion, its definitions and constructions, is also guided by the prevailing sexual ideal. In the 1930s the figure-hugging clothes which tightly encased women emphasised tension in their bodies and implied prudishness or sexual unavailability. Conversely, loose clothes and relaxed body posture is often used to emphasise availability or portray a 'loose woman' who lacks control over her sexuality. Both, seemingly contradictory, images reflect that a woman's sexuality is male-defined and restricted to male-sanctioned expression. Within the fashion industry domination by male designers has contributed to and perpetuated what James Laver (cited in Neustatter, 1990b p. 92) terms the 'Seduction Principle'. Male designers create garments which ignore a woman's needs, or comfort, but emphasise her seductiveness and desirability, packaged for male consumption.

Through history, women's clothes have been tailored to emphasise body shape and restrict efficiency of movement. In addition, fabric texture and colour are represented as signals of femininity so that silk, wool or suede, for example feel 'sophisticated' or 'sensuous'. Class and status are also reflected both in fabric and design. 'Continental chic' designs connotate 'style', and ultimately wealth, in contrast with the mass-produced fashions of the so-called 'Rag Trade'. However, even the 'well dressed' Chanel or Jaeger wearer is invariably perceived as reflecting the wealth or status of her male provider. While some women are personally and financially independent, Wendy Chapkis (1988) argues that expensive fashion perpetuates the male defined 'dress as success' principle. Women reinforce an element of competition and this reinforces the power relations of class and 'race'. The packaging of attractiveness and ambition is sold as a guarantee to beauty and success, thus maintaining the construct that failure to succeed as a woman is personal, not structural.

Chapkis states that although it has been challenged by indigenous cultures, the 'beauty trade' has expanded to reach a world-wide market. Beauty and fashion have become universalised and the standard value is white, 'Western' and wealthy, regardless of women's ethnic or economic position. The impact of American magazines, television and films, bought by countries throughout the world has consolidated a single version of beauty and success. In the predominantly white 'Western' world, the images of women of colour represent sensuality, adventure and eroticism to advertise travel, tourism and entry into the world of the exotic. The myths of the promiscuous, lascivious black woman or passive, subservient Asian woman persist in white, masculine, sexual exploitation. This is perpetuated and reinforced by the media, in advertising and in pornography where, amongst other things, torture and humiliation of black women is celebrated.

The norms and expectations of femininity embodied in the beauty and fashion industries have not gone unchallenged. Elizabeth Wilson (1985 p. 245) proposes that: 'fashion is one among many forms of creativity which make possible the exploration of alternatives'. During the 1970s feminists actively rejected clothing or artifices that exaggerated gender differences in an attempt to symbolically break the 'seduction principle'. Joan Cassell (1977) describes how the 'women's liberation uniform' varied according to political commitment. As Angela Neustatter (1990 p. 104) states: 'opting out of the adornment game was an important political and emotional gesture for many women. It allowed them to feel free of the competitiveness as well as the sense of being male fodder'. The response to such action was vociferous. The media subjected those who dared to cast off their male-defined sexuality to punishing criticism and ridicule. Their appearance and behaviour were cruelly caricatured in cartoons. Male comedians' jokes and tabloid headlines referred to 'bra-burners', 'man-haters', 'women's-libbers' and 'lessies'. These terms gained serious currency within male culture and reaffirmed the power of definition in the subordination of women. They have been extended to include *any* woman who proclaims her allegiance to feminism. The consequence has been to reinforce the ideal of femininity and to demand that truly 'feminine' women require male approval or face marginalisation and denial.

Feminists are united in their struggle against the sexual objectification of women and artificial gender divisions. But there is a debate over the politics of fashion and cosmetics as traditionally defined. The issues raised lead to questions about the need for separation and development of a 'new' or 'different' construction of 'woman', or the need for adaptation and reworking of existing constructions to promote positive representations of women. Chapkis (1988 p. 8) suggests that, initially, women were empowered by resisting gender stereotyping in appearance and creating their own images of womanhood. However, she notes that the standards by which women are judged, and critically judge themselves, alter little. Writers such as Angela Neustatter (1990) and Elizabeth Wilson (1985) suggest that one of the principles of feminism is to help women feel strong in and for themselves. They propose that women should enjoy creating their own images and gain pleasure from experimenting with their appearance. This does not mean 'selling out' but can contribute to the reclamation of the positive aspects of adornment. Their argument is that once women know what they want to be they can reclaim clothes, make-up and 'fashion' as expressions and emphases of this self.

Frigga Haug (1987 p. 258) suggests that women should separate their actions into those performed for a self-related purpose ('for me') and those that involve giving themselves away to another person ('for others'). What becomes important is the pursuit of 'the autonomous purpose'. The difficulty is knowing whether an individual woman is able to 'dress for herself'. More often than not, identities are constructed beyond the 'self'. 'Alternatives' are also packaged and there are limitations on the products available within which women can establish personal identities. Thus, debate continues over the ability of women to establish personal identities, on their terms, within male-defined parameters. Highly publicised examples are used to illustrate opposing positions. For example, is Madonna's *Sex* (1992) obvious pornography for men developed by a woman, or is it a collection of ideas and photographs in which a woman explores complex images related to her sexuality? Although Madonna claims control of the process, she cannot control how it is received by male spectators.

It is clear that powerful discourses reinforce and perpetuate stereotypes about both female appearance and **sexual behaviour**. From puberty to menopause women are seen to be 'controlled' or 'influenced' by changes in hormones and consequent development of their sexuality. The sexual character or morality of young women is used to define their behaviour and actions as 'normal', 'right', 'good' or 'abnormal', 'immoral' and 'deviant'. Sexual stereotypes, rooted in nineteenth-century medical and legal discourses, reflect and institutionalise this ideology. For boys, aggression, assertion and delinquent behaviour are deemed natural, part of their progressive development. For girls, however, any deviance has been viewed as a 'perversion' (Blos, 1969) or the result of individual pathology which rejects passive, naturally feminine behaviour and adopts anti-social masculine traits (Lombroso and Ferrero, 1895). Contemporary theorists have perpetuated such concepts with reference to the 'impaired health' of 'over-sized', 'lumpish', 'uncouth' and 'graceless' delinquent girls (Cowie, Cowie and Slater, 1968). Sexual character is a key factor in determining punishment and treatment for girls in the juvenile justice system (Griffin, 1993; Cain, 1989; Campbell, 1981). Webb (1984), for example, shows that care orders are applied for because girls have transgressed moral, not legal, codes and 'treatment' programmes centre on reclamation or development of femininity, homecare and motherhood skills. Professional discourses (psychiatry, education, social work, etc.) regularly reinforce the ideology of moral transgression by recommending 'protection' for girls from their own sexuality or that of others (Morris and Wilkinson, 1983).

In many institutions, violence against women is legitimated on the basis of accepted notions of male sexuality (Edwards, 1989; Kelly and Radford, 1987). **Violence against women** frequently occurs in the place where women feel they should be safe – their home (Gelles and Cornell, 1990). The perception that city streets hold the greatest risk for women and children helps to perpetuate the myth of the rarity of male violence in the home (Women's Aid Federation, 1989). The struggles of nineteenth-century feminists such as Frances Power Cobbe were, in part, struggles against their definition as the property of their husband and the physical brutality of 'wife battering'. Feminist activists who were directly involved with women survivors of 'domestic violence' revived this struggle in the early 1970s (Pizzey, 1974). The 'Women's Aid' movement has established that such violence is systematic and severe, that it is directly related to the position of women in society, and that the response of the state is complacent in the extreme (Women's National Commission, 1985; Pahl, 1985). The movement revealed evidence of a significant gap between legislative reforms aimed at providing protection (The Domestic Violence and Matrimonial Proceedings Act, 1976) and housing rights (the Housing (Homeless Persons) Act, 1977) for women sufferers of domestic violence, and their enforcement. Feminist studies have criticised the role of the police and their reluctance to interfere with domestic incidents, as well as the effects of this on women's willingness to report such incidents (Bourlet, 1990; Hanmer et al., 1989; Edwards, 1989; Horley, 1985; Hanmer and Saunders, 1984; Binney et al., 1981). Personal reactions and institution-alised responses to violence against women reinforce the acceptance and legitimation of the violence (Dobash and Dobash, 1980, 1992; Hanmer and Maynard, 1987). The language, ritual and conventions generally used in society, and embodied in the law, serve to reinforce and perpetuate dominant ideologies about female and male sexuality and cut across cultural and societal boundaries. More radical analyses of the violence perpetrated against women places routine violation within the broader contexts of the 'normalisation of terror' (Morgan, 1990) and 'femicide' (Radford and Russell, 1992).

The criminal justice system reinforces and perpetuates stereotypes of 'appropriate' role models for women – daughter, wife, mother – and 'appropriate' behaviour – passivity, submission, femininity. Courts are preoccupied with the 'moral character' of women and in cases of rape or sexual assault it is usually *her* sexual behaviour that is the focus of attention rather than that of the male accused. If a woman shows any sign of a positive sexuality *her* 'innocence' is questioned (Edwards, 1981). To qualify for protection (from men or the legal system) women have to abide by the rules of conduct relating to 'feminine' sexuality. A woman's sexual autonomy threatens the 'ownership' relationship implicit in compulsory heterosexual relations. Historically a woman's value has been determined by her father or husband and has depended on her economic status and desirability as the object of an exclusive sexual relationship (Brownmiller, 1976; Clark and Lewis, 1977). 'Virginity' and 'chastity' remain important issues in contemporary rape cases and this further ensures the relationship between exclusivity and value in women's sexuality. Male definitions of what constitutes rape prevail and relate to images of women's acceptable appearance and sexual behaviour. The issues of 'force' and 'consent' are linked to ideas about what constitutes 'appropriate' sexual exchange between women and men (Stanko, 1985). The traditional explanations and shared meanings which persist include: women enjoy rape (say no when they mean yes); women provoke rape (by the way they dress, by going out alone, by accepting lifts); only certain – unrespectable – women are raped; women make false accusations of rape (for revenge or to protect their reputation); rape is committed by maniacs (ill, sick, stressed, out of control); rapists are in the grip of impulsive, uncontrollable sexual urges; most rapists are strangers.

Feminist perspectives on sexual violence argue that male violence against women is a form of social and political control (Horsfall, 1991; Scully, 1990; Stanko, 1990; Kelly, 1988; Caputi, 1987). The fear or actual experience of violence/rape enables men to assert power directly and maintain patriarchal relations. All men are the beneficiaries of this physical domination and many participate to a degree (Stanko, 1985). Andrea Dworkin (1982 p. 46) claims that 'rape is no excess, no aberration, no mistake – it embodies sexuality as the culture defines it'. Men's behaviour is defined as 'typical' or, by contrast, as 'aberrant' and women's experiences of male violence are discussed and judged through an understanding of male behaviour that falls into one or other of these categories (Stanko, 1985). It is wrongly assumed that a minority of men behave in an aberrant manner and that rape is committed by untypical men from whom all other 'normal' men can disassociate. This construct helps to maintain what Susan Griffin (1971) termed the 'male protection racket' whereby a man argues that a woman needs protection, by him, from other (possibly aberrant) men. This fails to address the key issue that the most likely rapist, the most likely source of violence, is the 'protector' himself (Eisenstein, 1984). As Liz Kelly (1988) points out, the male protection racket creates dependency and vulnerability. Further, she proposes that male violence is a continuum in which its many forms are underpinned by common characteristics. These are abuse, intimidation, coercion, intrusion, threat and force. Yet much of this behaviour is seen as acceptable and typical by men. 'Their' wives, daughters, women relatives and 'friends' are seen to be the problem if they object. Feminist solutions to the sexual domination of women range from a rejection of heterosexuality in favour of celibacy, auto-eroticism or lesbianism (Bunch, 1986; Daly, 1984, 1978, 1973; Rich, 1980; Johnston, 1974) to androgyny (French, 1985; Millett, 1970) or a transformation in the institution of heterosexuality (Jaggar, 1983; Rowbotham, 1981).

Women's 'rightful' role as mothers has been espoused historically as 'natural' by virtue of their capacity to bear children. **Motherhood** is a 'rite of passage', invariably equated with 'womanhood' and glorified as women's chief vocation. This is reflected in the stigma and pity that is conferred on women who are childless – whether by choice or through infertility. Women who choose to deny their supposed 'maternal instincts' are frequently referred to as selfish – flying in the face of nature. This is because women, as mothers, have been exalted as selfless and altruistic nurturers of children (and their fathers). Moreover, the desire for children is seen as 'normal', but only in the context of heterosexual marital relationships. Such ideological assumptions are manifested in social policies and professional practices, whereby lesbian women lose custody of their children and gay and lesbian citizens and single women are denied access to reproductive technologies (Chesler, 1991, 1986; Ferguson, 1989; Smart and Sevenhuijsen, 1989; Stanworth, 1987).

Thus, women who become mothers achieve a prescribed status in society, providing that role is undertaken within fixed rules which are imposed by the ideology of motherhood and the family. Lesbian women and single women (with and without children) are perceived as 'deviant' and are stigmatised in a society where heterosexuality, marriage and motherhood are assumed. Moral, religious and biological reductionist discourses are regularly invoked to support such arrangements. Biology is presented as an expression of inevitability: 'what is biological is given by nature and proved by science' (Rose *et al.* 1984, p. 6). The message in sociological writings is that injustices and inequalities, sexism and racism, oppression and wars are natural and inevitable consequences of human evolution. Steven Goldberg

(1974 p. 105) suggests that male domination over women is biologically inevitable and functional. He argues that, at a particular phase of development, hormones 'masculinise' the foetal brain. Women are assumed to possess hormones which provide them with a 'greater nurturative tendency'. 'Femaleness' is implicitly the absence of 'masculinisation'. The 'scientific' exhortations of sociobiologists have become particularly important in the rhetoric of New Right social commentators such as Ferdinand Mount (1982) and Roger Scruton (1985) for whom women's 'liberation' is not only considered 'misguided', but also against nature. More insidious is the recent spate of novels and commentaries by women who identified themselves as feminists in the 1970s, but now suggest that women's biology really is their destiny (Marrin, Lee-Potter; cited in Heller, 1992). The reproductive argument infers that women can never fully enter public life as they are geared genetically to the needs of child rearing and home building. Entrance into public life is seen as being achieved at some biological and social cost.

Nineteenth-century feminists did not necessarily perceive as problematic the definition of women as 'natural' childbearers and rearers (Gordon, 1982). By contrast, in the late 1960s and early 1970s feminists challenged the definition of women by their reproductive status and pointed out how 'biology' is loaded with socially constructed meanings. Shulamith Firestone (1972) identifies biological sex as the root of all women's oppression by men. She argues that women's biological capacity to reproduce determines and maintains the division of labour between men and women, creating what she terms a 'sex class'. These reproductive roles are socially and politically imposed in order to support the biological family. Firestone envisages that women's liberation requires a biological revolution whereby women take control of the means of reproduction and eliminate the sex class system, thus undermining both biological and social motherhood. Similarly, Ann Oakley (1979) argues that motherhood is not a biological need for women – mothers are made not born. She advocates the reconstruction of 'motherhood', arguing that non-traditional childrearing and alternative patterns of living (such as collectives or communes) would free women from the constraints imposed on them.

Other analyses have focused on 'internal' processes and have suggested that it is not motherhood per se that is problematic. It has been suggested that patriarchy has distorted the experience of motherhood. Adrienne Rich (1977) argues that men are jealous and fearful of women's reproductive powers. For patriarchy to flourish, the power of the mother must be restricted. According to Mary O'Brien (1981) men create the social relations of patriarchy in order to compensate for their alienation from the process of reproduction. Psychodynamic analyses point to the process through which the 'need' to be a mother is constructed in a woman's psychic structure. For writers such as

Dorothy Dinnerstein (1976) and Nancy Chodorow (1978), equality in parenting is crucial since it should lead to men's and women's psyches being altered, and to a fusion of the public and private spheres.

O'Brien and Rich argue that women should not give up biological reproduction as it is potentially the source of their liberation. They suggest that a celebration of motherhood is necessary. If women regain control of their reproductive processes, then maternal 'experience' will be recreated and maternity used to transform social reality, hence consciousness. Such ideas have informed and been informed by an emphasis on 'women's culture' – a call for women to bring to the fore and celebrate their essentially female and maternal capacities (Daly, 1984; Griffin, 1978; Rich, 1977).

The danger with this position is that there is a tendency to infer a Utopian vision of womanhood and motherhood, where 'male' or 'masculine' equates with 'bad' and 'female' or 'feminine' with 'good' in an overly deterministic way. Moreover, the 'celebration of motherhood' implies the possibility that mothers can be naturally perfect if freed from patriarchal control (Chodorow and Contratto, 1982). The idealisation of mothers has paved the way for analyses which blame 'dominating mothers' for their daughters' oppression (Coward, 1992; Arcana, 1979; Friday, 1977; Dinnerstein, 1976).

Similarly, 'mother dominated infancy' has been constructed as the root of male oppression (Bly, 1990). Thus, mothers are identified as both powerless victims of patriarchal control and as the all-powerful agents and facilitators of that control. Such analyses are dangerously reductionist and are seriously constrained by dominant cultural, and post-Freudian psychological, assumptions about child development and 'mothering'. They also appear to continue to define 'woman' essentially as 'mother' or 'potential mother'. Many women, including feminists, want children and experience the positive and gratifying as well as conflicting and oppressive aspects of mothering. However, women should have the right to mother or not to mother as they desire.

Many feminist analyses perceive women's ability to give life to be the motivating force behind the male 'takeover' of **reproduction** by science and technology. A key concern has been identification of who controls reproductive technologies. Knowledge about, and control of, women's bodies has been appropriated by a relatively small, elite group of male medical experts (Faulkner and Arnold, 1985). The medicalisation of women's health in the nineteenth century played a crucial role in facilitating the transformation of social relations required to fulfil the needs of early capitalism. Women's allocation to the private, domestic sphere was directly related to the reconstruction of their normal, healthy bodily functions as 'problems' or 'illnesses' (Ehrenreich and English, 1979; Delamont and Duffin, 1978). In this, there were clear class and racial distinctions. Middle-class women were constructed as 'fragile', requiring inactivity, whereas working-class women and women from immigrant communities were constructed as 'sickening' – carriers of germs and diseases and prolific breeders of 'inferior' children (Showalter, 1987; Roberts, 1981). Yet, whatever the construction, all women became the focus of what emerged as an increasingly powerful, patriarchal medical profession, a profession whose discourses continue to legitimate and intensify the social control of women.

Knowledge of women's bodies has often been concealed from them by medical 'experts' (O'Sullivan, 1987). Feminists have been concerned to reclaim knowledge and understanding of women's bodies in order to challenge the distorted content of much 'western' medicine (Boston Women's Health Collective, 1978). The secrecy, mythology and ignorance inherent in constructions about women's biology are clearly evident in discourses which define menstruation and the menopause as 'problems'. Women's behaviour continues to be defined in terms of their 'deviant' biology or 'raging hormones', with little regard to the social as well as biological context in which it occurs (Edwards, 1988; Laws, 1985; Dalton, 1982; O'Sullivan, 1982). The impact of other life changes, which may be equally significant, is frequently neglected or rejected (Birke, 1986).

The denial of women's right to take control over their bodies has extended most emphatically throughout the reproductive process itself. Childbirth was once a home-based event, exclusively organised by female midwives and women from the local community. Increasingly it has been appropriated by male medical 'experts' within the disciplines of obstetrics and gynaecology (Stanworth, 1987; Ehrenreich and English, 1979). Pregnancy and childbirth have been placed within a hi-tech medical/scientific frame of reference. Women are perceived as patients and pregnancy is constructed as an illness. As each stage of the process of procreation is compartmentalised and medicalised, 'motherhood' becomes a disempowering and alienating experience for women (Pfeffer, 1993; Stanworth, 1987; Jaggar, 1983). Women have challenged this 'hi-tech' approach to childbirth, partly on the grounds that it is potentially harmful to mother and baby, but also in an attempt to regain control. Efforts to reinstate 'natural' methods of childbirth, and to act on the requests of women giving birth, have invariably met with resistance from the medical profession (Savage, 1988). There has been some response to women's demands by a few health authorities. However, the majority of women still experience childbirth as a procedure determined by the routines and regimes of hospital.

For Ann Oakley (1984), the management and control of childbirth is inseparable from the way in which women are managed and controlled. The 1960s and 1970s brought increased awareness of the impact of restricted access to contraception and abortion to women's lives. Issues relating to sterilisation and new reproductive technologies were also raised. The struggle for equality became inextricably linked to women's struggle for control of their bodies. Demands for access to safe and effective methods of contraception and abortion were prioritised. Feminist analyses exposed how the development of contraceptive technologies has been dominated by a male perspective and almost exclusively designed to ensure male gratification (Pollock, 1984). The Pill, for example, was marketed as a contraceptive which would 'free' women from the shackles of their biology so that they might participate fully in the 'sexual liberation' of the swinging sixties. However, it has been suggested that the extent to which the Pill has been liberating for women is questionable at a number of levels (Neustatter, 1990a). Not only has the Pill created an additional pressure for women to have sex by making it harder for them to say no, while placing responsibility for unwanted pregnancy firmly in their court, it has also put them at risk physically. Queries or complaints about side-effects are invariably ignored or dismissed by the medical profession. Additionally, the risk of HIV infection has underlined the significance of contracting other infections such as Hepatitis B and diseases such as cervical cancer. The Pill affords no protection against these and leaves women bearing the consequences of male irresponsibility.

The development of In-Vitro Fertilization (IVF), artificial insemination, surrogacy and antenatal screening opened up feminist debates in the area of **new reproductive technologies** (McNeil, 1990; Klein, *et al.*, 1985). New reproductive technologies are often related to infertility and are supposed to benefit women by giving them the 'gift' of life. Janice Raymond (1984) argues that the 'miracles' of test-tube babies hide the manipulation, and experimentation on, women's bodies. All of these technologies involve artificial invasion of women's bodies by 'experts' or 'techno-docs' (Klein, *et al.*, 1985). New reproductive technologies have been described as a form of violence against women which is new and frightening (Corea, 1985; Arditti *et al.*, 1984). Jalna Hanmer (1981) suggests that while new reproductive technologies are portrayed as 'therapies' for women, they actually reflect and substantially tighten men's control over women's reproductive processes.

Access to new reproductive technologies is greatly restricted, both financially and through dominant ideologies about class, ethnic background, marital status, age, sexuality, disability and the family. There are clear messages about who the recipients of such technologies should be. They are not equally available to all women (Pollack-Petcheskey, 1986, 1980) and there are serious eugenic implications involved in their use. Jalna Hanmer (1981) argues that screening and antenatal testing provides the choice to abort a less than 'perfect' baby. In a society which devalues people with disabilities, the potential consequences are obvious. Screening has also led to other innovations. In particular, it has opened up the possibility of sex selection which Marge Berer (1986) suggests could lead to the widespread destruction of female foetuses, as has already occurred in China and India. Thus femicide could be a more sinister facet of new reproductive technologies.

New reproductive technologies carry with them serious moral and political concerns. The basis of family life, particularly patriarchy, is threatened by the possibility of severing childbearing from sex and marriage (Smart, 1987). The possession of, and access to, new reproductive technologies has consequences for the legal status of children born through such methods. Given that established Western legal systems are founded on principles which reflect father right, male ownership and property inheritance (Stoltenberg, 1991), the issue of paternity within new reproductive technologies is brought into sharp focus. Yet it has also been suggested that as the functions of motherhood and reproduction are split into smaller parts, women could become redundant, and mothers obsolete. Through ectogenesis, men could become the perfect fathers of their artificially conceived, artificially carried and artificially delivered children (Rodin, 1991; Hynes, 1989; Stanworth, 1987; Corea, 1985; Dworkin, 1982).

Clearly, there is a need to distinguish between scientific research and interventions which help women, and those which undermine women at the most fundamental level. However, as long as reproductive technologies are developed within a patriarchal framework they are unlikely to increase women's reproductive rights or freedom. Perhaps it is more appropriate to talk of 'reproductive freedom' as opposed to 'reproductive rights'. This change in focus reflects the fact that material, legal and institutional empowerment is necessary before women can make informed and effective choices about reproduction as individuals. Rosalind Pollack-Petchesky (1986) suggests that the 'right to choose' does not mean anything if the social and material conditions affecting women's lives do not change. She states that an analysis which focuses on individual dimensions of reproductive freedom, such as control of their own bodies, is insufficient. It is also problematic since it is rooted in a framework of 'natural' rights and liberal philosophy, evading moral questions regarding when, under what conditions and for what purposes reproductive decisions should be made. She proposes that a broader analysis of the social relations of reproduction is necessary. This should take account of the wider political, social, legal and medical contexts in which 'choices' are made and how these change over time. True reproductive freedom is, therefore, simultaneously both social and individual (Davis, 1988).

The politics of reproduction are inextricably linked to the politics of **production**. Within feminism it is acknowledged that the social and cultural arrangements which contextualise reproduction act to centralise a woman's role as wife and mother. This serves to direct her towards primary responsibility for domestic work, childcare and family duties in the private sphere and restricts access to all activities in the public/civil sphere. It is precisely because men control the production and distribution of material goods, and maintain an institutionalised monopoly over social, political and cultural arrangements, that male power in the public sphere can be transmitted so easily into personal relations. This power is asserted, both interpersonally and collectively, by the use and abuse of women's sexuality. Men's physical and sexual power over women is maintained by an assumed right to keep women under the constant threat of violence. This control is not simply the sum total of the practices of social institutions. It also extends, often in a more subtle form, to the medical, moral, legal and political discourses which underwrite and legitimate such practices.

The assumption has been that women undertake domestic labour as a direct extension of their 'biological function' as mothers. In other words motherhood, childrearing, domestic labour and the servicing of, or caring for, others become part of the package ascribed to 'women's role'. The subjugation of women's labour forms the material basis for patriarchal relations within all societies. As Bob Connell (1987) concludes, this is the case whatever the cultural, social or political differences between societies. In non-industrialised societies based on subsistence economies, the family is often the focal productive unit whose collective labour is geared towards self-sufficiency. Women's work revolves around the direct production of crops, the production and preparation of food and drink, care of children and the elderly and the manufacture of clothing and household goods. It is a use of labour which is vital to the maintenance of the family and the immediate community and also part of a market-based exchange or barter economy. The expansion of industrial economies has encouraged a decline in subsistence economies. Many societies have been compelled to make a major transition from subsistence to industrial economies in a relatively short period of time. Consequently, economic systems are at different stages of development and dependency – from subsistence to advanced capitalist – within the world economic order. The assumption, borne out of a form of economic imperialism, is that the advanced capitalist economy offers the superior goal. This 'First World' ideology is fed by the pre-eminence of the US, European and Japanese economies on the world stage and the political and economic power vested within the industrial/military complex of these combined nation states.

'Western' feminist analyses illustrate how the segregation of home and work at the onset of the Industrial Revolution was an important factor in creating the sexual division of labour (Alexander, 1976; Rowbotham, 1973).

This was further reinforced and consolidated by state policy and union action. The division of labour was underpinned by a powerful ideology about women's primary roles as wives and mothers and this fitted with the emerging private/public split. Middle-class, Victorian, domestic ideology ascribed status to those men who were able to support a wife in enforced idleness. However, it was acceptable for her to become involved in charitable work among the 'deserving' poor and needy within the community. Working-class women were unlikely to be seen in the same light as their middle-class sisters. The reality of their daily lives was harsh and there were few concessions to their physical and mental well-being. However, definitions of their roles as wives and mothers were influenced by the domestic ideology, which reinforced and perpetuated the idea that their proper place was in the home, whether their own or in the service of a middle-class household. Women's involvement in paid work was considered to be temporary, secondary to their roles as wives and mothers. This was reinforced by the application of marriage bars in certain occupations and the expectation in others that women would leave paid work and return to the home once they were married. If a married woman undertook paid work it was expected to be part-time and her earnings were regarded as being supplementary to the 'family wage' which was the prerogative of the male 'breadwinner'.

Much of the critical theory concerning the politics of production in capitalist societies has been shaped, either in guiding principles or in critique, by Marx's three volumes on Capital. At the centre of this work is the idea that all social and institutional relations within capitalism are contextualised, if not determined, by the forces and relations of production. Undoubtedly, the Marxist legacy and contemporary neo-Marxist writings have been central to a critical grasp of class relations within developing capitalist societies. Women were acknowledged to be materially oppressed but only within the context of waged work. The political and ideological oppression of women was recognised solely in terms of the different social roles ascribed to women and men in the private and public spheres, as determined by the capitalist economy and its institutions. According to this position the overthrow of capitalism would end the oppression of workers and dismantle the political ideology of the family and women's role within it. Effectively this line of argument subordinated women's oppression to class oppression. It presumed that women would gain liberation from patriarchal relations if they put their efforts into fighting alongside men in the class struggle. Despite revised Marxist theory which identifies both the struggles of men and women as waged workers against economic exploitation and women against ideo-logical oppression, the persistent criticism levelled at Marxism is its neglect of gender relations as being of primary significance.

However, the work of Marx and Marxist writers has been usefully developed to analyse the role of women in the production process. In considering the key elements of historical materialism Friedrich Engels (1891) defined the connection between 'production' and 'reproduction'. By this he meant the production of food, shelter, clothing, warmth ('the means of existence') and the production of human life (reproduction and child-rearing). He argued that both processes are directly interrelated and shape the social arrangements within any society at any given historical moment. The debate has been most prolific over the political and economic implications for women of the relationship between production and reproduction within capitalism. Women were required as 'biological functionaries' to regenerate labour power for capitalist expansion but also to provide socially the domestic work implicit in the bearing and rearing of children and the running of households. Domestic labour remained unpaid but was essential to the maintenance and reproduction of the capitalist political economy. Further, although domestic labour could not be assessed through an actual product, it remained essentially productive labour. While domestic labour relations exist within the 'private sphere', and as such vary, they remain a site of exploitation which ultimately benefits capital.

Analyses which focus on the construct of 'women's work' and explore the economic value of this work – paid and unpaid – to capitalism have extended to the so-called 'domestic labour debate'. Central to this debate has been the division of men into 'breadwinners' who support the family by their participation in the workforce, and women into 'consumers' involved in private housekeeping and childrearing in the home. Yet as Margaret Benston (1969) argues, women remain primarily producers, with their consumerism obvious but secondary. The invisibility of women as producers is compounded by their lack of opportunity to sell the product of their labour. Much of the analysis that emerged was clear that unless women are freed from their onerous domestic duties, including child-care, their presence in the work-force creates a dual and often conflicting role. This led to campaigns for the socialisation of the private sphere, including child-care. Mariarosa Dalla Costa and Selma James (1972) claim that while women's domestic work is productive it is unpaid yet vital to the reproduction of society and therefore should be reflected in wages for housework subsidised by the state. This argument is supported by Wally Secombe (1974). However, Margaret Coulson *et al.* (1975) maintained that he, Dalla Costa and James, and Benston, each assume that 'women' and 'housewives' are synonymous. For Coulson *et al.*, the central feature of women's position under capitalism is the fact that they are both domestic and wage labourers. Discussion within the debate focuses on why and how women's domestic labour has retained such significance in the reproduction and maintenance of the labour force (Gardiner, 1975). Critics suggest that although the debate has made an important contribution to feminist analyses, it has not fully addressed the problems faced by women. It tends towards economic determination, and a narrow concentration on the labour performed in the domestic sphere, at the expense of theorising other significant dynamics within the wider familial household context (Molyneux, 1979).

Purely economic arguments around the value, productivity and location of domestic labour have been further developed to include the dynamics of family relations within marriage. Juliet Mitchell (1974) maintains that while economic aspects of patriarchy can be affected and altered, through changes in the mode of production, both biological and ideological aspects will remain in place unless the 'psychosexual drama' at the core of gender relations is changed. For Christine Delphy (1976) the 'main enemy' is the collective of men who appropriate and directly benefit from domestic labour. Even when they work in paid employment, women's labour power is controlled by their partners and their earnings are regularly appropriated. It is Delphy's concern that Marxism restricts its analyses to the 'industrial mode' and neglects this focal 'family mode'.

While agreeing that the family represents a key factor in women's oppression, Michele Barrett (1980) contends that the state also has a role in organising and overseeing the relationship which exists between the family, domestic life and the labour force. Like Heidi Hartmann (1979), she asks: who benefits most from the sexual division of labour – capital or patriarchy? In this context Iris Young (1981) considers that all forms or stages of capitalism are patriarchal. While accepting that patriarchy preceded capitalism, she argues that women's struggle should be directed against the 'dual system'. The unification of the structural relations of capitalism and patriarchy has provided the basis for a range of critical writing but, as Alison Jaggar (1983) states, the exploitation of women is distinct from the exploitation of paid workers. She argues that the elimination of capitalism in no way guarantees the liberation of women. Domesticity and sexual violence are crucial aspects of sexual oppression which are frequently ignored. Reproductive freedom for women is hardly recognised as an issue within critical male discourses. Her work echoes that of Hartmann whose widely publicised work on the 'unhappy marriage of Marxism and feminism' illustrates the neglect of gender-related issues by neo-Marxists. She maintains that Marxist analysis of capitalism has to be complemented by a feminist analysis of patriarchy, thus providing an integrated explanation of gender and worker relations within advanced capitalist societies (Beechey, 1987; Cockburn, 1981; Bruegel, 1979).

Class relations clearly play a significant part in women's lives – the opportunity structures are different for professional women than for working-class women and black women experience institutionalised racism whatever their class (Davis, 1981). But the literature also shows that the private sphere of domestic work and responsibilities is a major determining context for women. The overemphasis of 'sex class' (Firestone, 1972) as the primary determinant in women's lives fails to address mediation by the relations of production and neo-colonialism. To consider capitalism and patriarchy as dual systems proposes a distinction which is equally untenable. Patriarchies exist beyond the boundaries of capitalist political economies. There are no non-patriarchal societies. Consequently, as Cynthia Cockburn (1981) and Ann Ferguson (1989) have argued, analysis of advanced capitalist patriarchies must assume the interdependence of all structural relations without setting them into false hierarchies of oppression. In contemporary Western states these relations are those of production, patriarchy and neo-colonialism.

Conclusion

As with late nineteenth-century feminist analysis, often labelled the 'first wave', other feminisms have united in their critique of Liberal feminism's neglect of power in its analysis. Reflecting the development of other theoretical perspectives, there is no monolithic or homogenous 'feminism'. There is, instead, a range of feminist perspectives which locate power – its centre and its relations – as fundamental to substantive and enduring change. Put simply, the primary focus of Marxist feminism has been class relations and class struggle, while 'Radical' feminism has emphasised patriarchy, especially as its relations oppress all women regardless of class. 'Socialist' feminism has been concerned particularly with the relations between capitalism and patriarchy. Black feminist writers have criticised the women's academic and political movement for its ethnocentric and pre-eminently Western bias. The significance of 'Psychoanalytic' feminist writing has gained new direction with the work of 'Post-structuralist' or 'Postmodern' feminists who acknowledge the validity of diversity. In order to demonstrate that there is not one but many feminisms, many texts and research studies begin with the categorisation of feminism. Reference texts which overview feminist work in terms of its theoretical and political categorisation have consolidated this trend (Kramarae and Spender, 1993; Humm, 1992; Gunew, 1991; Tong, 1989; Williams, 1989; Lacombe, 1988). This process has not been without problems. As with any forms of classification, false boundaries have been created, resulting in the crude reduction of often complex work to caricatures.

What has become clear over the last three decades of feminist debate is that while there is a shared recognition of the oppression of women, women individually and collectively experience oppression quite differently and from quite different sources. Class divisions do matter, as does cultural difference and racism. Women who step outside the parameters of compulsory heterosexuality not only suffer personally for their sexuality but also institutionally. Yet each of these examples indicates that the oppression of women will not be negotiated away via liberal reform or equal opportunities. While recognising the importance of guarding against 'false universalism' (Eisenstein, 1984), it is equally important not to lose sight of common aims because of the diversity and complexity of the struggle.

As a mainstream position, born within and nurtured by social democracy, Liberal feminism is removed from the debates covered throughout this chapter. But, as Susan Wendell (1987) suggests, it has specific commitments to social and political change which are not necessarily incompatible with the objectives of critical feminist perspectives. These include: the promotion of self-esteem and pursuit of greater recognition; equality of opportunity in work and education; the ending of sex prejudice and *de facto* discrimination; equality of legal rights; the use of education as a means of social reform. Within this agenda Liberal feminism has impacted on social policy and law reform. Yet securing concessions through legislation and policy does not guarantee change through implementation. An alternative view is that the very concessions won by Liberal feminism underwrite the future success of patriarchal power relations through the political incorporation of women's resistance and opposition. Given that Liberal reformist objectives are implementary, its priorities are the process of socialisation and practices of discrimination. While the desire for equality of opportunity is rational and plausible, the assumption that it can be realised through identifiable legal and social reforms is naive. Access to, and involvement in, the public sphere is clearly significant for women. The political/legal changes of the last twenty years have benefited many women's lives. But this has not extended to include the range of oppressive relations raised in this chapter. In fact it has been the failure of Liberal feminism to address the questions and issues fundamental to women's subordination – and the assumption that equality can be achieved through reform – which has led to dissent and fragmentation within women's politics.

The debates within approaches identified as fundamental (Acker and Warren Piper, 1984) have created their own differences and tensions. Yet, as Lydia Sargent (1981) indicates, each perspective has the capacity to influence and support others. The concern to theorise power within the structural and institutional relations which subordinate women, and the development of knowledge which analyses power and its dynamic impact on the lives of women, have done much to deconstruct the patriarchal and essentially masculinist paradigms. Critical approaches have emphasised the need to develop analysis into practice. Whatever their differences and priorities, whatever the strength of the political disputes involved, these approaches lay the ground for an eclectic and synthesised analysis of women's oppression and subjugation in all its diversity. They provide the basis not only for a critique of Liberal feminism and the claims of 'post-feminism', but also for interpreting the daily experiences of women in 1990s Britain.

Part Two

Chapter 3

Patronising Rita: The Myth of Equal Opportunities in Education

Introduction: The Limitations of Equal Opportunities Reformism

The 1990s opened with persistent calls for an evaluation of the previous thirty years of the women's movement, including considered reflection on the advances made by and for women in all aspects of their lives. Central to this assessment have been the changes in education and the impact on opportunities for girls and young women. Much has been written and assumed about education as providing the most powerful means either to challenge or to reinforce accepted values, attitudes, behaviour and knowledge. Consequently, teachers and schools are often held responsible for social ills and failings, ranging from lack of respect for authority and indiscipline among young people to soaring crime rates and lawlessness. The most common criticism is that 'progressive' methods have undermined traditional values. Yet, ironically, educational institutions remain at the forefront in the transmission and reproduction of dominant, traditional ideologies.

Until the late 1980s, education institutions and Local Education Authorities were left to implement strategies and policies at their own discretion. Central Government made great claims for the concept of 'individual freedom of choice and action'. Consequently, little was done to initiate change within the education system. The Sex Discrimination Act (1975), although not requiring significant action from schools, made some challenge to conventions of differentiating pupils by gender. Yet the emphasis was on 'equal opportunities' rather than a concern for sex equality. It was an equal opportunities direction more concerned with the principles of supporting existing economic principles and Liberal democratic politics than with addressing structural issues concerning power and its relations. As far as the Government was concerned, greater investment in girls and young women at school would provide a useful source of skilled labour when they entered the job market. The philosophy of equal opportunity did not challenge those policies and conditions which supported and maintained traditional, patri-archal family structures in which the roles of mother and housewife remained dominant in defining women's experiences. In fact many of the 'new' policies directly reinforced those structures, with the ideology of 'the family' essential to the future well-being of Britain's social and economic status. During the 1970s, 'preparation for parenthood' was a key construct in maintaining the ideological primacy of the family. The DES and DHSS published a number of White and Green Papers highlighting the role of the school curriculum in the area of personal life. They emphasised schools as central in the preparation of pupils for parenthood, providing the means through which the transference of inadequate parent behaviour through successive generations could be broken (Grafton *et al.*, 1987). Such a curriculum was also expected to reinforce 'appropriate' behaviour in relationships. More broadly, Madeleine Arnot (1987) argues that policy shifts during the 1970s, prompted by the Equal Opportunities Commission and supported by Her Majesty's Inspectors, only superficially affected education. This was a direct result of underfunding.

The tension between 'grass-roots' campaigns and 'top-down' initiatives for reform in education has been marked. Securing reform in individual schools and colleges and extending this to other institutions, without support and innovation from central government, is a difficult objective. Debate in education has mirrored that within feminist politics and takes the familiar line of reform versus revolution. For example, Sandra Acker (1986) believes that top-down Liberal initiatives, embodied in equal opportunities policies, are a means by which change can be achieved. She suggests that they can be combined with radical calls from feminist teachers to consolidate the movement for sex equality. The objective is to transform education through challenging the teaching profession, the structure of educational knowledge and conventional teaching styles. In contrast, Mary O'Brien (1986) argues that feminist principles and Liberal policies of equal opportunity are incompatible since liberalism is fundamentally patriarchal in theory and practice, despite the lip-service paid to women's rights and some of the benefits gained by women.

Although many women had been striving for equality individually, the Sex Discrimination Act did provide the basis for a teacher movement which constituted a major challenge to educational ideas and practices (Weiner and Arnot, 1987). Initially, concern focused on micro-analysis and classroom interaction studies as feminists observed and monitored the daily events of schools. The focus was the impact of gender differentiation on girls and boys, and practical change within classrooms or schools. Using their personal perceptions and practice as a starting point for change, teachers concentrated on developing projects which would reduce inequalities between the sexes. During the late 1970s and early 1980s, feminist research in schools provided detailed accounts of girls' experiences of schooling. The research identified issues for necessary change and provided information which could form the basis of policy initiatives prioritising equality for girls.

The liberal reformism underpinning equal opportunities policies suggested that by challenging sex-stereotyped expectations of teachers and pupils, and treating the sexes equally, gender inequality would disappear. Feminist critiques, however, stressed the importance of the broader political and economic contexts in which education occurs, since schooling remains an essential institution in the maintenance and reproduction of advanced capitalist patriarchies. Gaby Weiner (1985) suggests that by the early 1980s there was a polarisation of teacher perspectives between 'equal opportunity' and 'girl-centred' education. The diversity of projects was a result of differences in goals, concentration of ideas and strategies. Teachers committed to equal opportunities developed initiatives which focused on making schools more responsive to the needs of female pupils, i.e. 'girl-friendly' schooling (Whyte *et al.*, 1985). In contrast, teachers favouring girl-centred schooling developed 'anti-sexist' strategies (Kenway and Blackmore, 1993; Whyld, 1992; Weiner and Arnot, 1987).

In practice it is difficult to identify clear differences as teacher perspectives and strategies cross boundaries, and alliances are formed between individuals and/or groups who hold quite different opinions. Nevertheless, distinctions can be made between what Gaby Weiner and Madeleine Arnot (1987) term 'egalitarians' and 'radicals'. 'Egalitarians' advocate equal opportunities in an attempt to redistribute the rewards of education. The main aim is to improve the life chances of girls and women by equipping them to move into more highly paid jobs, previously dominated by men. Further, it is assumed that improved schooling and counselling should help women acquire senior management positions in education and other institutions. Equal opportunities are promoted in the belief that equality in schools benefits *all* pupils. There has been a commitment to enhancing the job prospects of girls by encouraging them to study male-dominated areas of the curriculum such as sciences and technology, while encouraging boys to be sensitive and caring parents by following traditionally female subjects like child-care. There has been some emphasis on improvement in teaching methods and raising awareness of inequality through the dissemination of research findings about gender inequality and through in-service work. Pupil initiatives include widening subject choice at secondary level, improving motivation for pupils to take 'non-traditional' subjects, and encouraging 'academically able' girls to choose a career or full-time paid employment rather than domesticity or part-time work.

Within radical, anti-sexist approaches there has been disagreement over the focus and most appropriate strategies since the perspective includes teachers with different political affiliations. Black feminists are critical of 'equal opportunity' and other initiatives which appear to concentrate exclusively on the needs of white female pupils and teachers. Lesbian feminists are concerned about the heterosexual bias present in most initiatives on gender. Socialist feminists put emphasis on anti-sexist initiatives but also stress and critique the persistent correspondence between current curriculum initiatives and advanced capitalism. Crucially, this position rejects distinctive strategies focusing on gender if they fail to recognise the centrality of class inequalities. However, radical perspectives are unified in their shared aim of transforming the current education system. Instead of improving the inadequacies of the existing system their goal is the transformation of its power base. Anti-sexist approaches highlight the extent of female oppression, particularly in schools, emphasising strategies geared to the empowerment of girls and women. The twin objectives place girls and women at the centre of classroom life while challenging the dominance of male experience. This prioritises the transformation of schools' curricula, organisation and structures.

There has been some resistance by teachers, most notably in inner-city schools, to the hidden sources and processes of gender differentiation and power within schooling. Critical teaching methods, including significant feminist contributions, which question dominant ideological assumptions and focus on anti-sexist and anti-racist strategies have emerged (Singh, 1994; Gill *et al.*, 1992; Marshall, 1992; Massey, 1991; AMMA, 1987; Williams, 1987). Yet these have been the subject of a backlash inspired by successive Conservative Governments and their obsession with trendy 'left' ideas in schools. While sexuality has been placed on the agenda, particularly exploration of the relationships between heterosexuality, homosexuality, lesbianism and homophobia (Epstein, 1994; Khayatt, 1992; Sears, 1992; Szirom, 1988) the media-inspired backlash has led to draconian legislation and policy directives governing sex education. Undoubtedly, feminist critiques and research have influenced policy and practice and inspired individual teachers in their classroom practice. But the resistance from within Government, teacher-training (Siraj-Blatchford, 1993), 'the profession', and many schools, has curtailed progression towards anti-sexist curricula and practice.

Girls' Experiences of Gender Discrimination in Education

Despite the strength and extent of the backlash against progressive change within education, the overarching suggestion is that the main objectives of the implementary approach from within Liberal feminism have been realised. It is proclaimed that women's continual and persistent upward mobility into the professions of their choice, via successful school/university education, is indisputable evidence of the 'post-feminist' society. If these claims are sustainable, however, they will be evidenced not only in the material success of those women who have 'benefited' from this unprecedented access, but in their personal experiences 'on the way up'. The ultimate stereotype of the successful woman is young, white, middle-class, professionally employed, heterosexual and childless. She is the recipient of the 1970s reforms, policies and laws, a representative of the successful first generation of 'post-feminism'.

The research focused on the experiences of a group of professional women whose school/university careers spanned the early 1960s through to the late 1980s. In-depth interviews focused on their experiences of education, work and interpersonal relationships in order to assess the impact of equal opportunities legislation, policies and practice. Their experiences are integrated within an overview of the key themes of feminist research in education to provide an examination of the effectiveness of policies aimed at challenging gender inequality in schools and higher education. For it was precisely this identifiable group which were the supposed beneficiaries of 1970s change. From their experiences, the strengths and deficiencies of implementary reforms can be assessed.

Liberal feminists have prioritised equal opportunities, socialisation, sex roles, gender stereotyping and sex discrimination in schooling. Although the issues of discrimination, rights, justice and fairness as power relations are sometimes ignored by Liberal feminists because they imply the impact of structures, Eileen Byrne (1987 p. 29) recognises the impact of policies as well as attitudes in creating a structure of disadvantage for girls. Inequality in education 'has its roots in social history which records the stereotyping of expected adult roles for men and women and the translation of these into different curricula'. Although this is more obvious in mixed-sex schools, separate curricular routes also exist in all-girls schools. These serve to emphasise the differences between those perceived to be 'career' women, who will compete on equal terms with men, and the rest. In single-sex grammar schools subject differentiation was based on the perceived academic ability of the girls. As Karen stated:

It was really only the high-flying girls who were expected to do the sciences. The rest of us did cookery and needlework.

Jane, one of the 'high fliers' at her grammar school, found that:

> The assumption tended to be that because we were such a minority they didn't make any allowance for us. For example, I was doing pure and applied Maths when the rest of the sixth form were doing General Studies.

When it came to choosing options Anna noted that:

> If you were doing sciences you were streamed away from the more arty things.

Those women in the study educated in mixed comprehensive schools were expected to perform well in certain subjects but not in others, with the Arts–Science division a key issue. Girls were marginalised in Science subjects:

> A lot more was expected of the boys, especially in Sciences. The girls were treated with a kind of sympathetic indulgence.
>
> (Mary)

> In the hard sciences the expectations were different – Physics and Maths. It didn't really matter if you didn't achieve if you were a girl.
>
> (Hilary)

According to Kate, the differences in expectation were based on perceived biological differences between the sexes. She commented that there was 'definitely an underlying feeling that you couldn't expect girls to do well at Physics because they weren't made that way'. These 'feelings' were reflected in the teachers' responses:

> Certainly I did feel that the boys were taken more notice of in Physics than the girls. You know, we were just left to get on with it. A lot of other girls used to notice that as well.... There were more boys in the class anyway and only a few of us girls and we were always shoved to the back and left to get on with things whereas the boys, when they'd got problems, people used to always be helping them out. They used to always get to set up the experiments and all those sorts of things whereas we were just like the women at the back, writing it all down on pieces of paper.
>
> (Ruth)

In Maths I know the boys got a lot more encouragement.

(Mary)

A Maths and Science orientation for boys, and an Arts orientation for girls dominated 'O' level selections in most mixed comprehensives in the study. Consequently, the proportion of boys taking Science and Maths in mixed schools was higher, as was the proportion of girls opting for Languages and Arts subjects. Only two women felt that the timetable in school did *not* reinforce the Science/Art divide. Those at Grammar schools were offered a limited choice of subjects but could participate in all their chosen subjects without difficulty. In the comprehensives, however, Home Economics was timetabled at the same time as CDT or Woodwork in three cases and against Pottery in another. One of the women who followed Sciences courses could not take General Studies, another could not follow Modern Studies, Economics or Latin, and a third had problems when she combined two Sciences with English Literature at 'A' Level, although the school changed the timetable to accommodate her choice.

It is now well established that sex-role stereotyping and differential socialisation occur through the division of the curriculum into options and their designation as girls' or boys' subjects (Riddell, 1992; Whyld, 1983). Alison Kelly (1987 p. 138) highlights this in her discussion of the construction of 'masculine science'. She reviews previous work and presents the findings of the Girls Into Science and Technology (GIST) project, concluding that the masculinity of physical sciences is reproduced in schools in two ways. First is the curriculum packaging of science, which takes boys' orientation to life as normal 'by its emphasis on controlling nature and its apparent irrelevance to people's lives'. Second is the nature of interactions in the laboratory, 'which give scope for boys' bravado and disdain for girls to be transformed into superior competence at science'.

Ruth's experiences were typical of those reported in Kelly's research – in the Science laboratory boys dominated the lessons *and* the apparatus. Girls passively listened while boys talked to the teacher, often using incorrect technical jargon or giving wrong explanations. Kelly concludes that one of the central pillars of patriarchal society – the assumed intellectual superiority of males – is acted out in the Science classroom where boys take priority over the apparatus, teacher attention and physical space. This limits girls' opportunities to learn.

The socialisation of children into sex-stereotyped occupational roles through set assumptions and subject-orientation has a well-established history. As Kelly also points out, children from primary schools see the Physics and Chemistry classes in the senior part of the secondary school as predominantly male. Eighty per cent of Science teachers are men. This conveys the message that Sciences are mainly for boys. Lesson content and organisation then reinforce such perceptions. Additionally, sex-stereotyped views of occupational and family roles, learned from the school curriculum, encourage and reinforce gender divisions in interpersonal relationships. As Sandra Acker (1987) suggests, this process serves to sustain young women's dependency and deference while denying young men their caring and emotional potential.

In addition to these common-sense assumptions, sex-stereotyping is reflected in many resources used in schools. For example, Glenys Lobban (1978, in Weiner and Arnot, 1987) studied reading schemes and found the sphere of people's activities divided into 'masculine' and 'feminine' parts with few common characteristics. The number of masculine options exceeded the feminine ones and tended to be more active, and to relate more to the outside world, than did the feminine options. These revolved almost entirely around domestic roles. Kelly (1987) found a similar situation in her assessment of Science resources. Typically, there were between two and ten times as many illustrations of, and references to, men and boys than to women and girls, both in published Science materials and school-provided worksheets. When women and girls appeared it was in stereotyped roles which served to emphasise their marginalisation in Science (Hardy, 1989).

In all-girl schools intellectual ability also led to other forms of differential treatment. Susan pointed out that those seen as academically bright received recognition whereas those seen as less academic had a harder time and were given less recognition for other abilities. Joanne felt that some of the 'bright' girls were ostracised, that they lacked social skills and stuck together. Both Karen and Jane felt that the distinction between the 'very bright' and the rest was emphasised and often reflected differences in family background. This led to conferred status within school:

> There were definite cliques of people who didn't really need to compete in the 'brightness' stakes because they were socially established in school. They'd come up from the prep school or they were from backgrounds which were perceived to be of some sort of higher order anyway. For example, I remember a group of girls who were all doctors' daughters. To be academically bright outside one of those groups was quite difficult ... Being well outside that group of people I certainly felt resentment from some of the girls and some of the staff.
>
> (Jane)

The girls who did exceptionally well were thought of as 'swots' and they were always held up as examples. A resentment bred between those who always did well at everything and those who had to struggle to do quite so well ... The girls who were brighter than the rest of us did tend to look down because all the time it was being geared to which University you were going to ... I felt different because of the family background I had, which I'd say is normal working class ... A lot of the people at the school had parents who were doctors, solicitors, teachers or vets – the majority of the girls had 'professional' parents and the others were just ordinary. I don't think the teachers made a distinction but those of us who came from my sort of background felt it because of the people who were always on about what their fathers were doing or which college their mother was lecturing at this week. It was terrible because you just felt you couldn't compete with them. You felt awful feeling embarrassed about what your own parents did, but you did.

(Karen)

In mixed schools too there was a feeling of resentment between those seen as 'bright girls' and the others. Ruth recalled that, as 'the bright girl' in the CSE class:

You did feel like there was some sort of gang going on about it. They were never actually really unpleasant to me but you did feel like you were almost letting the side down. You felt like you were being a traitor.

Anna substantiated this:

Before you were banded, when you were all mixed together, it wasn't OK for a girl to be bright. Girls who weren't so bright were really antagonistic to the ones who were.

She felt this also to be true as far as boys were concerned:

In a group of guys, if one of the guys was academically bright that was OK but if one of the girls was academically bright I think some of the guys felt threatened by that so they used to alienate them from the rest of the girls by saying that they were boring or swotty. It wasn't OK for you to be bright if you were a girl from a guy's point of view.

However, she suggested that '... once you were banded and were all more or less the same intellectual ability it didn't matter much'. For Mary, streaming had a positive effect in the responses of boys to 'bright' girls in that 'you were an honorary boy'.

Liberal feminists argue that equality of opportunity is the solution to the under-achievement and under-expectation of girls at school. According to Susan Wendell (1987 pp. 84–85), equality of opportunity in children's education requires giving boys and girls the same: 'conditions for developing basic skills and knowledge', 'information about jobs and roles available', 'means of acquiring whatever specific (professional) skills and knowledge are necessary', 'conditions for physical development' and 'treatment in their psychological development'.

Byrne (1987) also suggests that 'equal' means 'the same', with equal opportunities in school enabling personal fulfilment. Thus individuals follow their chosen paths rather than being forced to follow girls'/boys' subjects. Both sexes would be educated for the best career opportunities rather than emphasising careers for boys and servicing, homemaking and personal relationships for girls. She proposes that, once identified, discrimination can be 'attacked at the active source, in the practices of a single, finally accountable group – the employers, the headteacher, or governors, the committees that authorise rules and practices' (ibid., p. 31). Byrne argues that other factors are inextricably interwoven with the influences of innate or conditioned inequality and subtle or overt discrimination. These include prejudice, role-conditioning, sex-role stereotyping, the influence of inherited assumptions from the (male) leadership of the past and the restrictive influence of practical factors (e.g. institutionalised sexism in education establishments, or the methods and administrative framework under which resources are differentially allocated). Nevertheless, Byrne concludes that equality of provision and delivery provide the route to elimination of under-achievement and under-expectation of girls at school, underwriting real freedom of curricular choice and aspiration.

Male Knowledge, Power and Sexuality

In education feminist work prioritising structural changes geared to the elimination of male dominance and patriarchal institutions has concentrated on male monopolisation of knowledge and culture, and the sexual politics of daily life in schools and colleges. Dale Spender (1982) suggests that mainstream 'academic' knowledge is, in fact, the record of decisions and activities of men in which women's contribution has been ignored or disparaged. Male dominance is seen as logical and natural, and schools contribute to its acceptance. The 'language of learning' controls the way that girls and women conceptualise themselves, their world and beyond. This process begins from the moment girls enter school, as Naima Browne and Pauline France (1985) illustrate in their discussion of sexist talk in the nursery (Attar, 1990; Spender, 1980). Sandra Acker (1987) identifies the 'gatekeeping' process in education which silences women and allows men to dominate decision-making. The social and political construction of male knowledge has implications for the school curriculum and power relations since access to power and policy-making are based on gender throughout education.

Teacher expectation plays a major role in defining gender stereotypes and marginalising girls. As discussed earlier, teachers' attention remains unequally divided to the advantage of boys. Michelle Stanworth (1981) relates how girls are marginalised in the classroom, how teachers have lower expectations of girls and respond less positively towards them. She considers pupils' experience of this behaviour and its effect on views about themselves and the other sex.

In contrast to Byrne, Pat Mahony (1985) argues that 'equal' treatment of boys and girls in education may produce unequal outcomes since prior socialisation ensures that girls and boys have differential competence or interest in certain subjects or activities. This suggests that through the very initiatives taken to redress inequalities girls may be set up to 'fail'. Barbara Licht and Carol Dweck (1987) discuss girls' lack of confidence, from pre-school age, in challenging intellectual tasks despite the fact that young girls consistently and generally perform as well as, if not better than, boys. They found that girls are more likely than boys to attribute failure to ability, while boys are more likely to blame lack of effort as the cause of difficulties in understanding a concept or performing a task correctly. Licht and Dweck point out that, if anything, girls should come to expect greater academic achievements since they receive consistently higher grades in primary school. Explanations for the persistent underestimation of their successes by girls include sex-role stereotyping and differential treatment by teachers towards girls and boys. Both sexes are encouraged to present themselves in a socially acceptable way so that girls are modest while boys are self-confident. Licht and Dweck suggest that girls are more sensitive to negative feedback while boys are more sensitive to positive feedback. Girls are likely to be neater, better behaved and will work harder to please the teacher and 'achieve'. Because girls receive less criticism over effort or discipline, both teachers and girls are more likely to attribute failures to lack of ability rather than insufficient effort. Yet girls' failure to achieve often reflects lack of effort or ineffective teaching methods. The long-term impact of girls' inhibitions is considerable and raises questions concerning the education and re-education of boys (Askew and Ross, 1988; Mahony, 1985; Deem, 1984).

As well as illustrating the differences in teacher expectation over subjects and ability, the research interviews also reinforced Dale Spender's (1982) description of the way girls receive messages concerning gender roles in the classroom:

> Girls were expected to conform a lot more to school rules, teacher expectations, standards of work. In the Sciences it was generally acknowledged that boys would be OK and they spent a lot more time with the boys explaining things to them because they were expected to be more intelligent about it. They were rather impatient about explaining things to the girls.
>
> (Mary)

> I think we were expected to run around a bit more and do things for people. You got praised for helping the teacher and that kind of thing.
>
> (Liz)

Katherine Clarricoates (1987) points out that girls are criticised for academic failure but ignored if they are successful. In addition, she describes the sexism in language used by staff, in books and by pupils at school, and the gearing of subjects or topics to the perceived interests of boys. The women interviewed were affected greatly by differential responses of male and female teachers at school:

> The sex of my teachers influenced the way in which lessons went. Certainly girls always felt much more comfortable with a female teacher and the boys with a male teacher. I always felt threatened by male teachers . . . I always felt they put me down, or they never took pains to notice my abilities. I always felt that some of the women teachers recognised the abilities I had and tried to bring them out . . . There was never a male teacher who did that, ever, in any subject I can recall.
>
> (Janet)

Mary felt that male teachers had higher expectations of the pupils and expected more contributions from them in class. She thought that they were more relaxed towards each pupil as a person. In the girls' Grammar schools the differences between male and female staff was even more noticeable:

> The male teachers were mostly young. The rest of the teachers in the school tended to be older, single women. The arrival of young men with different teaching ideas caused quite a stir. In the sixth form

there was certainly a closer personal relationship between the young teachers who were sixth form tutors in so far as, towards the end of the sixth form, we called them by their first names. There was a lot of teasing and so on ... There was a lot of flirtation and I feel, looking back, that they were really in their element as far as their egos were concerned. They were coming into a school which had no real behavioural problems, people who were reasonably bright so they didn't have to tackle any of those difficulties, and, of course, they were awash in a sea of sixth form girls.

(Jane)

A couple of the male teachers flirted with the older girls. They were in their mid-30s. I don't think any 'out of college' males would have been allowed in our school. It was all very much more jokey with the men than with the women teachers.

(Karen)

While Karen recalled that 'male teachers were definitely not as hard on us as the women teachers were' she went on to say that:

You would always quite readily go and talk to a female teacher if you were having problems with your homework or work but not so readily to a male teacher.

The feminist critiques of the broader dynamics of male power have placed sexuality and sexual harassment high on the agenda. The experiences of the interviewees exemplify the abuse of power by male teachers towards young female students, particularly in all-female schools. Jane described an encounter in which one of the male teachers asked her out while at a social event towards the end of her sixth form. Although she did not feel threatened, and was able to refuse without actually saying 'no', she remembered feeling uncomfortable whenever she subsequently met him in school. Susan also noted the changed dimension involved in being a 'young woman' at school:

In the sixth form you were certainly much more aware of male/female relationships and a sexual dimension in your relationship, being older. I don't feel this was ever abused with me. I think it was abused with other people.

In post-school education male tutors responded in a more overt manner towards female students:

> There was a reasonable amount of what I suppose they considered to be teasing which actually was ridicule ... There was a crude assumption that I wouldn't be able to handle a circuit board or reassemble something which had been taken to pieces. They [technicians] always intervened in what I suppose they considered to be the nicest possible way. It wasn't aggressive but a case of 'let me do that for you' and if I said 'no thanks' they did it anyway.
>
> (Jane, Metallurgy)

This often took the form of sexual harassment ...

> There were some who were very sexist. For example, there were some lecturers who would go on about legs and bottoms and things like that and therefore used to pay more attention to girls with nice legs and big breasts.
>
> (Mary, Osteopathy)

> If you were a woman it was OK to go along and get help and he'd spend all the time that you wanted. But there was some degree of sexual harassment attached to that.
>
> (Kate, Sociology)

The extent to which boys, often aided by male teachers, oppress, demean or harass girls, and sometimes women teachers, has been highlighted by other researchers (Skelton, 1994; Jones, 1985). Pat Mahony (1985) points out that it is not simply that girls receive less teacher time, but that their contributions in class are met with systematic ridicule from boys, and that their existence outside school is filled with non-verbal abuse and physical molestation. Half of the women who went to mixed schools remembered experiencing abuse from male classmates. The following statements are typical:

> The boys would make personal comments, especially once you got to the secondary school. I suppose now it would be thought of as sexual harassment really. It was verbal, not nasty, just comments about physical appearance.
>
> (Liz)

> I was actually assaulted by a bloke who came over and groped me. Lots of blokes used to grope me and make silly propositions during lessons. This happened to all the girls. Nothing was done about it. It was usually a female teacher trying to deal with it and she usually wasn't very effective. She'd shout at them or send them outside but

it certainly didn't stop their behaviour. I can remember that the boys used to abuse the female teachers as well, just verbally. It was accepted by other members of the class, by the school in general.

(Ruth)

In a study of boys' sex talk, Julian Wood (1987) shows the prevalence of girls' objectification in terms of physique and physicality. Focusing on the body, boys employ a 'sequence of invasions' to label girls sexually, using such categories as 'slag', 'whore', 'frigid'. Sue Lees (1993; 1987) also discusses the labelling of girls and relates this to an explanation of social behaviour in which girls should be attached to, and dominated by, males. Carol Jones (1985) describes a secondary school covered with woman-hating graffiti and pornographic drawings where, as in many schools, male violence in the form of visual, verbal and physical harassment is part of the daily routine for girls. Attempts to challenge this prevalence produced indifference or hostility from male staff.

For most women these circumstances continue in further or higher education establishments. Male students, often collectively, harass women students, both subtly and more overtly.

The women worked hard and got high marks. The men didn't generally, usually pratted around and actually behaved as a group in lectures so that they could get away with it. It was not the 'in thing' to ask questions or work diligently so they would back each other up to have a good laugh in lectures at other people's expense. I was harassed during my fourth year because it was predicted that I would get a first – verbal harassment. The sexual harassment was more just looking you up and down.

(Hilary, B.Ed. PE Secondary)

The other students, guys, got worse as we got towards the end of the course because, as they gradually turned into young doctors, they adopted what the tutors were like, although at the start most of them believed in equal rights and didn't see why women couldn't be doctors ... It was subtly done. It was definitely there though. Most female doctors complain about it afterwards.

(Anna, Medicine)

I do think some of the male students on other courses thought that they could do whatever they wanted with any of the girls ... a lot of the blokes on the campus thought that the women were there for their benefit and made this obvious in the way they spoke about them, related to them and sat in the bar and ogled at them. I mean just the whole treatment of women at college.

(Karen, B.Ed. Primary)

Sexual harassment and abuse take different forms when combined with racism (Suleiman and Suleiman, 1985) or when it is directed against both sexes who breach norms of heterosexuality (Jones and Mahony, 1989; Anon, 1986, cited in Acker, 1987). Writers, including Lees (1987) and Mahony (1989), propose the necessity of challenging the denigration of girls and the pervasiveness of verbal and physical abuse. In addition they assert that powerful and taken-for-granted assumptions about sexuality, which reflect and reinforce heterosexuality and the subordinate position of women to men, need to be contested.

The interviews provided strong evidence that post-school expectations of women were not confined to academic achievement and practical ability to perform tasks, but extended to gender-appropriate behaviour and personal presentation:

A lot of things in medicine are quite emotional and I think sometimes you wouldn't say things because you thought 'Well that's going to be constructed as a typically feminine response to something', even if you felt you were justified in saying something, because it was very much a masculine setting.

(Anna, Medicine)

With the exception of Andrea, who was encouraged to wear what she chose, the women who worked on professional placements were each given informal instructions regarding dress. Mary (Osteopathy) was instructed to wear a dark skirt and tights while the men wore dark trousers. Women had to wear 'proper shoes' (not sandals) and a white overall. Susan (Clinical Psychology) was told that women were not to wear denim and for men ties were essential. Ruth (Speech Therapy) felt that she was expected to be 'conservative', 'smart' and 'subdued'. For women teachers trousers were not permissible and men had to wear suits or jacket/trousers plus tie.

You had your pre-teaching practice pep-talk and during that you were told all the things you mustn't do and one of the things you were told was to dress in skirts and dresses and be smart, whatever that means. It was a general thing – 'look presentable'.

(Liz, B.Ed. Secondary)

An emphasis on the 'right' clothes was emphasised during Hilary's (B.Ed.

Secondary) training and students were marked on presentation. Women in medical training also were not allowed to wear trousers, and suits and ties were demanded of male students.

> You were expected to dress in a certain way, expected to look conventional. There was one girl who had her hair done purple and she was sent home. They didn't really approve if you had a sort of punky, spiky style. You were in danger of failing your orals if you turned up in 'alternative' dress. They didn't approve of big, dangly earrings either ... They reckoned that if you were conventionally dressed your patients would have more confidence in you.
>
> (Anna, Medicine)

Feminist research and analysis has promoted discussion about, and increased awareness of, the dynamics of male power in schools. For staff who strive towards reducing power differentials, emphasis has been placed on teaching methods which are non-hierarchical, less competitive and more participatory. In an attempt to provide a supportive and encouraging environment for young women some feminist teachers propose separate schools for girls and boys or segregation within mixed-sex schools (Hanefin and Nicharthaigh, 1993; Riordan, 1991; Whyld, 1986; Mahony, 1985; Deem, 1984).

Power and Class

The Marxist critiques of education (Bowles and Gintis, 1976; Dale *et al.*, 1981) emphasise the significance of 'correspondence' between the curriculum and the demands of advanced capitalism. In this work schools are seen to be institutions geared to the maintenance and reproduction of social divisions in the labour market, determined by the contemporary needs of capitalism. Socialist feminist analyses suggest that sexual divisions in the wage and domestic labour forces, the patterns of sex segregation in paid and unpaid work, and the division between the public (male) sphere of the economy and the private (female) sphere of domestic life are seen to be reproduced at school. The function of the education system is seen to be to satisfy the requirements of the labour market through the curriculum, the school organisation, and the teachers as agents (Gaskell, 1991; Shilling, 1989; O'Donnell, 1984).

Thus the division of the curriculum into options designated as girls' and boys' is not perceived to be simply the consequence of sex-role stereotyping and differential socialisation. Rather, it is viewed as being fundamental to the perpetuation of the sexual and social divisions of labour which underpin advanced capitalism. Girls form the majority of pupils taking child-care and parental role options and this has significant consequences for future roles (Attar, 1990; Grafton *et al.*, 1987; Mitsch-Bush, 1987). Marion Scott (1980 p. 100) suggests that the school plays a part in relegating girls and women 'to a unique place in the family and a specific place in the workforce'. At school, women (and also men) are taught what are considered to be appropriate skills as well as 'appropriate' behaviour. She suggests that educational assumptions are made about women. According to Grafton *et al.* (1987 p. 109) these include: priority of marriage and family; denial of full-time paid work or career; limitation of paid work to gender-appropriate jobs; insignificance of paid work, with income viewed as inessential. These assumptions are highlighted by the 'choice' of curriculum options open to girls at school and the expectations of staff regarding achievement and behaviour. They are also reinforced by the attitudes towards, and expecta-tions of, young women in post-school training. Where the women inter-viewed were involved in vocational courses taught by male tutors, in what were perceived as 'male' occupations, the differentiations were clear:

> There was a lot of patronising, a lot of unnecessary interest, put it that way, in my work. I felt particularly scrutinised. At the end of the two years I came out with some of the highest marks on the course and I felt from an early stage that there was a great deal of resentment about that and I certainly remember my work being scrutinised in a very critical way.
>
> (Jane, Industrial Chemistry)

Again, the women were marginalised and their abilities undermined.

> We were lectured by a lot of members of the dental and medical departments and they were totally patronising – didn't seem to think that we were capable of understanding anything and it was very very sexist. There were lots of connotations about the fact that we were silly females.
>
> (Ruth, Speech Therapy)

It was often suggested that the women were not fulfilling their 'proper' function in the private realm of the home and family:

> There were only ever two female medical consultants, the rest of our tutors were all men. They tended to be sort of – it was the guys who were going to get the consultant jobs, it was the guys who were going

to get on in medicine and girls were going to finish their course and probably go into general practice and if they didn't do that they'd get married anyway so there wasn't really a lot of point teaching them.

(Anna, Medicine)

As Marion Scott (1980 p. 97) points out, 'Within capitalism schools play a major part in the reproduction of the productive forces'. Thus, the division of labour is learnt in schools. This has a class basis, as consistent patterns of success or failure perpetuate the success of middle-class pupils and the failure of the majority of working-class children. Scott highlights the fact that only a few can succeed in meritocratic societies but that the ideology of the society is shared by all. Schools maintain the production of a workforce with a particular level (or lack) of skill and help to reinforce common-sense assumptions and expectations. The differentiation of the workplace is reflected and perpetuated through a division of the curriculum into 'mental' and 'manual', and through the separation of academic subjects (e.g. Arts and Sciences). Within this, girls and women are educated to enter the workforce as low-paid, low status part-time employees *and* to take responsibility for housework and child-care, simultaneously reproducing and nurturing the workforce.

The sexist ideology underpinning division of labour in the workforce and the home was the cornerstone of successive post-war educational reports. For example, the Newsom Report (1963 p. 37) stated: 'For girls too, there is a group of interests relating to what many, perhaps most of them, would regard as their most important vocational concern, marriage . . . many girls are ready to respond to work relating to the wider aspects of home-making and family life and the care and upbringing of children'. Even in professions which tend to be predominantly female, mainly so-called 'caring professions', the positions of responsibility were deemed inaccessible to women:

Their very attitude towards the female students was very patronising – 'the little teacher' – and they didn't expect you to have a thought in your head. You were going to be the teachers and you would never make the head because the few men on the course would always be the heads and deputies and we would be the classroom teachers for the rest of our lives.

(Karen, B.Ed. Primary)

Miriam David (1984) outlines how the structure of the curriculum and the gender emphasis of options are reinforced and perpetuated by pupil, teacher and parental expectations. These are also applicable to many women's experiences in post-school training. Although the families of the women interviewed were supportive and encouraging of their daughters' chosen careers, the misgivings of some were illustrated by Karen's grandfather, who could not understand why she had chosen teaching as opposed to banking 'or a sensible job where I'd earn a lot more money and use my brain!!'.

As Sheila Scraton (1989) argues, the strength of Socialist feminist analysis within education is that it has emphasised the significance of gender divisions as well as class divisions within capitalism. It is a 'dual' correspondence: to the needs of advanced capitalism and to the demands of patriarchy. Central to this is the role of school in reproducing or perpetuating a sexual as well as a social division of labour in the family and in the workplace. The main areas of concern are differentiation in training and links between school and motherhood. Hilary Gaskell (1986, cited in Acker, 1987) studied the notion of skill – often seen as a consequence of formal education and a determinant of occupational placement and its rewards. However, she claims that 'skill' is a socially constructed category limiting girls' access to training and experience on the basis of 'natural' differentiation. This differentiation starts in school where girls are trained in office skills, such as data processing, but not in allied areas such as computer science or management. Thus the partnership between education and the economy operates to confirm large numbers of girls and women in restricted, low-paid sectors of employment (Cockburn, 1985; Griffin, 1985). Miriam David (1984) argues that, because 'motherhood' places restrictions on paid employment, schools utilise, emphasise and perpetuate the sexual division of labour in the home by expecting mothers to be pre-school educators and unpaid helpers in school when their children begin to attend full-time.

In terms of a politics of reproduction, demanded by advanced capitalism and patriarchy, the issue is further complicated by the structural relations of neo-colonialism (James and Busia, 1993; Amos and Parmar, 1987; Carby, 1987). In complex, 'Western' societies it is no coincidence that institutionalised racism, founded on the international movement and exploitation of labour, has created and consolidated formerly immigrant communities as economically disadvantaged and politically excluded. This discrimination has been structurally maintained through schooling (Brah and Minhas, 1985). For girls, often experiencing patriarchal expectations within their own cultures and religions, the interplay of sexism and racism within the school has created a unique dynamic of oppression (Chivers, 1987; Foster, 1985; Suleiman and Suleiman, 1985; Swann, 1985). It is important here not to establish class, gender and race as a hierarchy of oppression but to underline the significance of these dynamics in the material and personal lives of young black women, whose marginalisation is a combination of all three determining contexts.

Current Directions in Education Policy

The education system has always been a priority in women's struggles for equality. Ironically, while schools and other education establishments perpetuate and reinforce gender inequalities, they *can* provide both the location to question and challenge these inequalities, and significant opportunities for women in their struggle for personal freedom. For Liberal feminists, strategies for change focus on attempts to alter the socialisation process, change attitudes and use legal and policy processes. They see the creation of conditions for equality as a long-term project, the accomplishment of which depends partly on state control (e.g. over public education institutions), and partly on personal-political efforts to change child-rearing practices, to inform young people of their choices, and to draw attention to positive role models.

Gaby Weiner (1985) points out that the move towards equality of opportunity in the early 1980s emphasised equal allocation of school resources and educational benefits rather than positive discrimination in favour of girls. This limited strategies for educational change; the main aim of such equal opportunities approaches being 'to encourage girls and women to move into privileged and senior positions in existing educational institutions rather than seek any fundamental changes in schooling' (Weiner, 1985 pp. 7–8). While this advanced discussion over gender issues, it had minimal impact on school life and neglected issues of power and decision-making in education. Further, an emphasis on individual attitudes led to a form of psychological reductionism in which the 'victim' was blamed for her (socialised) lack of perception or confidence. This left untouched the structural relations and institutionalised practices which embody power and its administration (Connell, 1985). Critics acknowledge that Liberal feminists are increasingly aware of 'internal' as well as 'external' barriers to women's achievement. They are beginning to recognise the effects of a total environment of male supremacy on women's perceptions of themselves and the way it moulds their interests, needs and wants, limiting their ambition, determination and perseverance. However, while the Liberal feminist critique of education recognises oppression it neglects the *roots* of oppression (S. Scraton, 1989). Although changes by individual teachers, schools or Local Education Authorities undoubtedly benefit girls and women, they remain short-term gains since the broader structural relations of patriarchy, capitalism and neo-colonialism are neglected.

Before 1989, the content of the curriculum was generally chosen and implemented at the discretion of individual teachers, usually in consultation with colleagues within the school. Although advice or recommendations were suggested by bodies such as county advisers and Her Majesty's

Inspectorate (HMIs), schools were not obliged to act. In the mid-1980s, HMIs showed an awareness of, although not always overt commitment to, equal opportunities in their 'Curriculum Matters' papers. For example, *Geography from 5 to 16* (DES, 1986 p. 4) states: '... fundamental is the need to ensure that geographical learning offers equal interests and opportunities to girls and boys ... As the content of geography focuses on people and places, teachers have a particular responsibility to ensure that they avoid bias and stereotyping in the images which they present and in the ideas and explanations they offer'. The *History from 5 to 16* (DES, 1988 p. 26) suggests that: '... history courses should ensure that women are not "invisible", that their changing social roles are made clear and that interpretations of the past which demean or obscure their experiences are avoided'.

The 1986 Education Act contained new statutory requirements but reinforced traditional assumptions and ideas about 'appropriate' education. Responsibility for the teaching of sex education, Religious Education and special needs provision was given to the governing bodies of schools. Although individual governing bodies now formulate the sex education curriculum, the manner and context in which sex education occurs must be clearly explained within school brochures. Additionally, the Government requires that courses are taught with 'due regard to moral considerations and the value of family life' (DES, 1986 Section 46). Circular 11/87 (DES, 25.9.87) emphasises this requirement and reiterates the aims of sex education programmes. These include appreciation of 'the benefits of stable married and family life and the responsibilities of parenthood'. It also points out that: 'There is no place in any school in any circumstances for teaching which advocates homosexual behaviour, which presents it as the "norm", or which encourages homosexual experimentation by pupils ... It must also be recognised that for many people ... homosexual practice is not morally acceptable ...'. Recent directives from the Secretary of State for Education reinforce such statements (Circular 5/94). With sexuality restricted to heterosexuality the potential for enabling students to understand sexual relationships is seriously restricted. Consequently, the ideology of 'compulsory heterosexuality' has been reaffirmed and the marginalisation of alternative sexualities has been guaranteed.

In her article Madeleine Arnot (1987) questioned whether there might be a move towards more centralised planning which could attempt to enforce policy on schools. Within two years, in 1989, the Conservative Government introduced the National Curriculum for English, Science and Mathematics for all 5 year-old children in England and Wales. It was envisaged that by 1993 all children up to GCSE level should have begun the three core subjects, and by 1995 the foundation subjects (Geography, History, Technology, Art, Music,

PE) should have been implemented at every age. Effectively, the importance of local autonomy, diversity of provision and an emphasis on the value of teachers as agents of change has been overturned. The introduction of the National Curriculum led to the implementation of policy 'from above'. From 1995 all pupils will follow the same curriculum, with no 'opting out' at age thirteen. The proposed aim of the National Curriculum is to ensure uniformity within and between schools. It is premissed on the notion of equal opportunity for *all* pupils.

In its 1989 document, *A Framework for the Primary Curriculum*, the National Curriculum Council (NCC) stated that, in addition to the National Curriculum core and foundation subjects, every teacher in each area of the curriculum should address the 'cross curricular' skills, themes and dimensions. These skills include communication skills (oracy, literacy), numeracy, problem-solving and study skills. The themes are those elements deemed to enrich the educational experience of pupils, such as Economic and Industrial Understanding, Careers Education and Guidance, Environmental Education, Health Education and Citizenship. The cross-curricular dimensions are the personal and social development of pupils throughout the curriculum as a whole, education for life in a multi-cultural society through awareness of cultural diversity, and equality of opportunity. In 1990 the NCC published *The Whole Curriculum* in which it is acknowledged that access to an 'equal' curriculum is often barred. When outlining what it saw as the way forward, the NCC suggested that 'a commitment to providing equal opportunities for all pupils ... should permeate every aspect of the curriculum'. It argued that the National Curriculum ensures that all pupils have access to the curriculum since a common curriculum is compulsory. Some of the 'more subtle barriers' standing in the way of access to the curriculum were acknowledged, with reference to gender, cultural diversity and special educational needs. The report recommended that 'schools need to take account of and challenge the attitudes present in society which consider that subjects such as mathematics, science and technology are less relevant for girls than for boys'. The proposed remedy was 'to foster a climate in which equality of opportunity is supported by a policy to which the whole school subscribes and in which the positive attitudes to gender equality, cultural diversity and special needs of all kinds are actively promoted' (ibid., pp. 2–3).

There is no obvious gender bias in the statements of attainment or programmes of study in any current National Curriculum documents (Smithers and Zientek, 1991) but it is only in the non-statutory guidelines that the significance of equal opportunities is mentioned. In the core subjects, even in the non-statutory guidelines, any reference is scant and generalised in terms. The non-statutory guidelines for the foundation subjects are more explicit and make some references to specific issues. For example, the

History document (1991c pp. C18–C19) includes a section entitled 'Equal Opportunities and Multicultural Education', which outlines the use of history to examine and challenge the views of women and 'minority groups' through past and present historical evidence. In the Geography document (1991b pp. 18–19) cross-curricular dimensions are also specifically mentioned. It is suggested that 'Geography helps pupils consider similarities and differences between individuals, groups and communities', and that 'Considering similarities first, and differences second, can help to promote positive images and challenge myths, stereotypes and misconceptions'. The proposals for Design and Technology (1989) and Physical Education (1991a) were more explicit, containing sections on 'Gender' and 'Sex and Gender'. Both emphasised the need to avoid stereotypes and extend pupils' 'capabilities and range of interests beyond conventional horizons' (DES, 1989 p. 6). The PE proposals were comparatively radical in their discussion of the positive effects PE can have in challenging stereotypes, masculinity and sex differentiated activities (1991a, pp. 57–58). However, the final documents were less detailed.

Generally, the non-statutory guidelines for National Curriculum documents refer to the need for consideration of equal opportunities and highlight the need to question stereotypes. Some also contain acknowledgement of past discrepancies, or omissions, and suggest possible strategies to overcome these and redefine subject content. In October 1993, the School Curriculum and Assessment Authority (SCAA) took over the role of the NCC and the School Examination and Assessment Council. SCAA is now responsible for dissemination of information relating to the requirements of the National Curriculum. The proposed alterations to the National Curriculum, due to be implemented in September 1995, focus entirely on subject content (SCAA, May 1994). Discussion, and the current recommendations revolve around the reduced number of attainment targets and a move towards general level descriptions rather than specific statements of attainment. The cross-curricular skills, themes and dimensions are not mentioned at all. Schools consequently depend on previous documentation from the NCC in these areas.

With the stated requirement that all schools should have agreed policies and practices on cross-curricular dimensions (NCC, 1989 p. 13), teachers of all subjects *should* be involved in evaluating current resources, lesson content and teaching practice to ensure that the cross-curricular dimensions are present, via a 'curriculum audit' for each subject which matches current provision against the requirements of the Education Reform Act, 1988. Whole-curriculum development plans, consistent with local/national guidelines and reflecting the needs of individual schools and their pupils, are the objective. They are proposed as working documents, subject to constant review and revision. The NCC (1990) recommended that a school should check whether it has policies for particular aspects of the curriculum, such as equal opportunities and multi-cultural education, during any policy review.

As Pat Hughes (1991) suggests, schools 'need to develop their own meanings for the catch-all phrase "equal opportunities"'. This can lead to substantive discussion over the need for policies which include equal opportunities and the kind of teaching strategies promoted by them (Rudduck, 1993; O'Brien, 1989). It also requires some agreement on what is meant by equal opportunities. Within this, consideration should be given to a number of areas. Organisational factors such as children lining up separately, the segregation of names by gender on registers and class lists, the use of boys for some 'jobs' and girls for others, each give official approval to differentiation between the sexes. Additionally, they affect children's views of themselves and what it means to be male/female. Classroom practice is often covertly sexist and discriminatory since much of the language used in school excludes women and children, and generic terms such as 'man' and 'he' are used to mean 'people', or 's/he'. As discussed earlier, resources, activities and subjects are often viewed as gender-appropriate. Stereotyped images, attitudes and expectations are presented to pupils in resources and by teachers, and boys receive more teacher attention than girls. Each issue needs to be raised, its occurrence questioned and then challenged. Discussion about gender issues is frequently heated since personal opinions form the basis of much educational practice and the teaching profession is often resistant to changes, particularly when 'traditional' common-sense assumptions are being called to account. Awareness-raising is an important first step in the discussion of gender equality but it is not possible to eradicate all sexist or discriminatory material from schools and introduce stereotype-free resources overnight. However, once it is a policy commitment to ensure resources are not discriminatory, teachers can actively seek out, purchase, or borrow resources which give positive images of girls and challenge other forms of discrimination. It is some measured success that 'packs' or schemes recently published to enhance, or cover, the National Curriculum have been written with a commitment to equal opportunities (Evans, 1988; Walker, 1988).

The limitations of such advances are raised by Alan Smithers and Pauline Zientek (1991) in their study *Gender, Primary Schools and the National Curriculum.* They found that 62.7 per cent of the teachers they interviewed considered that, while the National Curriculum would help lessen gender stereotyping because all children are compelled to take the full range of subjects, the 'National Curriculum will not bring all the benefits that it could, including counteracting gender stereotyping, if the teachers are not properly supported to make it work' (ibid., p. 24). They recommend that this support should take the form of provision of non-contact time, smaller classes and increased resourcing.

Clearly, the National Curriculum provides the basis to develop and implement equal opportunities policies which have to be understood, put into practice and monitored by all staff in each school. Some non-statutory guidelines are progressive, even radical, in their recognition that pupils do not start from equal knowledge and confidence and therefore separate strategies, including single-sex grouping, may be required. Realistically, the effective implementation of equal opportunities evident in mainstream directives, or more radical policies, depends on the allocation of time for teachers to become familiar with the guidelines, discuss their implications in school, assess current practice, evaluate existing resources, consider alternatives or additional material, and develop appropriate policies followed by effective monitoring procedures. This requires commitment on the part of the teaching staff, headteachers and governors of individual schools. Additionally, local and national education authorities must be committed to equal opportunities and to demonstrate this through the production of clear statements (for example ILEA, 1985) and the allocation of funding to enable the implementation of policies (Arends and Volman, 1992; Wilson, 1991).

The performance of girls and young women has improved, with greater numbers obtaining examination certificates and university degrees than previously (EOC, 1992a). However, as the experiences of the women interviewed shows, patterns of gender segregation run deep in education. The 1970s legislation had little effect on the 'hidden' curriculum, through which the opportunities open to girls and young women are severely restricted by negative gender dynamics, harassment and the attitudes and expectations of teachers. Extension of the curriculum to provide equal opportunities has been prevented by inadequate resourcing and a delay in response due to the administrative consequences of falling school rolls (Arnot, 1987). Women remain outside policy or decision-making and are excluded from the process of deciding what education should, or could, be (Spender, 1987). The economic strategies of central government continue to affect the perceived requirements of the labour market and, consequently, school leavers as future employees. Dominant ideologies regarding the roles of women and men at work and in the home persist, although references to social change are made within National Curriculum documents. Clearly the National Curriculum is the ultimate exercise in liberal reformism as it proposes reform via curriculum content, organisation and resources but fails to deal with other power-related issues (Davies *et al.*, 1990). The broader social, political and economic structural relations raised in the women's interviews are neglected, if not ignored and, as illustrated by sex education directives, such power relations have been reinforced rather than contested. While the effect of individual efforts should not be underestimated, change is required at an institutional level. The impact of feminist teachers on pupils, colleagues and education establishments can be dramatic but they walk a tightrope in terms of discussion of sexuality or challenging patriarchal assumptions. They also often endure hostility from colleagues, governors and parents.

Conclusion

The development of 'radical' and 'egalitarian' approaches to educational reform has increased awareness and discussion about many contentious issues, but teachers can be left in a dilemma about which strategies to employ. As Frankie Ord and Jane Quigley (1985 p. 105) point out, it is sometimes difficult to decide whether to concentrate on formulating whole-school policies or to focus on smaller, seemingly trivial, issues: 'When do we take on the more contentious issues, for example, sexual harassment or male discipline procedures, and when do we opt for "safer" issues, for example, registers in alphabetical order or girls wearing trousers all year'. Weiner and Arnot (1987 p. 359) note that different groups using anti-sexist approaches have been unified by a 'recognition of struggle as an inevitable by-product of attempts at social change'. Support groups and networks have emphasised the value of collective action and development of strategies to deal with the opposition and hostility prompted by feminist ideas. Weiner and Arnot suggest that, in an effort to support each other and maintain an optimistic belief that change is possible, radical and egalitarian teachers have formed alliances. Consequently, many teachers use strategies based on both equal opportunities and anti-sexist initiatives. The imposition of the National Curriculum need not hinder this and may, in fact, be used to reform education from within the system. Feminist teachers and parents could emphasise the cross-curricular elements to liberate and transform education (David, 1993; Acker, 1986).

The older women interviewed for this study were at primary school from the late 1950s to mid-1960s and had completed secondary schooling by 1970, continuing on to higher education. The younger women ended their primary education in the mid-1970s, secondary education in the early 1980s, followed by higher education in the mid-1980s. If the equal opportunities policies of the 1970s had succeeded, then it could be expected that the education of the younger women would be markedly different from that of the older women. In liberal terms, all the women in the study have succeeded. It seems that opportunities were provided for them at school, and in their careers, and they took them. Thus, they appear to demonstrate what women can achieve when given the chance to compete on equal terms with men. In fact, the interviews show that as girls each of the women experienced daily put-downs and harassment in institutions where the curriculum was male-defined and male-oriented, and where girls' and women's contributions, at all levels, were marginalised. The educational experiences of both the younger and older women emphasise that the education system has been, and remains, central in the reproduction of gender inequality and negative experience for girls.

When asked what they saw as future directions for the liberation and empowerment of girls and women, the majority of women in the study cited education as a major source of change and positive reinforcement of girls' abilities and opportunities. 'Our future lies in education and the value systems of the men of the future' (Hilary). What is required is 'education for equality' (Liz) so that children at school are not categorised as 'girls' and 'boys' who follow subjects defined as girls' or boys' and then move into jobs defined as women's or men's (Karen). 'There needs to be a recognition much sooner in people's education of what they're capable of, regardless of sex' (Janet). Many of the women believe that 'the attitudes of people start in childhood' (Karen). Like Janet, they concluded that 'education needs to be addressed because I believe that's the only way you can change the type of attitudes I have at work with some of my male colleagues'.

Acknowledgement of gender differentiation, and its social, economic and political basis, is an important step in challenging inequality in education at all levels. Girls and women teachers have always resisted dominant ideologies about the academic performance of girls, appropriate behaviour/dress/appearance, and predetermined roles (Robinson, 1992; Griffin, 1985; McRobbie and Nava, 1984). This has often resulted in considerable personal suffering and authoritative forms of sanction or punishment. However, individual and collective struggle against capitalist, patriarchal, neo-colonial ideologies cannot be underestimated. Combined with structural changes, it is possible to envisage the kind of educational institutions in which the recommendations and hopes of the women in the study are put into practice and realised.

Chapter 4

More Work, Low Pay: The Myth of Equal Opportunities in the Workplace

Introduction

The Equal Pay Act (1970) and the Sex Discrimination Act (1975) came into force in 1975. Both were intended to eliminate discrimination experienced by women in pay and employment. The effectiveness of both acts has been the subject of considerable debate in the women's movement, initially in the campaign to bring about legislation which would improve women's domestic, economic and political position. More recently the debate has focused on the limitation of the legislation in tackling the underlying structural inequalities which dominate women's lives.

The Equal Pay Act appears to legislate for economic equality, but its range is limited and narrow. For instance, women with children or those unable to work full-time are not covered. Without adequate child-care facilities it is impossible for many women to take advantage of the opportunities, albeit limited, of equal pay. Those women working under sixteen hours a week receive different conditions of employment from those working full-time, although a recent Judicial Review has resulted in a number of important changes (EOC, 1994). Mandy Snell (1979) illustrates how many employers have engaged in practices effectively excluding low paid women workers from the terms of the legislation. She also identifies a number of areas which, despite the Sex Discrimination Act (SDA), indirectly restrict women's opportunities at work. She claims that the restrictions are the result of well-established traditions which reflect male career patterns and 'illustrate the subtle way in which established structures, practices and attitudes interact to limit women's opportunities, often without an intention to discriminate on anyone's part' (Snell, 1979, p. 53 and see: Morris and Nott, 1991; Beechey and Perkins, 1987; Meehan, 1985).

Susan Atkins (1986 p. 62) is concerned with the wider implications of the SDA and, in particular, its failure to encompass fundamental aspects of women's oppression. She argues that women are profoundly affected by 'discriminatory treatment perpetrated by law and by government administrations such as the DHSS [now DSS], the NHS and social services departments of local authorities, all of which is outside the scope of the Act'. The SDA defines equality in terms of access to specific areas. It does not, however, make provision for individuals, or the Equal Opportunities Commission (EOC), to challenge inequalities in the private sphere. Atkins (1986 p. 64) argues that concentration on the public sphere directs attention from important issues: 'inequality based on the law's treatment and control of female sexuality, motherhood, women's financial independence and women's lack of power in personal and family relationships'. Sexual harassment and power relations in the workplace, both significant in reinforcing the inferior status of women at work, are also neglected by the Act. Although widespread, the impact of harassment has remained invisible, largely because many women regard it as a 'natural hazard' of working life (Wise and Stanley, 1987; Hadjifotiou, 1983).

Jeanne Gregory (1982) highlights the difficulties involved in bringing cases of contravention to industrial tribunals. The imbalance of power and resources that exists between the individual claimant and the defending organisation is intimidating and unlikely to encourage legal action on the part of employees. It is clear from the evidence that the success of the Equal Pay and Sex Discrimination Acts is limited. While there have been significant changes in pay and opportunities for some women, these advances have not been sufficiently sustained or broadly expanded. Consequently, the legislation deals with the results of discrimination rather than its prevention or elimination. A major obstacle is the inability of such legislation to dismantle those powerful forces which essentially prevent women from full and equal participation in the labour market. Given these conditions, legislation can provide the illusion of progress while driving discrimination underground. Meanwhile any challenge to the dominant order at its roots remains frustrated.

Women's Paid Employment

Contemporary feminist research demonstrates the need to identify how gender inequality is shaped and sustained by patriarchal relations outside the family, in the public sphere. Establishing the exact nature of patriarchal relations between women and men, together with the relationship between worker and employer, and how these elements interact remains a major concern within feminist analysis. This work emphasises the origins of occupational segregation and the designation of work as 'women's work' within the patriarchal industrial family

(Redclift and Sinclair, 1991; Crompton and Sanderson, 1990; Coontz and Henderson, 1986; Miles, 1986). While capitalism has emphasised and consolidated the division of labour between women and men in the public and private spheres it bears a pre-industrial legacy. In other words, capitalism inherited patriarchal divisions where women's labour power was controlled by men. Industrialisation substantiated and heightened this control (Alexander, in Mitchell and Oakley, 1976).

Once the capitalist mode of production was established craft-based organisations, or guilds, provided a strong foundation from which workers were able to resist incursions into their control of the labour process. The guilds, themselves powerful patriarchal institutions, regulated entry and apprenticeships. As a rule they excluded women, limiting their access not only to work but also to essential skills. Later, the guilds provided the framework for trade unions to develop. Women, unable to gain access to coveted skills and excluded from the protection of trade unions, were placed in a much weaker bargaining position. Their pay remained comparatively low and their admission to high status, managerial positions was barred or restricted. Yet they were central to the expansion of industry. Consequently their participation in the workforce was ensured, at least for a short time, by capitalists keen to reduce labour costs and at the same time gain control over skilled craftsmen. Skilled male workers, determined to maintain control over the production process and prevent the threat from cheap competition posed by unskilled male and female workers, resisted the extension of access. This was achieved, in part, by protective labour legislation which reduced the hours worked by women and prevented women's access to certain occupations. Male workers ran a successful 'family wage' campaign which affirmed the man as head of the household while ensuring that capital was supplied with a labour force which was produced, reproduced and sustained by women. Their contribution, at least in terms of payment, was never recognised (Hartmann, 1979).

The extent to which these developments were coincidental or due to the collusion of patriarchal and capitalist structures is difficult to determine, although it has been the subject of considerable debate. What is clear is that the role of women's labour power is maintained by the limited access women have to economic resources. It is also underpinned by the regulation of women's sexuality and reproductive capacities. In this sense patriarchy is not uni-dimensional, but the significance of restricted material access or opportunities is historically of major importance. The equal opportunities legislation and policies of the 1970s were heralded as the great incursion into the established material deprivation of women. If that legislation had proved to be effective, then some evidence of advancement in the public and private spheres should be identifiable in the lives of women two decades on.

Undoubtedly, the expansion of women in the labour market has continued unabated throughout the 1980s and 1990s while, relatively, unemployment overall has increased dramatically. Most women now expect to participate in the labour market throughout their lives, taking minimal breaks for childbirth. The women interviewed in depth for the studies – domestic, administrative and professional workers in a male-dominated institution and a group of 'successful', professional, career women – provide telling accounts of this period of change for women. Significant here is not only their experiences of the workplace, and the gender divisions within, but also their experiences of the relationship between the public and private spheres.

Occupational Segregation: Who Cleans the Toilets at Work?

The women interviewed for the following three sections work in a child-care institution which accommodates a small group of young men in secure conditions. The institution is responsible for the day-to-day care of the young men confined there, including education and work experience. Historically, the institution was managed by an exclusively male staff with the exception of the Principal or 'Headmaster's' wife, who was appointed matron and, together with a small group of domestic workers, was responsible for domestic arrangements. Since the mid-1960s women have been appointed on the teaching staff and as educational psychologists. The group of women interviewed represented all occupations within the institution, including teachers, residential social workers, an educational psychologist, domestic and administrative staff.

Catherine Hakim (1979) identifies several important changes in women's work patterns between 1901 and 1971. Most dramatic is the increase in married women's participation in paid work since the Second World War. She links this with the emergence of 'bi-modal' work patterns from the 1950s onwards, when married women started to return to paid work once their children reached school age. The majority of the women interviewed stated that their own mothers had returned to work after taking time out to raise a family. Many considered that women's involvement in war work was a significant factor in changing attitudes about married women with families taking on paid work, outside the home (Glucksmann, 1990; Braybon and Summerfield, 1987; Summerfield, 1984). Typical was this comment from Nina (Domestic):

The war was possibly the biggest change for women because they were actually encouraged to go out and earn a living.

Using the concepts of 'horizontal' and 'vertical' segregation in her analysis of occupational segregation, Hakim (1979) found that men and women were segregated horizontally into different occupations, although the degree of segregation was dependent on the nature of the work. It was among the semi-skilled, domestic and servicing-type occupations, many mirroring functions carried out in the home, that Hakim found the greatest degree of horizontal segregation. This proved to be a major area of friction for the women interviewed, particularly since much of the work involved in residential institutions is domestic or servicing. All stated that it was women workers who were expected to take responsibility for the domestic work, regardless of whether it was part of their job description. However, it was among the Residential Social Workers (RSWs) that the greatest conflict was encountered. Emma (Professional) recalled how, when she was first employed at the school, women were called 'housemothers' and the men 'housemasters', giving a clear indication of how men's and women's roles were perceived.

> I was allowed to take an equal position with my work partner, *but* I used to start work half an hour earlier to get the washing out of the way and try to do as much of the domestic work as I could to leave time for the counselling work.

Although there is evidence to suggest that horizontal segregation has diminished with the implementation of the Equal Pay and Sex Discrimination Acts, it seems that this is the result of men moving into areas defined as 'women's work' rather than women entering male-dominated occupations (Spencer and Podmore, 1987). There was concern that the advances, albeit limited, in the role of RSWs were gradually being eroded. Sally (Professional) stated that:

> If a woman Residential Child Care Officer (RCCO) grade three leaves the post, the managers get together and often they will recommend a male replacement because they feel that a man would be more appropriate (I know men here think that all male teams would be better). So they appoint a man to the position with the intention of giving them the same job description. He is shown what the job entails, including the domestic side of it. That will go on for a few weeks, but gradually they will be taken off those jobs.

A number of women felt that despite improvements, particularly since younger male staff had been employed and some managerial attitudes had changed, there was still some reluctance to ensure that work was shared out evenly between all care staff. Emma (Professional) recalled a discussion in which she and her colleagues were told that unless the women left the domestic work it would always be their responsibility. In her experience:

> Even if things are left because we are involved in taking groups of boys for activities, nobody else seems to step in and do the work. It will just be left. Nobody is prepared to push the issue.

Several women considered that the problem might be challenged if job descriptions clearly specified duties and were then monitored to ensure that all duties were shared equally. Sally (Professional) stated that:

> It should be made clear to all care staff that it is not solely women's work and team leaders should roster it if necessary.

Answering the constant male comment that women are 'better equipped' to carry out certain domestic duties she retorted:

> There is no reason why all care staff cannot be trained in the domestic side of the work when they start work here.

Her colleague Emma (Professional) stated:

> Although we have a progressive staff now (men are going up to do the washing or sort out the laundry, cleaning, setting tables and making supper), there are still those who say 'such a thing's not been done . . . because we had no ladies in'.

For her, a major barrier to long-term institutional change was the reluctance of senior managers to deal with the consequences:

> The reality of the situation is that there is no way it would ever be checked on or pushed. It would upset the status quo too much.

On a more optimistic note, many women identified a general and favourable change of attitude towards women in wider society. They considered that recent changes in grading at work had raised awareness of the possibility of change among women staff. While this in itself was identified as a major step forward, recognition of the difficulties and pressures encountered by women when major changes are introduced in an unsupportive workplace environment was highlighted by Carol (Professional):

> I think some of the women here don't want to change. They have

been brought up to expect full responsibility for domestic work and they are good at it. I think they feel comfortable and secure with that, and we need to respect that.

Resistance to change, by both men and women workers, was a clear problem for those women who had struggled to effect change through challenging sexist attitudes and institutionalised work practices. Susan (Professional) who was instrumental in implementing some of the changes, stated:

It was a battle both with men and women colleagues because it wasn't part of the work that women did within the school. I did get support from the older women, otherwise it was a case of 'I don't know what you're thinking of, women don't do that, you're causing trouble and why are you disrupting the place when we're all happy the way we are?' I couldn't get through to them that it wasn't because I wanted to be on a par with the men, it was because I wanted to take a proper caring role, which I couldn't the way things were.

Hakim's second category, vertical segregation, occurs within occupational groupings where women tend to be over-represented in the less-skilled and generally lower-paid jobs, while men are over-represented in highly-skilled, managerial jobs. Nina (Domestic) stated:

I still feel that this institution is a man's world. I think some of the men don't give any consideration to what the women who work here actually do. I don't think they value the work they do.

Within the institution there was virtually no change in the patterns of vertical segregation since the implementation of equal opportunities and sex discrimination legislation. This can be explained in part by the changes in the patterns of economic growth in certain areas, particularly private and public sector services, traditionally defined as women's work. Further, women tend to remain concentrated in industries and occupations which are predominantly female (Coote and Campbell, 1987; Sharpe, 1984).

Hakim considers that bi-modal work patterns have done little to improve the disadvantages experienced by women in paid work. Young women, new to the workforce, remain discriminated against because they are seen as undependable and a poor training investment. The myth prevails that they will give up work once married and/or pregnant. Older women returners are regularly treated as new entrants, but with all the assumed disadvantages of maturity in a culture where youth is linked with adaptability and resourcefulness. Several women in the study felt they were shunned by employers, and that their commitment to work was questioned, on the grounds that their family would take precedence over their paid employment. Julie (Administrator) stated:

> They wanted to know how old the children were? Who was going to mind them? What about school holidays? What if they were sick?

Part-time work and 'homework' have been cited as contributory factors to women's subordinate position in the labour market (Rowbotham, 1993; Coyle and Skinner, 1988; Mitter, 1986). The expansion of both has, undoubtedly, enabled women to re-enter the labour market. For some writers these changes are seen as a means for women to reconcile their dual roles. However, it would seem that rather than women benefiting from this access to paid work their unequal status is intensified. Elaine (Administrator) recounted how in a previous job:

> It was mostly women who worked there. Initially they were full-time, but company policy changed – it was cheaper to employ part-timers. I don't know how much they lost – holidays, breaks, etc. – but a lot of those women were the breadwinners anyway.

Olive Robinson (1988) states that the increase in part-time work has led to a reaffirmation of, rather than a decline in, occupational segregation. Additionally, much of the evidence available indicates that part-time work has been used to create a cheap, flexible labour force, adaptable to the needs of employers in a volatile and unpredictable economy.

Hakim's detailed account of the structure of the workforce, and women's place within it, provides essential background information, encompassing a period of seventy years from the beginning of the century to 1971. Her research, therefore, does not document the changes in occupational segregation expected from the implementation of equal pay and sex discrimination legislation, for example, increased parity between young women and men in terms of their participation in further/higher education, formal qualifications, and altered expectations relating to work for women and men. In fact all the indications suggest that, contrary to optimistic expectations, any changes that have occurred have been piecemeal and limited. This reinforces feminist claims that legislation is not sufficient to neutralise the patriarchal roots of discriminatory practices experienced by women in the labour force. Much of the occupational segregation outlined by Hakim's research remains intact. A thorough and detailed analysis of the structures which determine women's position in the labour force is needed to explain the underlying causes of this segregation.

Gender Segregation: Who Cleans the Toilets at Home?

Feminist debates concerning women's employment, emerging during the early 1970s, challenged and questioned prevailing attitudes about women in paid work. They sought to expose discriminatory practices and poor conditions which marginalised women in the workplace and made visible hidden and trivialised forms of work – homework and housework – which were generally the responsibility of women. It was the latter, the 'domestic labour debate', which predominated. Within this, feminist critics argued that by concentrating on the political economy of domestic labour, other issues were neglected. The debate shifted to include a broader analysis emphasising the complex interrelationship between the family and work: the 'family wage' and ideology of the family; the importance of women's paid work in sustaining the family; lack of adequate child-care and support for working women; the beneficiaries of women's domestic labour. Each issue received considerable attention in theoretical debates and was expanded into important research studies (Saltzman, 1990; Beechey, 1987).

Sylvia Walby (1988) argues that an understanding of the origins of gender segregation, and its maintenance at work, is the key to explaining women's subordinate position in the workforce. Conventional explanations such as 'Human Capital Theory', founded on the premiss that labour selection reflects the human capital accumulated by each worker (e.g. education, qualifications, training, skills and experience), connect women's position in the family to their position in the labour market. The implication is that if the best jobs and highest rewards are linked to an accumulation of human capital, women are inevitably disadvantaged because their process of accumulation is interrupted by marriage and childrearing. In the research Marjorie (Professional) gave a typical response:

> Things are stacked against women. The majority will have breaks to have children. They 'lose' work experience but also lose confidence.

The inadequacy of the Human Capital Theory is evident in considering those women who continue to work without breaks for childbearing and rearing yet remain in low status, low-paid occupations. Even where there is evidence of men and women starting with equal skills, qualifications or experience, the distribution of higher status and higher paid grades remains uneven (EOC, 1990a; Robinson, 1988). The concept of skills in the workforce has more to do with gender inequality and who is in a stronger bargaining position than actual job content: 'Women workers carry into the workplace their status as subordinate individuals, and this status comes to define the value of the work they do' (Phillips and Taylor, 1980, p. 79). All of the women interviewed highlighted the importance of training and skill acquisition, while offering different explanations. Many considered that although it was not an option open to them, either because of age or position, they felt training was important for women who wanted 'to get on'. Marjorie (Professional) remarked:

> I just see women as being the underdogs all the time, in work, at home, in everything. Although it's not the whole answer, at least it would give women some choice.

Emma (Professional) was less optimistic:

> Improved skills training would be useful, but I would still come back to the laundry.

Others were keen to endorse training which recognised and acknowledged their skills as being positive attributes. Improving women's confidence and self-esteem, as well as encouraging assertiveness, were identified as means to empowerment. Anna (Professional) felt that:

> Women themselves need to adopt a better attitude about themselves ... We need to make more demands and say what we want rather than wait for other people.

Cultural theories, in contrast, suggest that women make a rational choice about the type of work they seek out and that choice is based on an adherence to values associated with femininity and domesticity. Critics focus on the failure of cultural theorists to examine the underlying causes determining women's choices. It is argued that the ideology of the family, and women's role within it, indirectly limits women's involvement and choices regarding paid work. Several women interviewed felt that women's ideas about, and expectation of, their role are an important factor in forming attitudes towards paid work. For many, the domestic life – home, children and husband/partner – is very important and women often defer their personal needs. As Marjorie (Professional) commented:

> Married women are at a disadvantage because opportunities are restricted but also because they experience conflict between work and family. Women often want to have the experience of bringing up their children.

Ideologies about the family inform and influence at a structural level, maintaining and reinforcing the construct of a male head of household responsible for the financial support of dependent wife and children. This is embodied in the concept of the 'family wage', and enshrined in the servicing of male workers within the family. Some of the women interviewed recalled how their fathers were considered to be the primary breadwinner. Yet for several of the families, the mother's wage was essential – either because the father had become unemployed or was on a low income, or because the family was large and one wage was inadequate. For many the contribution made by the mother went unrecognised, or was trivialised, and rarely led to any help with household chores. Claire (Administrator) stated that:

> Although women worked, men still expected them to run the home efficiently. They were brought up to expect the women to have the meal ready, the kettle boiling and the shirts ironed.

Sharon (Domestic) and Ruth (Domestic) reflected on how women's paid work was regarded as secondary:

> As he walked in the door, if everything wasn't ready for him to sit down then it was wrong. He expected that. As long as everything in his life ran smoothly then she could do what she wanted.

> It's always been considered that women work partly to 'get out of the house' for a bit of 'pin money' and it's always been the case that if you can't cope you can always pack the job in. Women can do the housework and the job as long as you don't moan about it and because the woman's job is not that important.

From the statements it was clear that the special treatment received by fathers was passed on to the next generation with implications for future wives and partners. Claire (Administrator) felt that:

> My mother has sole responsibility for the home. My father is waited on hand and foot, as soon as he comes home she rushes into the kitchen to get his tea out. It's the same with my brother. So she has taught him to be like my father and he now treats his girlfriend the same way.

Clearly, women make a significant contribution to the family income and homes in which a man is the sole breadwinner are increasingly rare. With high levels of structural and long-term unemployment women's earnings are even more important to the financial survival of many families. The idea that women's earnings are peripheral, used primarily to provide luxuries, denies the necessity for women to work in order to avoid poverty. Estimates suggest that families living in poverty would quadruple if women were to relinquish paid work. Add to this the number of one-parent families, in which a woman is the sole earner, and the myth of a wife being supported financially by her husband is revealed (Coote and Campbell, 1987). Moreover, women rarely benefit from what Anna Coote and Beatrix Campbell call the 'patriarchal bonus': extra payments made for shiftwork, overtime, long-service awards or merit awards attached to posts of responsibility. As Emma (Professional) described:

> Until recently we had to take time off in lieu rather than claim for overtime. Senior management felt that women care staff shouldn't claim pay for overtime.

There is little evidence that the gender divisions within domestic labour have changed, with the double day remaining a reality for most women in paid work. This was a feature of daily life endorsed by the majority of women interviewed. The following comment from Marjorie (Professional) was typical:

> Marriage affects women's paid work, in particular the problems and conflicts associated with the 'double-day'. Also, if it is a traditional family life, with children, they will have breaks in their career. Long, very demanding breaks that militate against them going back into paid work. And if they do go back they are also bound to be burdened down with all these guilt feelings about abandoning their 'proper career' i.e. their children.

Although feminist research has argued that women's traditional role in the family is not the main reason for their subordination in the workforce, the pressure to find work which accommodates domestic responsibilities remains an important contributory factor (Barrett, 1980). Those women who were, or had been, married or in a relationship with children, worked until the birth of their first child. Their individual work profiles after this varied con-siderably, some returning to paid work, others remaining in the home for many years. Many worked temporarily until the birth of a second child, some returned to paid work once their children were of school age. Those with young children who were able to gain paid work felt that the opportunities for women in their situation were restricted, as Deirdre (Domestic) pointed out:

When I first started back it was a case of doing something I didn't really want to do, but I did it just to get back into the swing again ... At the moment it's a case of taking on work which is convenient.

In contrast, male workers persistently achieve higher status and better paid jobs as a result of lesser involvement, and responsibility, within the domestic sphere. Men's work patterns have the expectation built into them that work requirements will be prioritised over domestic arrangements. Claire (Administrator) recognised the significance of this:

A man, because of the way that society perceives his role, can follow whatever career he wants to and give the amount of time he feels is necessary towards that. Where, if a woman in a relationship has a career, she can only in reality pursue it to the same extent with the tacit consent of her partner.

Gender, then, is central in the determination of structural arrangements in paid work, including skills and training, and the social, interpersonal arrangements within the domestic sphere. For women this raises important issues concerning strategies for coping with what is effectively a double workload – home and job. Do women have to adopt 'male' work practices if they are to enter management positions? How easy or difficult is it to resist when individual commitment is measured by the length of time women can devote to work? For the majority of married women there will be periods in their working lives when they are unable to work, or are restricted in the type of work they are able to do. For them, the domestic role continues to underpin their unequal status.

Equal Opportunities: Jobs for the Boys?

In the mid-1970s Audrey Hunt's survey of management attitudes provided an insight into how male managers perceive women workers and added a further dimension to the problem of women's lack of status in paid employment. As Hunt's (1975) work preceded the implementation of legislation on equal opportunities and sex discrimination it could be expected that its findings are outdated. However, the women interviewed nearly two decades later indicated that little had changed – at least for them and their colleagues. The responses to questions relating to promotion and equality of opportunity elicited an overwhelming consensus that women remain less likely to be promoted into positions of responsibility, even when they hold equal or superior qualifications to men. The following quotations are typical of the responses:

I think the reasons are mixed but mostly lack of opportunity and lack of confidence. But, I think because of the attitude of many of their colleagues, a lot of women don't push for higher grade positions. Even if they are capable, they don't want to rock the boat. In the end there are more men – women are outnumbered.

(Helen, Professional)

Men have more chances when it comes to promotion. Employers assume women will have children and that family commitments will interfere with their work.

(Marjorie, Professional)

Margaret Thatcher – she hasn't opened any doors for women, I thought she might have done. It's still a man's world. If you look at jobs, 9 out of 10 have men in top positions.

(Nina, Domestic)

Many of the women considered that lack of prospects was partly due to the institution being male-dominated, particularly at senior levels, and partly because opportunities for promotion were restricted anyway. Yet Marjorie's (Professional) response typified the broad opinion: 'all things being equal, women didn't have the same chances of promotion as men'. She also thought that there were other factors which prevented women seeking out promotion:

It's something to do with women as well. I'm a classic example of someone not wanting a power position. If I'd have been ambitious I could have been a head of department.

She considered her own choices reflected a rejection of male values. Sally (Professional) felt that, despite equal opportunities, a bias towards employing men prevailed and she gave an example of how legislation can be evaded. She recounted that when she first applied for her present position she discovered there was an informal, 'unwritten' agreement to fill the position with a man. The position entailed overseeing and coordinating the work of a group of men. Given the predominance of men in senior positions, the employment of men by men further reinforced and reproduced inequalities and assumptions made about women workers. As Sally said:

It's only recently that women have managed to get the higher grades. I don't believe that in all the years this unit has been open, only one woman has been capable of doing the work associated with that grade.

Emma (Professional) recounted her experiences in pursuing promotion:

> When I applied I was discouraged by the senior staff and I felt that the questions at the interview were unfair. I didn't get the job. I felt the men had all clubbed together to keep me out and I think senior management were worried about the reaction they would get from the men if I got the job.

Although eventually promoted, she continued to experience hostility and obstruction. However, she was determined, despite the personal stress this caused, to confront the situation and as a result the situation was eventually resolved. Those responsible for creating the difficulties acknowledged their part in the prevention of her promotion. Her account highlights the difficulties encountered in implementing policy decisions concerning equality of opportunity which challenge deeply entrenched attitudes about women's abilities at a grass-roots level. Helen (Professional) felt that women's visibility in positions of responsibility was an important factor:

> Opportunities aren't equal because the women are only ever seen to be doing menial domestic work. They don't assert themselves enough to be included in areas of greater responsibility.

Iris Young (1981) argues the significance of women's sexuality to a full understanding of the gender-based division of labour. She maintains that sexual abuse and sexual harassment are central to how power is manifested interpersonally and sanctioned within capitalist patriarchy. Dany Lacombe (1988) raises the crucial question: who benefits from the gender oppression women experience at work – patriarchy or capitalism? As more women have resisted harassment and related their personal experiences of victimisation, there has been some attempt to address the issue. Trade unions have taken some positive action to eliminate workplace harassment and the Trades Union Congress (TUC) has introduced guidelines. However, many women are sceptical of the effectiveness of unions, which often exhibit many of the sexist attitudes and behaviour that women are fighting against. There are also doubts about how effective such initiatives can be in eliminating behaviour which is widely condoned or ignored and which affects women in all areas of their lives, not just work.

The women interviewed gave mixed responses to the issue of sexual harassment in the workplace. Most of the women had experienced, or witnessed, harassment and cited examples of sexually derogatory verbal statements or sexually discriminatory comments. Anna (Professional) recalled being asked embarrassing, personal comments by boys in the unit:

> Boys often have preconceived ideas about women, which are
> reinforced by male colleagues. It's difficult to tackle because,
> generally, there is a lack of support over these sorts of issues.

Others had experienced sexual harassment in other work situations, but not
in their present employment. One woman stated that following her experiences of harassment elsewhere she had 'learned' to distance herself from
male colleagues as a measure of self-protection. Another felt that women
were used in many situations 'to bolster men's egos' and as a result would
find it difficult to make it an issue. The women's responses to harassment
also varied. Emma (Professional) stated:

> I tend to confront it directly and say that it's not acceptable. And OK,
> I was a miserable cow, I was this, I was that. But I made it clear that
> I wasn't there to be touched or played around with!

In discussing sexist comments from the boys in the unit Anna (Professional)
felt that this could be excusable because it was the result of:

> Feelings that the lads have expressed due to the fact that they are
> adolescent and resolving their sexual identity and learning to interact
> with the opposite sex.

However, she stressed that when such comments were overtly direct she told
the person involved that it was unacceptable. A number of women felt that
if incidents of sexual harassment were reported to senior staff they would be
trivialised or treated as a joke, although others were confident that they would
be dealt with.

Issues concerning personal presentation and 'appropriate' behaviour also
elicited mixed responses. Claire (Administrator) commented:

> There is pressure. Even people who think they are quite liberated still
> exert certain kinds of pressure with respect to all sorts of things –
> appearance, dress, general manners, activities you engage in.

Most of the women felt that they were expected to accept 'moody' behaviour
from male colleagues without question, but if women showed their feelings
they were labelled 'hysterical'. Helen (Professional) highlighted this point:

> Women tend to show their emotions in a different way. I've seen men
> slamming doors and having temper tantrums and I've seen women
> in tears. It's how these two things are viewed. It would be seen as

a weakness in a woman and therefore you're unstable, not suited to the work and unreliable.

It was clear that female staff were expected to behave in a feminine and subordinate way. This manifested itself in 'unwritten rules' about how women should behave and dress, depending on their role. Marjorie (Professional) felt that:

In certain situations you have more credibility if you wear a skirt, but I see my main purpose as working with young men, and informal clothing is less intimidating to them.

From the interviews it can be seen that the institution continued to operate on a range of assumptions concerning 'gender-appropriate' behaviour. This extended beyond job expectations to promotion, presentation, behaviour and included an acceptance of harassment. While not always overtly intimidating, there is no question that such systematic and institutionalised practices impacted on all women employees. It is this, often hidden, agenda which has proved elusive to legislative and policy reform.

The Experiences of Professional Women

The preceding research considered the significance of equal opportunities and sex discrimination reform on women of all ages involved in domestic, administrative and professional occupations within one institution. The following section concentrates on the employment experiences of professional women. The intention is not to establish direct links between the two groups of women interviewed. In fact, it could be assumed that given their age, professional status, and the supposed benefits of equal opportunities legislation, the experiences of the professional women would be quite different (Witz, 1992). The interviews, however, reveal the danger implicit in such an assumption.

When asked about the conduct of job interviews it was obvious that equal opportunities legislation, which outlaws questions about marital status, the likelihood of motherhood and child-care, was blatantly and regularly contravened. The following responses were typical:

They want to know whether you're married ... And they're always quite interested in whether you're planning to have a family. They have asked me about that in a couple of jobs I've applied for – 'What are your long-term commitments to medicine?'

(Doctor)

> If you'd not been single or if you'd had children I think, in the jobs
> I've applied for so far, there would probably have been discrimina-
> tion against you as a woman.
>
> (Clinical Psychologist)

> I know when, for instance, Linda joined she practically had to give
> an undertaking that she wouldn't have children.
>
> (Solicitor)

Andrea (Local Government Officer) felt that, had she been male, her job
would have been presented to her in a different way. She was re-deployed
from one job and manoeuvred to another by being told that her skills were
'transferable'. It was presented to her as a favour and a career opportunity
whereas she believed that with a man the employers 'would have been more
straight'. Ruth (Speech Therapist) felt that there would be a 'reaction to
anything from a male' since Speech Therapy is female dominated. However,
Jane (Industrial Chemist) experienced the converse:

> At one interview I was told quite bluntly that I wouldn't be
> physically capable of doing the work they expected. At another they
> made the point that I would be expected to do some physical work
> and that they were taking a chance employing me. The plant manager
> at the time claimed to be an ardent socialist and always said that was
> the reason he took me on but I have reservations about that. I suspect
> that they were just very short of candidates.

Some of the women interviewed recounted the experiences of colleagues
concerning pregnancy and discrimination:

> Somebody I'm working with . . . is just going off on maternity leave
> and I know the head of department came in and said to her, without
> realising it reflected his attitude, 'Oh I don't know whether we're
> going to get money released for your job because you're still getting
> paid'.
>
> (Clinical Psychologist)

> Basically, he [the boss] made the decision that if one of the women
> managers gets pregnant she will be moved sideways and a new
> manager appointed and then she could return to the sideways-moved
> position but she could not return as a manager.
>
> (Programme Development Manager)

> We had a receptionist who's just, literally, had a baby but our firm has unfortunately got into a bit of difficulty in the last few months so I think they were going to keep her on and pay her maternity leave, or whatever, and have her back, but, due to the recession and God knows what else, they're not keeping her on.
>
> (Solicitor)

The interviews elicited a variety of responses to questions relating to promotion opportunities within the different professions represented. Several of the women experienced discrimination in promotion. Management positions were predominantly, or only, occupied by men in clinical psychology, primary education, speech therapy, higher education, the secure unit, medicine and industrial chemistry, even though the first three of these are female-dominated professions. Liz (Teacher in a Secure Unit) summarised the response of many women:

> I suspect because they [male managers] think their way of doing things is the right way they won't entertain any different approaches which might challenge their power.

Perceptions of women's approach to work affects promotion. For example, as Liz pointed out, women's skills are not recognised and stereotyped images (e.g. that women are good organisers) are seen as negative or unimportant. Andrea (Local Government Officer) felt that the amount of work expected of her was more than that expected of male colleagues. Although it was acknowledged that she had skills, abilities and an academic training, she still had to prove that she could do a range of things. But it is not only at a practical level that women's performance influences promotion prospects. Jane (Industrial Chemist) highlighted the effect of women's behavioural response to male colleagues:

> I started to take exception to the behaviour of a lot of the men towards me and this was perceived as me being awkward, odd, peculiar, ungrateful, unsociable. I think, although my job description changed ... my status remained exactly the same. I'd reached some sort of ceiling which I'm convinced was a direct result of my lack of willingness to comply with being one of the boys.

The majority of the women worked in organisations which had adopted equal opportunities policies. However, many considered that workplace practices indicated these were no more than statements of intent, rendered

93

meaningless by the reality of routine practices and behaviour.

> They state that they're Equal Opportunities employers ... but I don't
> think there's a great understanding of what that means – it's more a
> statement than anything else.
>
> (Clinical Psychologist)

> I think it's far easier to get to be a head, a deputy head or an adviser
> if you're male and it's proven every time ... I think males find it
> much easier to get to the top, and I don't think their progress up the
> career ladder is based very much on their teaching ability in the
> classroom.
>
> (Primary Teacher)

Susan (Clinical Psychologist) considered that her chosen profession had
changed, from one in which the numbers of men and women were equal, to
one where women outnumbered men. This was the result of a reduction in
pay and increased opportunities in the commercial sector, which led to
people choosing alternative options and men, in particular, deciding to follow
financially lucrative routes. In osteopathy the number of women has
increased in a previously male-dominated profession. However, in higher
education, industrial chemistry and the secure unit, men dominate at
managerial and non-managerial levels. In all of the women's experiences
secretarial and domestic staff were exclusively female.

Three of the women stated that men were promoted faster to higher
levels in their professions. In Kate's (Programme Development Manager)
company there was no salary structure and men were often employed on a
higher basic wage. At the same time there were male colleagues who earned
the same salary as her even though she was 'two steps ahead of them'. Jane
(Industrial Chemist), found that although no two people were doing the same
or equivalent job, the man whose job description was nearest to hers was paid
in excess of £10,000 p.a. more. When she asked why, she was informed that
'men are the breadwinners'. Mary proposed that because male colleagues are
often more ambitious, they work longer hours to earn more whereas she saw
her occupation less as a job and more as part of her life. Although Janet
(Hospital Administrator) and Joanne (Solicitor) did not feel their opportunities for promotion were restricted by their sex, all the managers except one
in Janet's workplace were male and in the firm of solicitors where Joanne
worked none of the eight partners were female. Andrea, in local government,
argued that more than 50 per cent of the workforce were women, but only
one out of four senior managers was female. In medicine too, at junior doctor

level the proportions were even. But, typically, there was only one female consultant in the hospital where Anna worked. Primary teaching, speech therapy and programme development are all female-dominated professions although, as already mentioned, management positions were dominated by men.

Many of the women considered that while in theory conditions of service were sufficient, in practice women suffered because of lack of flexibility (e.g. around family holidays), poor provision for women returning to work and inappropriate conditions in the workplace. Only Janet (Hospital Administrator) considered that her conditions were favourable in theory and practice, although it is interesting to juxtapose her view with that of Susan (Clinical Psychologist):

> The health service, in my experience, doesn't give any real recognition for the needs of women.

Janet also felt that an Equal Opportunities Policy was applied 'to the letter' although she was aware that:

> If you did a job evaluation on the basis of equal pay for work of equal value, there are still women's jobs in the NHS which are undervalued.

All of the women considered that their sex definitely affected the response of colleagues to them, mainly in a detrimental way:

> The consultants do it all the time, they're dreadful ... They make remarks about women in general.
>
> (Doctor)

> I get patronised every day by a young man who's head of the section next to us. He thinks he's being friendly and is so thick-skinned that even when I've told him and demanded apologies for the way he's treated other women ... he's laughed at me or just ignored it and become embarrassed because he thinks I've gone over the top. And he thinks that he's a really cool, young, with-it type of bloke ... The Chief Officer patronises all the women. He thinks that if he can flatter you, give you compliments that then you'll work extra hard.
>
> (Local Government Officer)

The men Hilary (Senior Lecturer in PE) worked with could be divided into two groups:

> The 'old guard' still treat me like they always have – condescending, authoritarian, sexist . . . and overt and covert harassment every single day of my working life in this particular course team. That's one group, but the other, which is fortunately increasing . . . is a group of mature professional men who come from a totally different culture. It's a complete culture war between the two groups' very different ethos. That group treats me normally, as a professional.

In a school with sixteen female teachers, Karen (Primary Teacher) described an appalling situation where:

> The male head continually comes into the staffroom and thinks it extremely funny to make sexual innuendos, continually refers to parts of his anatomy which we're not really interested in, and the size, thinks nothing of putting his arm around you, which he does often . . . He certainly does take liberties being a man on an all-female staff.

Janet (Hospital Administrator) illustrated the effect on women of the over-confidence of male colleagues:

> I've found I have an awful lot of problems with the egos of the male managers. It's like there's still a great deal of one-upmanship going on and I always feel, even though it's ridiculous, inferior. I know very well I'm not but I still feel it at times and I still question my confidence.

Jane (Industrial Chemist) described how her colleagues responded differently when she did not adopt gender-appropriate behaviour:

> They liked me quite a lot when I was trying to be one of the boys and were very disgruntled and aggressive when I asked people not to call me love but to call me Jane. I complained quite strongly when I was actually touched quite intimately one day and I didn't get any support. I was just seen as being awkward and having no sense of humour . . . What I found was that every single time that a new person was employed on the shop floor, or even in management, I had the same battle . . . people who were new to the company were warned about me . . . that I was awkward, that I had no sense of humour.

The response of colleagues often reflected their expectations of, and assumptions about, women at work. Liz's (Teacher in Secure Unit) experience exemplified the effect of stereotypical assumptions:

> When I started work there they were very protective, over-protective to the point where I was stifled really. For instance, I wasn't allowed to do certain things. I couldn't take a group of boys to teach them science because the only facility for teaching science was in the garden area which was outside the security of the building and that wasn't acceptable ... Until two years ago I was never given the opportunity to run the shift (I finally was just as they changed my hours to days). There was the idea that these young men might try and overcome me in some way to try and let themselves out. The fact that we had, and still have, grossly overweight men and people that are near to retirement, or on virtually permanent sick, doing the job has nothing to do with it. So one reason was the security aspect. The other, I would imagine, would be that they just didn't think it would be possible for a woman to be able to operate the timetable and generally keep the place running smoothly.

Most of the women felt they were not taken seriously, and that their decisions were questioned by colleagues:

> ... being young and female doesn't go down well with a number of men so it tends to be the slight put down if you like: 'Alright love I'll do that for you' as if they're doing you a big favour, as opposed to, not fulfilling an order but, following through a policy decision which really has no option attached to it.
>
> (Programme Development Manager)

> ... being a young woman I was responded to differently. You were responded to not entirely seriously. You were responded to in terms of how you look. People introduce you as 'charming', 'lovely' in a way that they certainly wouldn't for a man ... people would think they're being complimentary to you but don't realise that they're negating you as a professional.
>
> (Clinical Psychologist)

Only Mary (Osteopathy) and Anna (Doctor) felt unequivocally that their decisions were taken seriously. Ruth (Speech Therapist) and Andrea (Local Government Officer) both thought this to be the case 'generally', and Joanne (Solicitor), Susan (Clinical Psychologist) and Kate (Programme Development Manager) each believed they were eventually taken seriously after years of having to 'prove themselves'. They experienced particular male colleagues persistently undermining them in various situations:

> There's one partner who turns round and says 'No, that's totally wrong' and you sit there and listen to what he's saying and then say at the end 'Well, Michael, you've just said exactly what I said at the beginning'. I feel sometimes he just likes to overrule.
>
> (Solicitor)

For these professional women, as Joanne (Solicitor) pointed out, 'A lot of it comes back to confidence'. Susan (Clinical Psychologist) summarised this point:

> I can think of examples of where a woman has been experienced and had sound ideas and I've heard afterwards people being disparaging of her point of view or feeling that she's talked too much. Although there are a lot of men doing that people don't talk about it in such a negative way. It takes quite a lot of time to build up courage to do that.

In Karen's (Primary Teacher) experience, the male headteacher did not bother to listen to any of the female staff and thought he was the only effective and efficient person. Hilary's (Senior Lecturer in PE) decisions were constantly questioned by the 'old guard'. These men stuck their chests out, pointed their fingers at her and prominently invaded her physical space. Their non-verbal communication in response to anything she suggested at meetings was obvious and extremely off-putting. They habitually sat together in a confrontational position in the room, leant back on their chairs with their hands behind their heads and looked at the door while she spoke. One of them had not spoken to her for four years, except for a line of verbal abuse when she was appointed course team leader for validation of the course. He wrote letters to senior colleagues criticising all aspects of her work. The group consistently undermined her work with students. In addition, they worked together in meetings to ensure that her initiatives were blocked.

Janet (Hospital Administrator) felt her decisions were often not taken seriously and she had to write specific memos to one manager to ensure that he did what she asked. Jane (Industrial Chemist) described how it was difficult to 'get anything through' in her workplace. This was exacerbated by one colleague who could not override her decisions but won assurances from others that certain decisions were blocked. When she was asked to set up a department a major battle ensued with another colleague about whether there was sufficient finance for equipment, space and resources, although it was outside his brief to comment on the situation. The result was that Jane was placed in his department, whereas had she been male, she would have been in charge of her own department. Liz (Teacher in a Secure Unit) felt that her colleagues were not interested in her comments or judgements. In their contact with others outside the workplace, half the women felt they were patronised. The expectation was that they were secretaries and Kate (Programme Development Manager) was expected to pour the tea at her first meeting!

The problems involved in socialising with colleagues outside the workplace were recognised by most of the women in the study. Of particular concern was the situation where colleagues, predominantly male, manipu-lated the 'agenda' in order to exclude women co-workers. This strengthened the 'male networking' system and prevented women from participating in informal decision-making. Most of the women either joined male colleagues in social events or spent time with female workers. Jane (Industrial Chemist) found that she was excluded from social events, and the decisions taken there, once she decided not to participate as 'one of the boys'. For staff working in the secure unit social events were, in theory, open to all. However, the chosen venues often excluded women:

> There have been occasions when things have been planned. I'm thinking of things like sportsmen's dinners, visits to a strip club, the races, binges.

Sport provides opportunities for collective male participation where work is a common bond but also a reason for joining the team. The men at the university where Hilary (Senior Lecturer in PE) worked had regular hockey, cricket and lunch meetings at which work was discussed, although more recently these had declined and a group of women had developed their own activities and support network. Janet (Hospital Administrator) described the situation at her workplace:

> In particular they play football on a Friday night after work ... with some of the senior managers at district, who are all male. And they have this five-a-side thing ... and they do discuss work because I've been in the office when one has rung another and said 'Are you going tonight? Oh yes, we'll discuss it there then' ... It's known throughout the organisation and among the office staff as 'the boys club', it's that obvious.

Such groups also existed at a more formal level in institutions:

Within the district department the overall head was male and a couple of heads of department were male and they gave you the impression of an exclusive club. Overall sexism was evident in the way they carried on, so even other women in senior positions were excluded from this exclusive group.

(Clinical Psychologist)

Most of the women experienced comments and assumptions about their personal life. The majority tried to keep work and private life separate. However, Kate's (Programme Development Manager) boss, on finding out that she was 'living with' a man commented: 'I hope this isn't the kind of thing you discuss in your work outside the company'.

Gender-based assumptions were reflected in comments such as 'Isn't it time you were getting married?' (Karen, Primary Teacher); 'I don't know what's wrong with you. Why haven't you got a boyfriend?' (Joanne, Solicitor); 'Did you make the tea last night?' (Anna, Doctor). Situations in which women were not meeting with traditional expectations regularly invoked comments. This often related to marital status and to motherhood:

Obviously it was expected that I would give up work to have children and certainly when I initially started working that was commented on . . . I wonder whether they think 'Maybe she can't have children, we'd better not say anything just in case she can't have them'.

(Teacher in a Secure Unit)

Pressure to conform to unspoken rules about appropriate dress for women was a common experience. Only two of the women dressed as they pleased to work. Andrea and Ruth were aware that they did not 'conform' as far as 'presentation' was concerned, and that this affected the way they were seen by others:

Sometimes I feel conscious that I might look scruffy in comparison with other women. There's some who wear make-up, look really smart, wear high heels and all that. I've never wanted to dress like that – I'd feel uncomfortable and wouldn't be able to work properly. But I do feel conscious that, somehow or other, they're being smarter than me so they may be treated as being better employees.

(Local Government Officer)

I feel ashamed when I don't put on make-up or look smart. Our district is very much into power dressing – shoulder pads and that sort of thing. I always feel a bit embarrassed and a bit 'naughty' because I don't participate and am not dressing up as a glamorous smart woman. It's this idea of being a '90's woman'; power dressing and walking around with a briefcase sort of attitude.

(Speech Therapist)

Typically, it was expected that the women wore clothes of a particular style. Janet (Hospital Administrator) was expected to wear a business suit, to look 'official', 'professional', 'formal'. Susan (Clinical Psychologist) liked to look 'smart' although she felt the choice of clothing was hers. In contrast Kate (Programme Development Manager) was informed, when she started work, that she was to wear 'business dress and no trousers' and was later asked to 'dress older because you look too young to be doing the job'. 'Making an impression' was seen to be important to Joanne (Solicitor), who wore make-up and dressed smartly 'because it looks good and if I want to get on there's a certain standard of dress and way of presenting yourself ... If you look smart you perform better'. Hilary (Senior Lecturer in PE) tried to achieve a balance between being casual but acceptable for visiting schools, and Mary (Osteopath) dressed in a way that would 'present the right impression' to patients. Liz (Teacher in a Secure Unit) was aware that she tried to make an impression in meetings, whilst Jane (Industrial Chemist) made a conscious decision to 'dress down rather than up'. If she wore a skirt the inevitable response was 'I didn't realise you had a pair of legs'.

The women interviewed also pointed out that their behaviour was determined by being a woman:

I tend to go into work deliberately smiley and am expected to do this while in work. I also think I probably touch more. It's quite acceptable for me to put my arm round somebody if they need comforting.

(Teacher in a Secure Unit)

Anna (Doctor) felt that female doctors are more likely to be physical, and respond sensitively, than male doctors. However, she suggested that to enhance career prospects some female doctors consciously stop themselves behaving in this way:

You see some women doctors and you'd never know they were women doctors ... They become very masculine in the way they make decisions, in the way they interact with patients and nurses ... A lot of women feel that in order to get on in medicine they have to become masculine because it's male dominated. Often they're right, actually, because they're the women who do best.

The majority of women felt that women's health was not seen as an issue in their workplace. It was either never mentioned, or it was discussed in a negative way which some women found offensive, uncaring and insensitive:

> The odd partner, if you're grumpy or whatever will probably turn around and say 'Oh time of the month?'.
>
> (Solicitor)

> 'You can't have your cake and eat it' is I think his [the boss'] favourite expression. 'If you want to be treated as equals you have to behave as equals. Men don't create once a month because they're unwell. Men don't demand additional care and consideration because they're pregnant therefore the same must apply'.
>
> (Programme Development Manager)

> You get sly comments – 'Oh it must be the time of the month' or something like that if you say something that's out of turn . . . I think they'd feel upset if they knew how unsympathetic they came over. I think a lot of men that work there like to think of themselves as being very liberal and not too traditional but I don't think that's true at all. They're totally unsympathetic about issues like that.
>
> (Teacher in a Secure Unit)

Those women who worked in a predominantly female environment experienced more sympathetic acknowledgement of menstruation or PMT and its effects. Three of the four women in that situation found that it was informally acceptable for women to go home if necessary.

When questioned about women managers, not one of the women considered that male colleagues would be, or were, happy working for a woman as their senior manager. Anna (Doctor) suggested it would depend on who the woman was, but that some men could not cope with a woman further up the scale and argued or questioned all her decisions. The interviewees recalled that when male colleagues had a woman senior their responses were obstructive. Kate (Programme Development Manager) described how two men, who resented the position of the female centre manager, initially were subtle in their undermining of her authority, but were increasingly uncooperative and eventually left. When the only female senior manager was appointed at her institution, Hilary (Senior Lecturer in PE) stated that the male staff were 'completely disorientated . . . It was the biggest culture shock of their lives'. After 54 years of male management in the institution, her appointment had a major impact. But once she faced serious management problems the men adopted an 'I told you so' mood. This attitude was unjustified, since the woman manager proved to be better than any previous male managers. In addition, the problems she faced were related to restructuring of the institution and involved issues which had not occurred previously – a male manager could not have coped better.

The personality of the senior manager was quoted as an important factor by two women. Half of Janet's (Hospital Administrator) male colleagues were 'definitely uncomfortable' with their female boss. They stated that this was because of her personality but Janet felt that it was because she was a woman and that this was reflected in the way they treated other women staff. The other half respected the boss but she had to earn this respect. Ruth (Speech Therapist) felt that the personality of her woman manager affected the way others perceived and responded to her. But she recognised that her sex was a major contributory factor:

> ... she's an example of a woman who's got power and uses it in a totally callous and unjust way. She's a very good manager in that she's good at fighting for people's rights and everything she says goes. But she's very insensitive to people on a personal level. She's very good at organising people but has no compassion about her. She totally loses all that side of a female that is supposed to be the good and positive side, and has developed that side of her that's very assertive and ruthless ... I think she's had to do this to survive.

Andrea (Local Government Officer) felt that woman managers were scrutinised more stringently. She recounted how this had happened in a different section of her workplace:

> Because a woman has been outspoken and creative and acted like a really good manager but in a 'feminist' way, the male top management can't cope with that so they're going to restructure the service and put the man who's her deputy in charge of it all and move her sideways so she doesn't have any direct operational management ... 'yes men' are moving up so the Equal Opportunities Policy is taking a step backwards.

Joanne (Solicitor) said that she would like to think that having a male or female director would not have made a difference to her colleagues, but she was unsure. Mary (Osteopath) imagined that traditional male osteopaths would find it difficult working with female osteopaths 'because traditionally men are not used to being in a subservient role when women are around, however liberal they may feel they are'. Liz's (Teacher in a Secure Unit) male colleagues would make their feelings of discontent clear to a woman manager even though these would be unjustified. The majority of male staff would question the security of the unit because they assume a woman is physically unable to control people, despite the fact that there has never been an incident to substantiate their fears – in the unit boys have attacked male staff but never females. Karen (Primary Teacher) was adamant that the male headteacher at her school could not cope with a woman manager 'because he is full of his own importance and thinks men can do everything better than women'.

Conclusion

The research reveals a range of significant features concerning women's experiences of employment and the persistence of discriminatory practices in the workplace, regardless of class or status. Jobs remain segregated, often informally, with women expected to perform certain jobs or duties solely because they are women. Their work profiles and promotion opportunities are restricted and there is clear evidence of considerable resistance by men to women managers. Further, the undermining of women's authority encompasses sexual harassment and intimidation at a range of levels. Regardless of their job, the experiences of women are clear: it is through their womanhood, their femininity, their physicality, that they remain judged. While much discrimination endured by women is subtle, it remains damaging and debilitating.

Although there has been a marked increase in the paid employment of women over the last decade, the dual role experienced by women workers remains onerous. Women in well-paid employment or living in substantial double-income households can, to an extent, be freed of this pressure by employing other women (usually at low pay) to carry out their domestic work and child-care. However, this is not an option for the majority of women in paid work and, despite rising male unemployment, women in heterosexual relationships continue to juggle the responsibilities of their job, housework and child-care.

The pressure on women to succeed in the public and private spheres is marked. Many of the women interviewed indicated their guilt or the feelings of inadequacy that result from not realising the objectives which they set for themselves. These were compounded by their awareness of the 'super-woman' construct via advertising and the media. This research demonstrates, that without shared responsibility for domestic labour and good quality child-care, the problems faced by women in employment will not be resolved. It is this frustration which impacts so heavily on women's lives as they seek to combine paid work and domestic responsibilities.

The combination of social and interpersonal forces governing women's experiences of the domestic/paid labour relationship represents a fundamental, material and political barrier to equality. With the notable exception of some middle-class women, their experience of paid work has become institutionally restricted to low-paid, part-time and unprotected jobs. This process of institutionalisation, however strongly resisted by women who refuse to be its victims, continues to affect access, status, pay, conditions, promotion and self-esteem. The advances that have been made are important. But their proclamation as a new dawn for women, as representing an era of 'post-feminism', is both unsustainable and premature.

Chapter 5

Fatal Abstraction: The Myth of the Positive Image

Introduction: Critical Theory and Media Analysis

Representation of the world, like the world itself, is the work of men; they describe it from their own point of view, which they confuse with the absolute truth.

> (Simone de Beauvoir, 1949 p. 175)

The effect of constant stereotyping and misrepresentation is to project an inaccurate and damaging view of women, providing the rationale for keeping us 'in our place' ... This unfair media treatment also conditions the way we women view ourselves ... We end up 'agreeing' to a greater or lesser extent that male means normal, superior, more important.

> (Dickey, 1985 p. 4)

The imagery associated with femininity, which defines the 'ideal' woman, is so all-pervasive, in newspapers, magazines, on television and radio, at the cinema and theatre and throughout advertising, that its messages are taken for granted. To the unprobing mind these images appear 'natural' and inert, interlocking almost imperceptibly with the same categories of images men and women have been socialised into creating since early childhood. This implies the existence of a relationship binding together the *specificity* of the process whereby images of women are produced and presented with the *generality* of the social relations which give rise to women's position in society.

Increasingly, feminist politics has appropriated and transformed existing knowledge and knowledge-in-process in order to inform its political activity. In so doing it has created a new vocabulary opening up a dialogue on previously unexplored areas of women's experiences. Significant develop-ments around the concept of ideology, especially in semiological and structural analysis (e.g. Barthes, 1973, 1967; Althusser, 1971; Levi-Strauss, 1966) have provided a rich theoretical source for feminists. The Althusserian notion that personal identity and social action are governed by ideology and that ways of thinking about the world become 'naturalised' had an obvious relevance to feminism given the taken-for-granted assumptions underpinning social constructions of femininity.

Directly related to its unprecedented growth and concentration during the 1960s and 1970s, the media increasingly became identified as the 'machinery of representation' in modern society – an institution of ideological control with the power to construct meaning about the world and represent it to the public in many different and conflicting ways (Hall, 1986 p. 9). Feminists began to prioritise the media's treatment of women, focusing on its part in reflecting society's preferred view of women. This work demonstrated that any analysis of media representations of women could not be divorced from the wider context of ownership and control as, increasingly, the ownership and editorial control of the media was concentrated in the hands of a very few white, rich men. Thus, imperialist, capitalist and patriarchal interests dominated media agendas. With women media workers under-represented throughout press and broadcast institutions, all aspects of media coverage, particularly media images of women, carried a legacy of male priorities and definitions.

As previously argued, a central proposition of 'post-feminism' is that sex discrimination legislation and equal opportunities policies have virtually eradicated inequality between the sexes. When applied to the media it is a proposition which cannot be sustained. An Equity report (March 1992) disclosed that on average women actors earn less than half the pay of their male counterparts. Women have less opportunities to work, have shorter careers and find acting jobs much harder to come by once they reach their 30s and 40s. This preoccupation with the 'use' of young women in theatre and film roles is institutionalised throughout the media.

In terms of appointment to senior positions within the media, a survey of journalists carried out in 1980 by Roger Smith (cited in TUC March 1984) revealed that 80 per cent of women in journalism were concentrated at the bottom of the organisational hierarchy, usually as news reporters, feature writers, writers for women's pages, etc. Moreover, although women accounted for 10 per cent of general news reporters, they tended to be assigned to lower status 'human interest' stories. Ten years later Gillian Dyer and Helen Baehr (*GH*, July 1990) state: 'News gathering is competitive and hierarchical – a job for the boys hunting in packs – and deeply implicated in the male worlds of politics, economics, business and industry'. Very few women rise to be specialists in industrial and political reporting or foreign news, with some notable exceptions such as television news journalist Kate Adie, who is single and without children. Similarly, Polly Toynbee, BBC Television's Social Affairs Editor, explained that when she was 24 and a newspaper journalist she had to choose between 'a career in hard news and remain childless, or stick to feature writing, columns and home news and start a family' (*GH*, July 1990).

The male dominance within broadcasting has been recognised and monitored by the European Broadcasting Union and the UK media unions over a long period. Their findings reveal that since the mid-1980s there has been relatively little change despite a surge of 'interest' in equal opportunities issues. Figures compiled from the 1990 survey by the Commission of the European Communities Steering Committee for Equal Opportunities in Broadcasting reveal that women represent just 36 per cent of the total broadcasting workforce (Gallagher, 1990). However, analysis of the occupational and hierarchical distribution of men and women within these organisations shows that 69 per cent of all permanent administrative posts are occupied by women, while 93 per cent of all permanent technical posts are occupied by men. Within every professional category women's share of employment is concentrated at the bottom of the hierarchy and is progressively reduced at each salary band, while for men it is precisely the reverse. The research shows that although women represent 69 per cent of the total workforce in administration, only 2 per cent are in the top salary bands nine and ten, while 21 per cent of the total 31 per cent of men employed in administration are in bands nine and ten. The study indicates that only 11 per cent of those employed in senior management are women and in terms of decision-making, the male membership of internal and external committees is 91 per cent and 88 per cent respectively.

Margaret Gallagher (1990) explains that these broad statistics confirm that careers in broadcasting are dominated by men. Statistical evidence from the Broadcasting Entertainment Cinematograph and Theatre Union (BECTU, 25 August 1991) concerning the occupational and hierarchical distribution of men and women employed in the BBC clearly supports the findings of the European Communities Commission. The full significance of these statistics is that they were researched *six years* after the BBC launched what it proclaims as one of the most progressive equal opportunities campaigns. It was not surprising, therefore, to hear one female employee, attending a conference on the future of women in British television (14 March 1991), comment that if she waits for equal opportunities strategies to bite, her opportunities will arrive with her bus pass! (BBC, 1991).

The Independent Television Commission (ITC) was unable to provide comparable statistics for its member companies or Channel 4, but it can be deduced from the *Final Report and Accounts* of its predecessor, the Independent Broadcasting Authority (IBA, 31 December 1990) that two of the nine members who sat on the Authority were women; three of the Authority's 24 senior staff were women and three of Channel 4's 14 senior staff were women. The last available information concerning male/female distribution of senior jobs in independent television companies published in 1984 demonstrated that the number of women represented in senior posts in commercial television was extremely poor. The issue is not simply about equality in employment, but concerns the roots of discrimination and inequality, buried much deeper and operating at the ideological level of attitudes and behaviour. This was forcefully illustrated by comments made by women in British television in March 1991. Anna Ford, BBC newsreader, stated that 'a great many men espouse the cause of women, but they do not yet feel it in their guts' (BBC, 1991 p. 7). Liddy Oldroyd, freelance producer/ director, described her experience as the first woman director of *Spitting Image*, working with 120 men and greeted by a puppeteer who yelled 'Hey we got some pussy on the floor. How d'you feel about that, boys?' (BBC, 1991, p. 8). Janet Street-Porter commented that the BBC 'is like a Masonic League with its own rituals' (BBC, 1991, p. 10).

Alan Parkhurst, Group Director of Personnel, Central TV, described typical boardrooms as male clubs where sexist attitudes are betrayed by chance remarks, e.g. 'It's essential to get the right person and when *he* starts ...'; 'Your policy on sexual harassment. I just told the young lady I knew Spring was coming because the skirts are getting shorter. Is this sexual harassment?', 'You know I support your ideas on this sexual equality thing, but when the money gets tight, we have to consider the priorities' (BBC, 1991, p. 10). Jenny Russell, Producer, *Channel 4 News*, pointed out that 'women who speak out are penalised by being ignored, demoted or denied good assignments' (BBC, 1991 p. 11). Jini Rawlings, Chair of the Committee, *Reel Women*, stated that 'women often don't speak up because they will be seen as aggressive' (BBC, 1991 p. 11). Janet Street-Porter referred to this as being part of elaborate rituals where 'women are not very good at speaking the language'. What is clear from these comments is that superficial attention paid to equal opportunities fails to acknowledge the entrenched attitudes and behaviourial codes underpinning women's oppression and marginalisation within the media and its organisation.

The portrayal of women in the media denies them strong, powerful, independent images. They have been systematically excluded from 'serious' roles or coverage and are invariably consigned to 'women's pages', 'women's fiction', 'day-time television' and 'supporting' or 'servicing' roles. Further, black women and lesbian women, conveying the most threatening images to white male supremacy, are rarely represented positively (Dickey *et al.*, 1985). Any aspect of womanhood which does not correspond to the traditional, male-defined image is ignored or marginalised. Women's marginalisation also derives from the media's use of the English language in all its maleness, e.g. 'mankind', 'manpower', 'chairman', 'man-made', 'man-in-the-street'. As Simone de Beauvoir wrote in the late 1940s, women are treated as 'other' – alienated from a world in which they represent over half the population (de Beauvoir, 1949).

At best, media treatment of women can be described as narrow. Typically, women's interests and activities are limited to the confines of home and family as doting wives and mothers, passive servers (servicing both domestic and sexual functions), dependent on men. Alternatively, women's bodies are frequently exploited for their sexuality and physical appearance. In advertising women's bodies are used unremittingly as 'bait' to sell a whole range of commodities. Margaret Gallagher (1979 p. 11) argues that underlying most media images of women are the dichotomous definitions of 'woman as virgin' or 'woman as whore' – 'good' women or 'bad' women. The 'virgin' image may vary in the form of its presentation, but 'throughout the imagery runs a consistent stress on subordination, sacrifice and purity.' The 'whore' image is also diverse, but connections with dangerousness, insensitivity and unscrupulousness predominate. She considers that 'this points to a fundamental paradox in female imagery, and an inability to cope with women's real sexuality'.

Ultimately, women are instructed that conformity to weakness, passivity and self-sacrifice will encourage male love/approval but that independence, strength and self-confidence will be punished by castigation, desertion and physical abuse. In this context stereotyped images of women in 'acceptable' roles are presented as 'natural'. Socially constructed gender differences are constantly manipulated and confused with biological differences. To 'be a woman' is to be defined beyond the biological, representing 'a whole process in which individual and gendered identity are acquired' (Betterton, 1987 p. 7). With women defined and judged by physical appearance, their 'emphasised femininity' (Connell, 1987), the media '. . . reinforce the ways of acting, thinking and feeling "characteristic" of the female role, femininity and womanhood . . .' (Smart and Smart, 1978 p. 2). Stereotypes of femininity are constructed through appearance – 'the visual image'.

Discourse analysis, derived from the work of Michel Foucault (1977), has been developed within feminist analyses of the functioning of ideas and ideology as essential components within the relations of power and domination. Medical, legal, political and religious discourses emerge and consolidate within key institutions (the family, the church, the school, the media) each transmitting and reproducing 'knowledge' about women and women's sexuality. They are derived within and supportive of 'hegemonic masculinity' (Connell, 1987), their ideas and constrictions universalised, reflecting taken-for-granted or common-sense assumptions. They legitimise male dominance over women through social forces, defining and institution-alising 'desirable' roles and relationships for women.

Ideologies are not static, they represent a process of reproduction of ideas, with no clear historical beginning or end. They are 'timeless' and self-perpetuating because they are part of an inheritance and retain a 'purpose'. As Judith Williamson (1978 p. 99) states, '... obviously an ideology can never admit that it "began" because this would be to remove its inevitability'. Thus, the 'knowledge about women' portrayed in the media is always produced from something believed to be 'already known', acting as its seal of approval, endowing it with truth. Media claims for neutrality and objectivity, for coverage as reflective of 'reality' depend on context. When media messages coincide with and reinforce existing ideas and values widely held in society, the effect is cumulative and powerful. Thus, 'images of glamorous women or perfect mothers may not correspond to the experience of most women, but they do define femininity in ways which are perceived as actually existing' (Betterton, 1987 p. 22).

As Foucault argued, the relationship between power and knowledge is central. Patriarchal knowledge defines women and subordinates their experi-ences and knowledge to the margins. However, this process is not simply deterministic. Liberal democratic thought has always proclaimed the 'right' to opinion, free speech and protest and more critical analysis has identified the revolutionary significance of resistance. However, such freedoms are differentially experienced, reflecting differentials in power. Those who are not in a privileged position, having limited access to the formal means of mass communication, endure reduced and limited freedoms (Hall, 1986). Yet it is precisely the illusion of freedom which is essential to the maintenance of ideology. Competing ideas are taken up and reworked in a different context, over time. Struggles around the content of media images of women seemingly have succeeded in establishing 'new' and more representative images but such shifts are possibly no more than accommodation, incorpora-tion or distortion. For instance, since the 1970s the notion of 'liberation' has been co-opted from the women's movement and reworked so that a 'liberated woman' is portrayed as a paid worker, still managing to service her family and to look ultra-feminine. Thus, while the content of the image has changed, the fundamental definitions of femininity have not.

The 'visual', the significance of 'looking', is of particular importance in defining femininity because, as already stated, a woman's character and status is invariably judged by her physical appearance. John Berger's (1972) analysis of the female nude draws some interesting conclusions regarding the relationship between images and their spectators:

> To be born a woman has been to be born, within an allotted and confined space, into the keeping of men ... Men look at women.... Women watch themselves being looked at. Women are depicted in a quite different way from men – not because the feminine is different from the masculine – but because the 'ideal' spectator is always assumed to be male and the image of the woman is designed to flatter him.
>
> (Berger, 1972 pp. 46, 47, 64)

The culture of looking is different for women. While the image can be reversed, portraying a male nude, the relationships of power and control are *not* reversible. In fact '... the male spectator's enjoyment is not solely erotic. It is connected to a sense of power and control over the image' (Betterton, 1987 p. 11). Therefore representations of men and women through formalised imagery demand an analysis of power, particularly in representations of male and female sexuality (Morphy, 1984). The construction of ideal types or images of women's bodies serve to make men feel more secure and powerful and women insecure and powerless. As Virginia Woolf so eloquently put it more than sixty years ago, 'Women have served all these centuries as looking-glasses possessing the magic and delicious power of reflecting the figure of man at twice its natural size' (cited in Cline and Spender, 1987 p. 18).

In 'Western' societies white, middle-class, male action, thoughts and words represent the 'norm' and women are constantly defined in relation to men. However, meanings do not simply live in images – they circulate between the representation, the receiver of the image and wider society (Kuhn, 1985). The application of semiological analysis in feminist media criticism has opened the possibility of exploring more closely the contribution of media practices. Camera techniques, lighting, particular forms of media presentation (e.g. news, documentary, light entertainment, drama, comedy, advertising) collectively structure images as a preferred signification.

Semiology has sought to explore the nature of sign-systems going beyond the narrow rules of grammar and syntax, opening up and revealing underlying meanings within a text. This has resulted in a concern with connotation and denotation – those associations and images called upon and made known by certain usages and combinations of signs. Central here is examination of familiar or latent myths and images alive in the culture of those who make and receive media content. According to Olivier Burgelin (1972 p. 317) '... the mass media clearly do not form a complete culture on their own ... but simply a fraction of such a system which is, of necessity, the culture to which they belong'. This indicates a value in semiological analysis over conventional content analysis, directed towards uncovering the latent ideology and 'bias' of media content, rather than purely manifest content. In this the receiver of the 'sign' plays an active role in the process of creating meaning (Williamson, 1978).

Thus, ideology sustains its impetus and becomes precisely that of which we are not aware. It is not received from above – it is constantly recreated through people. In this sense the signifying practices of the media are inextricably connected to personal and collective identity. Stuart Hall (1973) develops a similar analysis in his work on television discourse, proposing that the audience is both the source and the receiver of the television message. Images are, therefore, recognisable by the viewer in a way that is widely shared within a culture. They are both denotative and connotative. Yet it remains important to acknowledge the scope for the formation of alternative understandings of a message at the connotative or contextual level. The notion of 'resistance' is important here. Hall (1973 pp. 14–15) suggests that such 'misunderstandings' of the 'dominant' code have a societal basis – that is they are identified not as a defect in the process of communication as such, but as a feature of fundamental 'structural conflicts, contradictions and negotiations of economic, political and cultural life'.

Hall's typology of 'hegemonic', 'professional', 'negotiated' and 'oppositional' codes was concerned with identifying 'certain broadly-defined societal perspectives which audiences might adopt towards the televisual message'. The 'hegemonic' or dominant code for Hall represents the ideal 'perfectly transparent communication' whereby the audience 'decodes a message in terms of the reference-code in which it has been coded'. The 'professional' code refers to those technical operations and skills employed by media professionals in the process of production and presentation. To a certain extent this code is independent/autonomous in its functioning. Yet it does operate '*within* the hegemony of the dominant code', serving to reproduce dominant definitions. When an audience decodes a message within the 'negotiated' code, it acknowledges the legitimacy of the dominant, hegemonic code while reserving the right to negotiate an alternative position. This relates to Roland Barthes' (1973) concept of 'inoculation' in which 'the dominant ideology is able to ensure its continuance by neutralising threats from oppositional ideologies, through acknowledging some of their elements in an apparent show of tolerance' (Baehr and Dyer, 1987 pp. 9, 10). The 'oppositional' code represents the point at which the audience rejects the dominant, professional and hegemonic codes and arrives at a different reading of a message – a 'ripe' moment for political action or resistance.

Women's resistance in the private and the public spheres has been constant over the last 150 years, but the enormity of challenging media sexism cannot be underestimated. When women are continually portrayed as 'objects' and servicers to men and children, this not only reinforces the unequal treatment of women elsewhere in society, but more invidiously impinges on the views women hold of themselves, as well as their expectations (TUC, 1984). Just as equal opportunities legislation has lagged behind reality, so social and cultural representations of women have lagged behind the law. Beneath the veneer of equality and 'alternative' images of 'new liberated women' lie the established misogynist messages. Media sexism cannot be divorced or isolated from other oppressions. However, a critical feminist analysis provides a framework within which the apparent unity of ideology (reinforcing and transmitting classist, racist and sexist images) can be deconstructed.

Critical work must pursue its analysis at both the visible, transparent level of appearances and content and also at the less obvious, below-surface level of hidden meaning and context. By focusing on a specific set of representations, those of Liverpool women, and moving between the ideas and assumptions which informed the writing of those women's lives in theatre and television, and the reality and experiences of those women represented, the research was concerned to assess the derivation, definition and maintenance of the stereotype. It concentrated on television, film and theatre since these have been the key vehicles used in popularising contemporary images and representations of Liverpool women. Interviews with scriptwriters, authors, women actors and the women whose lives have been subjected to stereotype were used to consider whether the claims of 'post-feminism' towards a redefinition of women's lives are sustainable.

'Liverpool Mams': The Patriarchal Construction of Motherhood

A consistent theme in writing parts for Liverpool women is the matriarch. Such women are characterised as wives and mothers whose attention centres on the home and family. The character Nellie Boswell, in the situation comedy *Bread*, portrays a Liverpool woman in her 50s whose energies are almost exclusively tied to servicing and holding together her crisis-prone family: a cantankerous father who lives next door; a wayward husband who gravitates between his wife and Irish mistress; four sons and a daughter who drift in and out of romantic relationships but always return to the security of the 'nest'; an Irish nephew who has to be kept on the 'straight and narrow'. Nellie is strongly defined as the lynchpin of the family – the emotional pivot through which the action takes place. As daughter Aveline stated when she returned home after leaving her husband, 'Oh Mam, what would we all do if there wasn't you. This house is like a little church, all warm and welcoming and you Mam, you are the altar' (*Bread*, BBC TV, Autumn 1990). Alongside runs the notion of the self-sacrificing mother who subordinates her own needs to those of her husband and family. Thus Nellie struggled with her desire to enhance her relationship with Derek (a stranger she met in the park) against her 'duty' as a wife and mother. She was identified as true to her own needs and desires (albeit with guilt) by going away to the Cotswolds with Derek overnight. It could be argued that this gave a positive portrayal of a woman breaking out of the compassion-trap. However, that opportunity was lost since the script went on to 'punish' Nellie for breaking the rules by having Grandad fall and break his leg whilst she was away.

A similar tendency can be identified in the television soap *Brookside*. In a glossy public relations brochure (1988 p. 27), Phil Redmond (*Brookside*'s creator and Executive Producer) states:

> ... the soap opera genre, heavily centred on domestic, 'maternal' events, has typically provided strong women characters of special interest to its presumed female audience. *Brookside* ... does not fit easily into the sex-stereotyping formula ...

However, closer examination of the central women characters such as Chrissy Rogers reveals obvious stereotyping. Chrissy was wife of Frank and mother of Sammy, Geoff and Kate. She, as with many of the married women characters, was always seen in relation to her family. A female scriptwriter for *Brookside*, when asked about examples of sex-stereotyping commented:

> Chrissy Rogers is the worst one in my view. She's always this slightly ratty, but underneath it, loving mother, and I wish she'd fucking well stop it!
>
> (Interview, 20 September 1990)

Storylines focused on Chrissy's struggle to keep the family going in the face of financial hardship since Frank was out of work. Thus, Frank, in conversation with his daughter Sammy, bestowed the virtues of his wife's self-sacrificing nature:

> ... she'll take on anything your mum. Look at me, there she was waiting to become a teacher and she ends up with me, Frank, the steel erector ... and I was made up to get her.
>
> (*Brookside*, Channel 4, Summer 1990)

A hint that Chrissy might be heading for an affair was quashed within the *Brookside* storyline conferences. Again a female scriptwriter revealed:

> Chrissy was not allowed to have an affair because we had to present
> her as the perfect wife, essentially, in this perfect marriage.
>
> (Interview, 20 September 1990)

Similar problems can be identified in other married women in *Brookside* –
Sheila Grant and Doreen Corkhill were obvious examples. It was Doreen
who seriously considered sleeping with her employer in order to keep her
family's finances afloat. However, this was set in the context of her
husband's (Billy) financial troubles. The 'story' was Billy's. Doreen's
actions were reactive to that story. Sheila Grant was always portrayed as a
woman of strength, with views of her own, often faced with difficult
decisions in her life. Yet again the attempt to convey a 'positive' woman was
undermined by storylines which continued to define her role within the
family even as she fought against it. Thus Sheila's commitment to her Open
University course was regularly challenged by storylines which pulled her
back into her role as wife and mother. Sue Johnston, who played the Sheila
Grant character, commented:

> I was really sad that it ended up her becoming even more of an
> appendage to another man and the studies disappeared. I felt that was
> when I started to lose my interest in Sheila Grant.
>
> (Interview, 27 October 1990)

In the development of her character beyond her eventual divorce from Bobby
Grant, Sheila was portrayed, on the surface, as a more 'liberated' woman in
her relationship with Billy Corkhill. However, an opportunity to see Sheila
establishing an independent life for herself was not grasped. As Eithne
Browne (the actor who played Chrissy Rogers) commented (Interview, 1
August 1990) the story was written in such a way that Sheila needed a man
to be able to leave Bobby and set up home again in 'the Close'.

Willy Russell's character Shirley Valentine exhibits similar proneness to
domestic martyrdom. Even as she decided to take positive action in search
of her lost identity, she was not allowed to do so without the compulsory
agonising over husband and children:

> Just . . . just do me a big favour God, an' don't make me have to pay
> for it durin' this fortnight. Don't let anythin' happen to our
> Millandra, our Brian . . . Three weeks secretly ironin' an' packin' an'
> cookin' all his meals for two weeks. They're all in the freezer. Me
> mother's gonna come in an' defrost them an' do his cookin'. With
> a bit of luck 'he' won't even notice I'm not here.
>
> (*Shirley Valentine* script, 1988 p. 16)

There is an implicit assumption in much of the material analysed that these women wield the power in their families. Hence, Freddy Boswell in *Bread* described his wife as 'tough as a butcher's block, son' and Theresa in *Letter to Brezhnev* commented 'I've only got me mam's wages and if I don't give them to her she'll chore the face off me'. Such dialogue is reinforced by references made by women actors and scriptwriters:

> It's [Liverpool] a matriarchal society ... It's not open that they [mams] hold the reins to the power base, but they do.
> (Margi Clarke, actor, 12 July 1990)

> The person who made me who I am was me mam ... Women handled the money well – kept the family together ... they're resilient, tough ...
> (Jimmy McGovern, scriptwriter, 6 August 1990)

Elaine's mother in *Letter to Brezhnev* is portrayed as domineering and loud. She swears a lot and insists that no daughter of hers is going to Russia. Nellie Boswell appears to dominate her children in much the same way. Billy's wife Julie shouted at him as he retreated to the fold:

> That's right, Billy, run away, run to yer mam! Jump into her apron pocket and hide.
> (*Bread*, BBC TV Autumn 1990)

What is not acknowledged within this discourse is that whatever power is given to these women is confined to the private, domestic sphere. As Chris Bernard (Director of *Letter to Brezhnev*) stated, 'the women have matriarchal power, not political power' (Interview, 9 August 1990). It is Joey Boswell who is acknowledged as having responsibility for overseeing the daily interactions of the Boswell family with the outside world. Hence his father stated:

> Look son you're the rock here, the family anchor is hanging on to you, so don't let go.
> (*Bread*, BBC TV Autumn 1990)

Women who hold powerful positions outside the family are frequently portrayed negatively, as hard, uncaring, even dangerous. This is well illustrated in the characterisation of women 'officials' such as the 'frustrated spinster' in charge of the fraud squad, the stony-faced psychiatrist and the glove-fisted social worker in Alan Bleasdale's *Boys from the Blackstuff* and

Martina, the DSS clerk in *Bread*. Sue Johnston (27 October 1990) expressed it this way:

> I think there's still something that frightens men about strong women. They don't mind strong women around, but they don't want *their* women to be strong.

There is a clear contradiction between dialogue which portrays existing 'mams' in a heavily sentimentalised fashion and dialogue which deals with women as potential wives and mothers. This can be seen in Willy Russell's *Stags and Hens*:

> EDDY: I've seen it before. Once they get married the edge goes ... it's the beginnin' of the end for him.
> BILLY: I'm not gonna get married Eddy. I'm stayin' at home with me mam.
>
> (*Stags and Hens* script, 1985 p. 24)

It is clear that a difference emerges in the way men relate to their 'mams' and their girlfriends/wives. It was legitimate for Nellie Boswell in *Bread* to shout and bawl at her sons, but when Julie, Billy's wife, attempted to shout back at her husband she was portrayed in a negative light. In response to Julie's behaviour Billy exclaimed to his solicitor:

> It's humiliation isn't it, it's trespassing on a man's pride ... It's breaking and entering a man's ego. It's homicide of the homo-sapiens.
>
> (*Bread*, BBC TV Autumn 1990)

Another recurrent theme in the material is that of the 'naturalness' of motherhood. The portrayal of Aveline in *Bread* as being obsessed with 'having babies' from the moment of her marriage is a clear example. She hounded her husband at every available opportunity, bringing him persuasive 'little treats'. In one scene she implored 'It's not unusual to want a baby is it ... every woman wants a baby'. Similarly, Rita, in Willy Russell's film *Educating Rita*, is admonished by her father 'I don't know why you bothered getting married, you're not pregnant yet'. Her husband eventually gives her the ultimatum 'It's dead easy, Susan, you pack that course in and stop takin' the pill or you're out'. Beryl, in Carla Lane's *The Liver Birds*, criticised Sandra for 'not knowing the first thing about babies' as if it should come naturally. Even more contentious is the denial of women who reject motherhood. Discourse around the sanctity of motherhood is very powerful.

Two female scriptwriters for *Brookside* explained how this was a potential problem with a female character on *Brookside*, Patricia Farnham. They described the anxieties of the male scriptwriters in the storyline conferences who feared Patricia would become an antipathetic character if she was seen not to be very good with small children. However, as the women scriptwriters explained, not all women particularly like or are good with small children, but this does not mean they do not love their children.

Although aspects of the characterisations of Liverpool women as mothers appear 'familiar', and have some basis in the history of those women's experiences (such as qualities of strength and spirit in the face of adversity) they are lifted out of the context of their historical reality. As Noreen Kershaw stated, '... it only needs notching up a few inches and you're playing something that isn't real' (Interview, 1 August 1990). Decontextualised from their historical reality, images of Liverpool women as mothers have been reconstructed firmly within a patriarchal context.

'Tarts with Hearts'?: The Politics of Sexuality I

Television and theatre representations of Liverpool women's sexuality are dominated by the assumptions of heterosexuality. The 1993–94 *Brookside* storyline of Beth Jordache's lesbianism was the notable exception. Otherwise the sexuality of the women characters is consistently defined from a male perspective – woman as sex object; woman as 'other'. Pauline Duggan in Alan Bleasdale's *The Muscle Market* is portrayed as a sex-starved wife and has little dialogue other than the regular overtures she makes to her husband for sex. Husband Danny, on the other hand, is seen to rebuff Pauline's advances with such one-liners as 'it's quarter to seven and we're both 41'. Danny, it seems, is far more interested in his vampish secretary and mistress Susan Baxter. It is Danny who chases the relationship while Susan is portrayed as 'cool' and reluctant, and supposedly powerful, because of her sexuality. Yet her sexuality is defined through Danny's experience, not her own. Frustrated at her refusal to have sex with him in the woods after he gave her a gold bracelet Danny says, 'You've had the wages, what about the sin?' Here Susan is instantly defined as 'whore' – existing only to service Danny's sexual needs. This portrayal is reinforced in the continuing storyline when it is revealed that Susan has embezzled some £43,000 from Danny's business and plans to flee abroad with her 'real' lover. Women's sexuality in this characterisation is defined as dangerous and emasculating. She is portrayed as the villain while Danny is the victim of her sexuality and the script ensures that Susan is punished. When Danny learns of her 'betrayal' of him he butts her in the face and kicks her several times while she lies helpless on the floor.

There is a tendency to dichotomize women's sexuality into images of Madonna/whore, good/bad, passive/unchaste. A double standard of morality is evident as women's sexuality is regulated through male definitions of the legitimacy of particular expressions of that sexuality. Legitimation not only has meaning in terms of the servicing of male sexuality. Women's sexuality within the home is defined within the contextual primacy of motherhood. Aveline's sexuality in *Bread* was given expression solely through her obsession with becoming pregnant from the moment she was married. Similarly, in *Educating Rita*, Rita's sexuality is confined by her struggle to avoid becoming pregnant, indicating selfishness for so doing. The expression of female sexuality through motherhood is portrayed as taking precedence over other expressions of that sexuality. In *Bread* Nellie Boswell faces the dilemma of balancing her needs and those of her family. The script restricted Nellie to the 'acceptable' female fantasy of temptation, not allowing her to succumb to that temptation. A decision taken at a *Brookside* storyline conference not to allow Chrissy Rogers to have an affair illustrates the point. A woman scriptwriter believed that Chrissy having an affair would threaten the male scriptwriters, 'at a personal level ... if Chrissy could, so could their wives' (Interview, 20 September 1990).

The dichotomy between 'acceptable' and 'unacceptable' expressions of female sexuality is reinforced by women characters conforming to the 'acceptable' stereotype and being given the dialogue with which to berate other women portrayed as possessing that 'dangerous' female sexuality which exists outside the bounds of marriage. In *Bread* it is Nellie Boswell who repeatedly castigates 'Lilo-Lil', her husband's mistress, whom she blames for his unfaithfulness: 'and I know that Irish tart is back because it's her chest that causes all these adverse weather conditions' (*Bread*, BBC TV, Autumn 1990).

Similarly, Nellie disapproved of her son's attraction to a sophisticated 'older' woman living across the road, 'Our Jack's mixed up with thin Lizzie over the road, old enough to have given birth to everybody in the entire planet' (*Bread*, BBC TV, Autumn 1990). In Willy Russell's *Stags and Hens*, Linda, the prospective bride is condemned by her women friends for daring to 'break the rules' by dancing with her ex-boyfriend on the eve of her wedding:

BERNADETTE: Yes, an' we all know where talk leads ...
CAROL: Y' don't see ex-fellas the night before y' gettin' married do y'?
BERNADETTE: But, I'll tell y' what, if y' ask me she's up to no good. That girl is playing with fire. We're her mates, I reckon we

better sort out a way to stop her gettin' burnt ... I think she's immoral, I do.

(*Stags and Hens* script, 1985 p. 55)

The women then, are equally constrained by other women who deliver the message of patriarchal ideology. There is a parallel here to the reactions of women spectators to images of women characters breaking the rules. Those interviewed indicated that portrayals of Liverpool women which express a very positive, proactive female sexuality make them feel uneasy. In particular the bawdiness and up-front sexuality of the women in *Letter to Brezhnev* and *Stags and Hens* was met with ambivalence. A woman scriptwriter for *Brookside* (Interview, 20 September 1990) suggested that this need to dissociate as a woman from such images with the reaction 'I'm not like that', reflects women's conditioning not to find them acceptable. By contrast, 'If you had a male character who was sexy and raunchy and broke the rules men wouldn't necessarily want to dissociate themselves from it'.

Yet male sexuality is consistently portrayed as positive. Aveline's husband in *Bread* put it:

Man is the force, the power. Man's libido is all mixed up with his pride. Man likes to see himself as the great begetter of life.

(*Bread*, BBC TV, Autumn 1990)

Implicitly, women's sexuality is limited, presented as passive or submissive. In *The Liver Birds*, Paul and Robert pursued respective girlfriends, Sandra and Beryl, primarily for sex. In contrast, Sandra and Beryl were flattered by the attention, predictably struggling not to succumb to temptation. The following exchange is typical:

ROBERT: Beryl, I'm trying to ask you a question.
BERYL: I know, and I'm trying to avoid answering it.
ROBERT: Look, it's not like you think – at least not entirely. There are lots of reasons why a chap asks a girl back to his flat you know.
BERYL: Me mum only warned me about one.
ROBERT: The truth is I ... I want to have breakfast with you.
BERYL: That's the one ...
ROBERT: And I bet you don't know what I'm looking forward to most of all.
BERYL: I'll bet I do Robert.

(*The Liver Birds* script, 1975)

Beryl confided in Sandra,

> Besides it's wrong and I'm not happy doing wrong things, it's against my nature. All I needed was one little thing to stop me, and put me back on the straight and narrow.
>
> *(The Liver Birds* script, 1975)

There is a tendency in the material for female sexuality to be 'legitimately' expressed through the fantasy of romantic love. In *Stags and Hens*, Carol tries to draw a distinction, as she sees it, between 'blue' films and the film *Emmanuelle*,

> ... with the blue films it's just sex, y' know for the sake of it. With Emmanuelle it's like beautiful an' romantic, all in slow motion, now that's how sex should be. All soft an' in colour ... I'm not interested in fellers who want to make sex. I want a feller who makes love, not a feller who makes sex.
>
> *(Stags and Hens* script, 1985 p. 16)

Similarly, a contrast is drawn between the characters of Elaine and Theresa in *Letter to Brezhnev* in terms of their expressed sexuality. Theresa is portrayed as loud and confident with an openly expressed desire for sexual gratification. Yet from the outset her friend Elaine is portrayed as searching for romance. Out on the town in Liverpool both girls' expectations are fulfilled when they meet two Russian sailors. Theresa happily exclaims to Elaine that Sergei 'had me going all night'. By contrast Elaine tells a shocked Theresa 'it didn't seem to matter' that she and Peter didn't make love since they spent most of the night talking. While Chris Bernard, director of *Letter to Brezhnev* was keen to make the point that Theresa and Elaine were each 'perfectly legitimate in their desires and wants' (Interview, 9 August 1990), the storyline ultimately favours the woman who plays by the rules – Elaine. It is she who is seen to 'get the man' at the end of the film and go off to live 'happily ever after' while Theresa is left at the airport, a tearful and pathetic figure. The moral of the story being, of course, that 'good' girls are rewarded with romantic bliss, while 'bad' girls are punished by being left on the proverbial shelf. Attempts to portray a positive female sexuality frequently fail because of the habitual tendency to include a negative comment or consequence that tips the balance back towards disapproval. In *Shirley Valentine* although Shirley takes positive action in pursuing her personal needs and desires after years of prioritising her husband and children, voices of disapproval are constantly heard – most significantly, Shirley's own:

I suppose y' think I'm scandalous – married woman, forty-two, got grown up kids. I suppose y' think I'm wicked.

(*Shirley Valentine* script, 1988 p. 28)

In *Brookside* Tracey Corkhill's decision to terminate her pregnancy, while representing a genuine attempt to deal sensitively with the issue of a woman's right to choose, was purposefully counter-balanced by Sheila Grant's heavy religious sermonising (woman scriptwriter: Interview, 20 September 1990).

Brookside has made serious attempts to deal sensitively with men's physical and sexual violence. Inevitably these are difficult issues for an early evening soap and the expectations of drama-documentary analysis are sometimes too demanding. Yet it remains important that they are dealt with knowledgeably and that they challenge stereotypes. To that end there was a commitment to a storyline which did not 'blame' Sheila Grant for the rape which she suffered. Yet there was a danger that the script,

... could be accused of fulfilling every working-class male's nightmare – if you let your woman do an Open University course, some slick bastard's going to be at her – therefore keep your woman barefoot and pregnant.

(Jimmy McGovern, scriptwriter, Interview, 6 August 1990)

Similarly, the 'date rape' storyline involving Diana Corkhill and Peter Harrison was acknowledged for its attempts to deal with the emotional turmoil of a rape trial. The outcome, however, in which Peter was acquitted, reinforced a range of popularly-held prejudices about the validity of women's experiences and testimonies relating to male violence. It was broadcast at the precise time that women in real life were experiencing a backlash over their 'date rape' allegations against 'respectable' men who were known to them. Further, the 'routine' events and 'ordinariness' (Stanko, 1985) of male violence can be diminished by storylines which either focus on isolated or comparatively rare examples, or attribute causation to deviant, pathological individuals and families. The storylines involving the Jordache family reflected this tendency. Trevor Jordache was presented as the 'sick' wifebeater of Mandy and 'perverted' sexual abuser of his daughter, Beth. The characterisations of Mandy and Beth were problematic with Mandy the stereotypical, weak, passive, 'appropriate' or inevitable victim of verbal and physical violence who failed to protect her daughter from Trevor. Eventually her 'rescue' was due to the intervention of another man – Sinbad.

Beth's character initially conveyed the genuine courage and determination of a survivor of sexual violence. But this was undermined by a storyline involving the development of her lesbian sexuality. Had this storyline focused on another woman character it might have been a more positive portrayal but the choice of Beth inferred that she had 'turned into' a lesbian (for lesbian read 'man-hater') solely as a consequence of surviving sexual abuse from the man closest to her in her childhood. The first real attempt to develop a lesbian storyline was effectively undermined by connecting developing sexuality to childhood damage. Even within those scripts which seemingly are committed to representing positive and alternative images of Liverpool women's sexuality, therefore, there have remained powerful undercurrents of patriarchal discourse. From the interviews with actors and scriptwriters it is clear that this is a direct result of those scripts being conceived, written and presented within a patriarchal context.

'The Dolly Birds!': The Politics of Sexuality II

The overwhelming message within the texts and productions analysed is that stereotypes of femininity portray, even demand, women's subordination through the accommodation of men's interests and men's desires. Liverpool women's appearance and behaviour is constructed through male definitions. Aveline in *Bread* is one extreme example. She struts in high heels wearing tight, multi-coloured, gaudy clothes inferring a distinct lack of 'taste' or dress-sense. Her dialogue, delivered in a high-pitched, child-like naïve fashion, centres on an obsessive concern for her appearance and the desire for a career in modelling. Her only other concern is the equally predictable portrayal of her desire for motherhood and her pathetic attempts to become as efficient a wife and mother as her 'mam'. Aveline's character remains trapped within a classic patriarchal stereotype.

Consistently the women characters are seen to be concerned with their appearance *for* men. In *Letter to Brezhnev* Theresa arrives at a nightclub and goes directly to the 'ladies' dressed in her working clothes: white overall, turban and wellies. Within ten minutes, to the astonishment of her friend Elaine, she emerges in a red dress, black high heels, blond hair, bright red nail varnish and lipstick. Elaine asks her how she managed such a transformation, to which Theresa replies:

> I never go anywhere without me bits ... I'd rather go into work lookin' plain then it surprises the fellas when they see me lookin' like this.
>
> (*Letter to Brezhnev*, film, 1985)

When asked about her portrayal of Theresa, actor Margi Clarke suggested that flash clothes and heavy make-up can be important tools through which women can express their sexuality:

> It's a valuable part of our sexuality and it can be used as a cloak – the cloak of glamour. You can be a hag crone behind that cloak. It's protective for women I find, it can help build confidence, give your ego a boost, and I don't think we should ever sacrifice them.
>
> (Interview, 12 July 1990)

The difficulty is, of course, how exactly does a woman know whether she is adorning herself for herself? In adopting the expected codes there can be a denial of the subtle process through which women come to internalise the social construction of their identity, perpetuating an ideology which defines a woman's worth solely through her attractiveness to men.

The portrayals of Pauline Duggan and Susan Baxter in *The Muscle Market* represent a construction of female characters whose identities hinge on their attractiveness to one man, Danny Duggan. Pauline uses all the predictable 'womanly skills' in a vain attempt to rouse husband Danny's sexual interest in her. She gets his breakfast, sees him out, punishes her body on an exercise bike, cooks him dinner with his favourite pudding, and then waits patiently at home in front of the television, draped in a long black evening gown, for Danny to return. In contrast, Susan Baxter, Danny's mistress, does not need to work at gaining Danny's interest. She is slim, dressed in a tight slit skirt, an open-neck blue silky blouse and wears no make-up. Her non-verbal communication speaks volumes. She is either stood smoking with hand on hip 'Miss World-style' or sat at her desk cross-legged revealing a fair amount of leg. Both women are given the stereotyped identities which react only to the main character, Danny Duggan.

Beryl and Sandra in *The Liver Birds* operate within the same constraints:

> BERYL: Hey, Sandra, I've just thought, I look awful in the morning.
> SANDRA: Don't be silly. Men prefer natural beauty.
> BERYL: I know but I haven't got any. Even my eyelashes are bought by the yard.
> SANDRA: Well take them off.
> BERYL: But I'll have nothing to flutter at him.
>
> (*The Liver Birds* script, 1975)

Sandra went on to assist Beryl in 'beautifying' herself for her evening with Robert. Beryl had her hair ironed, a pedicure and face and eye masks applied. Sandra encouraged:

> Never mind Beryl, it's all in a good cause, think how beautiful you'll
> look for Robert.
>
> > *(The Liver Birds* script, 1975).

When Robert arrived prematurely, Sandra took it upon herself to explain:

> There's something you ought to know about women. During the
> course of making ourselves look beautiful there is a period of
> looking positively ugly. We usually manage to keep it a secret until
> we've married you.
>
> > *(The Liver Birds* script, 1975)

Here there was no indication that Beryl suffered all this for 'herself', because
she wanted to, in the way Margi Clarke referred to earlier. Rather this process
reflected a response to a male expectation of women and the comment about
the mask revealed after marriage has been a vehicle for so many male
comedians.

When a woman character attempts to cast off male expectations, other
women characters are used to speak the words of disapproval which define
her as deviant. In *Stags and Hens*, for example:

> LINDA: Come on . . . let's go.
> FRANCES: You haven't done y' make-up.
> LINDA: I can't be bothered. Come on.
> FRANCES: Y' not goin' into a dance without y' make-up on!
> LINDA: Why not?
> BERNADETTE: We'll wait for y' Linda . . . go on, do y' make-up.
> Y' don't wanna look a mess.
>
> > *(Stags and Hens* script, 1985 p. 31)

Similarly when Linda asks for a pint of bitter Bernadette chastises her:

> Linda love, no come on. A joke's a joke. I've seen you do that before
> love and we all think it's a good laugh. But not tonight. It's a hen
> night you're on, not a stag night. Now come on, something a bit more
> lady-like.
>
> > *(Stags and Hens* script, 1985 p. 32)

Shirley Valentine suffers an onslaught of disapproval from her daughter,
when she tells her of the imminent trip to Greece:

> I think it's a disgrace . . . two, middle-aged women goin' on their

own to Greece – I think it's disgustin'.

(Shirley Valentine script, 1988 p. 20)

Shirley reacts with a predictable loss of confidence and severe self-criticism:

I'd spent three weeks tellin' meself I could do it, that I'd be all right, be able to go, be able to enjoy meself. I'd even convinced meself that I wasn't really that old, that me hips weren't really as big as I thought they were, that me belly was quite flat for a woman who's had two kids. That me stretch marks wouldn't really be noticeable to anyone but me. I'd even let that salesgirl at C & A sell me a bikini. But ... I suddenly had thighs that were thicker than the pillars in the Parthenon. Me stretch marks were as big as tyre marks on the M6 an' instead of goin' to Greece I should be applyin' for membership of the pensioners' club.

(Shirley Valentine script, 1988 pp. 20, 21)

The issue of age and diminution of sexual attractiveness is a constant theme. While discussing the decision to deny Chrissy Rogers an affair, it was suggested by a female scriptwriter for *Brookside* that the male scriptwriters had difficulty in seeing Chrissy as a sexually attractive older woman (Interview, 20 September 1990). Supporting this observation another script-writer for *Brookside* recalled a previous storyline conference when it was planned that Barry Grant would begin an affair with an 'older woman'. It seems one of the men said 'Yes, make her about 28'! Similarly, when Sheila Grant and friend Kathy had a 'heart-to-heart' about 'love', prior to Sheila's wedding, Kathy told Sheila, 'you're lucky to find it once you're in your 40s'!

In Willy Russell's *Stags and Hens* the male characters are depicted through the cultural ideals of masculinity and femininity:

ROBBIE: I was goin' out with this crackin' tart once, y' know, nice smart girl she was. We went out on a foursome with Dave an' his tart. I got the first round in, asked them what they were havin'. This girl I'm with she said er, Babycham or a Pony or somethin', y' know, a proper tart's drink. Know what Dave's tart asked for eh? A pint of bitter! ... I was dead embarrassed. I'm out with this nice girl for the first time an' Dave's tart's actin' like a docker.
KAV: She's a laugh though isn't she?
ROBBIE: Laugh. The one I was with, she never came out with me again after that. I said to Dave after, 'Fancy lettin' your tart behave

127

like that'. 'She's always the same' he said. 'But she'll settle down when she's married'.

(Stags and Hens script, 1985 p. 20)

The male dialogue projects powerful images of misogyny. The discussion between 'the lads' about women's appearance before and after marriage is a striking example:

ROBBIE: When y' get married y' spend longer looking at them than y' do screwin' them, don't y'? I'll tell y' la, when I get married she'll be a cracker my missus will, beautiful.
KAV: She might be a cracker when y' get married to her Robbie but she won't stay that way.
ROBBIE: She bleedin' will!
KAV: Go 'way Robbie. Y' know what the tarts round here are like; before they get married they look great some of them. But once they've got y' they start lettin' themselves go. After two years an' a couple of kids, what happens, eh? They start leavin' the make-up off don't they, an' puttin on weight. Before y' know where y' are the cracker you're married's turned into a monster.
ROBBIE: My missus isn't gonna be like that. If any tart of mine starts actin' slummy she'll get booted out on her arse. A woman has got a responsibility to her feller. No tart of mine's gonna turn fat.

(Stags and Hens script, 1985 p. 23)

The relegation of woman to the status of 'object' or 'other' in this piece is unmistakable. Strong images of hegemonic masculinity underpin much of the writing. In *Educating Rita* her father supports her husband's view of his daughter's behaviour as deviant:

If that was a wife of mine I'd drown her.

(Educating Rita, film, 1984)

Similarly, in *Brookside* the storyline around the characters of Terry and Sue Sullivan was contentious. Inadvertently, Terry discovered he was not the father of her child. Sue's 'betrayal' threatened Terry's sexuality especially as he discovered his infertility. He reacted violently towards Sue, throwing her and the baby out of the house. Sue Johnston, who played Sheila Grant, recalled how Brian Regan, who plays Terry, received many letters following that episode of *Brookside* from men who applauded his violent behaviour towards his wife (Interview, 27 October 1990). His dialogue was tinged with misogynist phrases for several weeks afterwards such as 'life's a bitch and then you marry one'.

Class Unconsciousness: The Depoliticisation of the Working-Class Liverpool Woman

It has become usual for Liverpool women to be depicted exclusively as working-class women. However, this does not translate into any positive sense of the women as political. This is very much left to the male characters: the Boswell men in their encounters with DSS officialdom; Bobby Grant and Frank Rogers with their trades union struggles; the *Blackstuff* boys' soul-destroying experiences of unemployment. The women do not feature as active participants in class struggle. They are merely represented as providing unthinking support for their men. They are never seen organising, either in terms of jobs or a trade union. In *Brookside* Bobby Grant was the shop steward while his wife Sheila was not even a union member! Such representations reinforce the separation of men's and women's roles and responsibilities into the public and private spheres. As one of the women from the Liverpool Women's History Project stated:

> The establishment says it's okay for men to talk about politics, but 'nice' girls and women don't. It's not feminine or ladylike.
>
> (Interview, 19 July 1990)

Some attempt to redress this imbalance was carried in *Brookside* when Sammy Rogers developed a keen commitment to environmental issues – not exactly radical politics within the context of the contemporary consensus around 'going Green'. As a young, single woman in the 1990s there was a concession to giving Sammy access to some political dialogue. It is interesting to note that Jimmy McGovern (ex-scriptwriter for *Brookside*), although responsible for the more hard-hitting storylines about white, working-class males in Thatcher's Britain, stated his decision to leave *Brookside* was influenced by the rejection of a script he wrote which politicised the character of Tracey Corkhill (Interview, 6 August 1990). This involved Tracey organising a ceremonial burning of thousands of copies of *The Sun* newspaper on the first anniversary of the Hillsborough Disaster.

It seems that women are allowed to be narrowly political only in the compartmentalised and marginalised area of 'women's issues': infertility, menstruation, rape, housework. As such, this lumps together all women and underestimates differences generated by 'race' and class. The scripts reflect a clear tendency to neglect the perspective of working-class Liverpool women. They sentimentalise the experiences of these women and represent their lives negatively. The heavily sentimentalised character of matriarch Nellie Boswell, for example, distorts the reality of the struggles faced historically by working-class Liverpool wives and mothers. There is an exploitation of a mythology which romanticises such women as 'hard' and 'earthy', but with heart and moral purpose. Writer Carla Lane commented:

> I love Liverpool mams. I love the days when they wore black shawls and sold celery on the streets, with pink faces.
>
> (Interview, 9 August 1990)

As one of the women from the Liverpool Women's History Project commented about Carla Lane's *Bread*:

> I find it a very funny programme. She has got a gift for knowing what people can laugh at, Carla Lane, but it's got to be emphasised that it's just a funny programme – *it's not life.*
>
> (Interview, 19 July 1990)

This emphasises the point made earlier by actor Noreen Kershaw (Interview, 1 August 1990) when she highlighted the risks involved in exaggerating particular traits for dramatic effect. This tendency is something Margi Clarke referred to as 'TV Scouse' – the greatly exaggerated use of working-class Liverpool idiom and accent for comic effect. She feels that there is a definite trading on that 'forced' working-class Liverpool identity which subsequently has consequences for Liverpool women actors like herself, who can often become type-cast, and for the stereotyping of working-class Liverpool women.

In the texts there is a condescending middle-class subtext which underpins the storylines governing the lives of working-class Liverpool women. In *The Liver Birds* much of the comic effect relied heavily on the stereotyping of Beryl as a young, common, loud-mouthed, scatty, working-class Liverpool woman who was constantly reminded of her inferiority by middle-class Sandra. The strength of the storyline lay in the humour generated by the juxtaposition of such an unlikely pairing. The following extracts of dialogue illustrate the point:

> BERYL: And you know Sand, he's not like any other feller I've had, he likes books and paintings and talks posh. He's one of your lot.
> SANDRA: Well at last you're going in for a bit of culture. It makes a change.
>
> SANDRA: He loves you for what you are.
> BERYL: That's right, it's what I am. What am I?
> SANDRA: Well. You're – small – blond – noisy and er . . .
> BERYL: Common.
> SANDRA: Yes – no – well nice common.

BERYL: What's nice common?
SANDRA: Well it's honesty, sincerity and friendliness with a funny accent.

(*The Liver Birds* script, 1975)

A subtext of middle-class commentary can be identified in much of Willy Russell's work. As actor Eithne Browne suggested, many of the central female characters in Russell's work (especially Rita in *Educating Rita*, Linda in *Stags and Hens* and Mrs Johnstone in *Blood Brothers*) are given essentially similar 'class' based storylines:

... always the girl who wants ... 'I am working class but I want cheese and wine'. 'Somewhere over the rainbow there's a place for me and it's better than this one' ... They are always grasping for that middle class.

(Eithne Browne, Interview, 1 August 1990)

For Rita, her 'way out' was to 'better herself' through education. Towards the end of the play she states:

I'm educated, I've got what you have an' y' don't like it because you'd rather see me as the peasant I once was ... I've got a room full of books. I know what clothes to wear, what wine to buy, what plays to see, what papers and books to read.

(*Educating Rita* script, 1985 p. 228)

In *Stags and Hens* there are constant negative references to working-class life in Liverpool. In the film version, *Dancin' Thru' the Dark*, the tone is set immediately with the opening shot showing the pop group driving into Liverpool for their evening gig, gazing at scenes of dereliction. The driver is heard to comment, 'it's like Beirut without the sun'. Quickly into the storyline the 'girls' make similar comments:

BERNADETTE: I suppose we'll live and die round here.
CAROL: It's a dump isn't it eh ...?
BERNADETTE: The life's just drainin' away from the place, but no one ever does anythin' about it.

(*Stags and Hens* script, 1985 p. 17)

However, it is Linda who agonises with feelings of restlessness for something other than her current existence and a sense of loyalty to her home town. Meeting her ex-fiancé Peter, now a famous pop star living in London, brings her dilemma into sharper focus, especially as they inadvertently meet on the eve of her wedding. As if to strike a prophetic chord, before she is reunited with Peter, Linda is heard to say to her friends as she emerges from the toilet:

> 'But if we do not change, tomorrow has no place for us'. It says so ... on the wall in there.
>
> (Stags and Hens script, 1985 p. 31)

Predictably, although Linda is seen as a deviant woman deserting her fiancé on the eve of her wedding, her aspirations for better horizons win the day and are implicitly the legitimation for her otherwise unacceptable behaviour.

Class antagonism is undoubtedly the central theme of *Blood Brothers*. Again there is an obvious restlessness in the key working-class characters. In particular Mrs Johnstone is burdened by a sense of inadequacy and inferiority. In fact she is portrayed as so irresponsible that she becomes pregnant with twins when she cannot afford, as a single parent, to feed her existing seven children! Well and truly caught in another version of 'the working-class trap' Mrs Johnstone is coaxed into an illegal agreement by the childless, middle-class Mrs Lyons, whereby one of the twins is handed over at birth. The suggestion is that at least one baby would have a decent life.

> MRS JOHNSTONE: If my child was raised in a place like this one, [He] wouldn't have to worry where the next meal was comin' from. His clothing would be [supplied by] George Henry Lee.
>
> (Blood Brothers script, 1985 p. 87)

It is not just Willy Russell's work that conveys such classist stereotypes. *Letter to Brezhnev* carries a very similar theme of working-class 'girls' who are bored with their dreary existence and long to 'break free'.

> ELAINE: I'm sick of the men 'round here – they've got no romance in them.
> THERESA: Well, Kirkby isn't the most romantic place in the world is it, Elaine?
>
> (Letter to Brezhnev, film, 1985)

It is Elaine's restlessness which is the focus. She confides in Peter, the Soviet sailor:

> I used to wish I was a bird so I could fly off ... I dreamt about you ... the typical, bored teenager's dream ... you know the handsome

man from the mysterious East comin' and whisking you away . . . but it doesn't happen like that does it?

(Letter to Brezhnev, film, 1985)

For Elaine it does happen in fairy-tale tradition! Once given the opportunity to fly to Russia she has no qualms about leaving Kirkby:

If I stay around here I'll live to regret it.

(Letter to Brezhnev, film, 1985)

It is Theresa, the working-class girl with no dreams beyond 'Drinkin' Vodka, gettin' fucked and stuffin' chickens' who is left behind 'trapped' in working-class Liverpool.

Whatever defence the writers offer there exists a contemptuous treatment of working-class Liverpool women in their material. By focusing on individual women's personal relationships as wives, mothers, girlfriends, mistresses, women's economic exploitation is conveniently side-stepped, neglecting all recognition of women's potential as a powerful, political force within society. It also plays to packed houses nationally or is given prime-time national TV coverage. The appeal is one which trades in stereotypes and which persistently presents a negative image of Liverpool and a diminished image of the City's women.

'A Case of Whitewashing?': Reflecting a Legacy of Racism

Conspicuous by their absence from the texts are central women characters from Liverpool's ethnic communities. In *The Liver Birds*, *The Muscle Market*, *Educating Rita* and *Blood Brothers*, there are no black characters. In *Letter to Brezhnev* there is the token appearance of a black, male, working-class Liverpool taxi driver for five minutes. In the film of *Shirley Valentine*, Shirley's daughter's friend, Sharon-Louise, is tokenistically cast as a black woman. She is seen once and has no dialogue. In the film version of *Stags and Hens* (*Dancin' Thru' the Dark*) one of the more silent members of the girls' group is again cast as the token black woman. In *Boys from the Blackstuff*, there is one black, male, working-class Liverpool character, Loggo. While he is given considerable dialogue in the script, that dialogue bears no significance to his ethnicity. It is essentially a white, working-class man's dialogue about the experiences of unemployment, coming from a black man's mouth. No issues about black people's experiences of unemployment are dealt with. There are only four significant female characters in the material represented with an ethnic background other than white Anglo-Saxon.

Lilo-Lil in *Bread* is a middle-aged, single, Irish woman, living in Liverpool. She is portrayed negatively as Freddy Boswell's 'mistress' and as such, through a predictable double-standard of morality, she is defined as deviant – an 'Irish tart' who lures Nellie Boswell's husband away with her wild and wanton ways. Lil is given no depth to her character aside from this stereotype of 'dangerous', 'uncontrollable' sexuality. She only has significance in the servicing role she has to Freddie Boswell's sexuality. When asked by DSS clerk Martina why she accepts being treated so badly, Lil stoically replied 'It's written in the stars and in our knickers'. The significance of her 'Irishness' can be understood only in terms of the long-standing anti-Irish feeling that is part of Liverpool's history, and popular mythology surrounding the fecundity of Irish Catholic women. It is significant that, according to actor Noreen Kershaw (Interview, 1 August 1990), Eileen Pollock, who plays Lilo-Lil, had difficulty getting an interview with *Spare Rib* since playing the character. Noreen related that Eileen Pollock accepts such a stereotypical role in order to have a 'bread and butter' income while she writes and directs feminist theatre productions. Such conditional acceptance, however, does little to nullify the impact of the portrayal.

Brookside, with its commitment to 'issue-writing', has attempted to deal with the issue of racism. Sammy Rogers' friend, Nisha (a Liverpool-born Asian girl) and their respective white boyfriends, Owen and Pete, were enjoying a picnic in the local park when a group of white male youths physically attacked Nisha, calling her 'a Paki'. Nisha's boyfriend Pete ran away while Sammy and Owen were assaulted in defending her. As well as portraying the reality of white, male, racist violence, the storyline went on to deal with the tension created in Nisha and Pete's relationship as a result of the attack. Pete's decision to end the relationship saying, 'I didn't think it was going to be that risky' provided an opportunity to explore and challenge racism in a less obvious, but equally oppressive form. Nisha's experience as a young woman having to deal with the many faces of racism was sympathetically handled. Similarly, a more recent storyline attempted to explore the dynamics and brutality of organised racism. Mick Johnson and his brother endured an onslaught of threats and violent attacks on their new pizza business. Although both storylines were handled with sensitivity they remained 'issue-led'. The point being that once the 'issue' had been written and broadcast there was an implicit assumption that the story was complete. This demonstrates no commitment to representing the permanent, ordinary, everyday life experiences of racism in the context of what Lord Gifford (1989) termed the 'uniquely horrific' extent of racism in Liverpool. While such storylines are undoubtedly important, the representation of racism only in its more extreme, overt expressions colludes with the assumption that racist attacks are isolated, rare aberrations perpetrated by sick or pathological individuals.

Other black women characters in *Brookside* include Josie Johnson and Marianne Dwyer. Josie was portrayed as the archetypal slack, black working-class woman who did her husband, children (and gender) wrong in her preference for 'freedom' over domesticity and motherhood. In deserting the duties of marriage and motherhood she was duly 'punished' via a heavy moralistic dialogue from other characters, both women and men. The portrayal was negative and distinctly male-centred, evoking sympathy for the long-suffering and ever-patient Mick. Her punishment was institutionalised as she lost custody of the children and Mick was further rewarded with a 'new' woman, worthy of him. Marianne was presented as an articulate, ambitious, middle-class black woman. The contrast in her character with that of Josie was unmistakable and effective, yet Marianne also developed negatively as a scheming, whining, hard-nosed and selfish woman. She dumped Mick's brother at the altar in preference for Mick, revealing her deceitful nature. There followed a 'sexual harassment at work' storyline which focused mainly on Mick's angst over the situation ('is she another Josie?'; 'has she given her boss the "come on"?'). Mick's response was stereotypically spontaneous, aggressive and confrontational. The black working-class 'male protector' of 'his' woman was set against Marianne's cool, scheming, feminine guile, through which she eventually turned the tables on her (black) boss. In fact her character emerged as a white, middle-class 'superwoman' giving a distorted representation of the dynamics of male violence and power. It reinforced the idea that it is primarily the responsibility of women to put an end to harassment.

The subtext of these storylines carried clear expressions of misogyny and racism. Should women, particularly black women, want to compete in the 'white man's world' they should be prepared to take the consequences. It was a theme confirmed in Marianne's characterisation: could she really 'hack it' in taking tough decisions in the world of business? In this struggle she became the 'tortured', 'unhappy', 'whining', 'post-feminist' woman of the 1990s. She wanted a career, she wanted a relationship with Mick, but she rejected marriage and was consistently impatient when dealing with Mick's children. This was constructed as both selfish and deviant. Her 'punishment' was the introduction of a competitor for Mick's affections – Carol, an uncomplicated, bubbly, white, working-class Liverpool woman with no aspirations above those of her class or gender. The women were locked in a tactical struggle for Mick and, unsurprisingly, Marianne was compelled to sacrifice her successful job away from home in order to 'keep' her man. Ultimately, to secure the relationship she gave up her independence and became engaged to Mick.

Overall, the few images of Liverpool women from ethnic communities that can be identified in the material studied relegate those women to the margins of the storyline, represent them as negative stereotypes, and offer a one-off tokenistic acknowledgement of one dimension of their oppression: black women as victims in need of paternalistic intervention. It is only in marginalised or fringe media productions (such as the work of the Liverpool Black Women's Media Project) that positive images of black women are seen. This affirms the institutionally racist nature of mainstream media production, which racially stereotypes black men and women and 'ghetto-ises' material of interest to black people or material which deals directly with the experiences of black people.

Brookside Revisited: Reconstructing the Illusions

One of the clearest examples of the power of hegemony is evident in interviews relating to *Brookside*. The account given by two women scriptwriters of their struggles to establish more positive representations of women characters mirrored the oppressive relationships of the women characters within the scripts. The scriptwriters gave vivid descriptions of how their voices were silenced within the storyline conferences. They described their feelings of intimidation by male scriptwriters. During one meeting one of the women was 'brave' enough to make the point that male scriptwriters were constantly interrupting the women when they tried to make important contributions to the discussion. This challenge to male dominance resulted in her being 'punished' by constant jokes and jibes from the men, such as 'Ssh **** is about to speak'. This woman recalled how the ridicule continued for much longer than she considered funny. Indeed, it had the presumably desired effect of further silencing her through the fear of attracting additional ridicule. This is a clear example of how 'professional codes' (Hall, 1973) operate firmly within the hegemony of the 'dominant code', in this case ultimately reproducing a preferred representation of Liverpool women.

Some eighteen months after the original research was completed follow-up interviews were arranged with Eithne Browne and the two women scriptwriters at *Brookside* (31 March 1992 and 13 April 1992) for, inevitably, the storylines had moved on, including the subsequent transformation of Chrissy Rogers from '... the perfect wife, essentially in [the] perfect marriage' (Interview, 20 September 1990 above) to a discontented, dissat-isfied woman who had 'out-grown' her husband, eventually to leave her family and resume her long-abandoned teacher-training career. This was of particular interest since there had been unanimous agreement among the women actors, women scriptwriters and administrative/production personnel originally interviewed at *Brookside*, that Chrissy Rogers was 'the worst example' of sex stereotyping (Interview, 10 September 1990 above). So what had inspired this metamorphosis? The truth was that Eithne Browne had had enough:

> There are only two ways round it – you just keep going on, trying, with your character, and the women I've admired there in the past have done this themselves, or you just keep your head down and take the money, and I couldn't do that and it did come to a head to head conflict . . . 'if you don't like it, go'.
>
> (Interview, 31 March 1992)

Eithne's explanation was supported independently by one of the women scriptwriters (Interview, 13 April 1992) who said:

> I'm very interested in what's happening to our women characters actually. The minute they get uppity they get elbowed out it seems to me . . . I'm not sure she wanted to go so much as she was bolshy as an actress.

Eithne expanded further on her disillusionment with Chrissy:

> She started off as a really strong mother who would go and fight for her children and who would fight for a better education when she believed she was right. That was for about the first eighteen months and then I thought she was a good character and I believed in her and fought for her all the way. Then after that they seemed to just stop writing for her, you never saw her out of the kitchen and it was very lacklustre and very unbelievable.
>
> (Ibid.)

The scriptwriters were confronted with a *fait accompli* – Eithne Browne was leaving the programme and they were told to begin writing Chrissy's demise:

> It was more or less presented to us that she was going. It was not a decision made by the writers . . . I think . . . there are certainly other precedents for this . . . if the actual actress is very difficult.

> The brief at times was impossible, I mean dramatically, the brief was that she walked out on her daughter's wedding day which was almost impossible to do, how to motivate it . . . absolutely absurd really.
>
> (Interview, 13 April 1992)

137

One of the women writers commented that ironically she felt a great sense of freedom in this situation, although it was always tempered by the dictat that Chrissy was going to walk out on Sammy's wedding day. To this extent she felt that she made the script 'half-work':

> The way that we had led her up to it, her dissatisfaction with Frank, her longing to move on intellectually and her feeling that now that the children were more or less off her back, she was *beginning* whereas he was ready to put his slippers on and *end* seemed to me a very valid and truthful account of what actually does happen.
>
> (Interview, 13 April 1992)

Eithne Browne agreed but felt angry that such a strong characterisation could only be written after she had decided to leave:

> They suddenly wanted Chrissy to have this outgoing life when they knew I was leaving ... I just felt complete betrayal of the character ... My argument would be they could have written these things months back, years back.
>
> (Ibid.)

The other woman writer felt cautious about the eventual storyline:

> The previous marriage in which the marriage broke up because the woman was 'getting ideas above her station' was the Grant's marriage and I think it does represent something of what's happening, so I think it is a fair reflection. I'm just anxious we shouldn't do it too often because I think the danger is that what we will be saying if we do it too often is something like 'marriages can only survive if women are compliant, obedient and subservient'.
>
> (Interview, 13 April 1992)

Eithne was also concerned about this:

> If you take an overall picture of the way the women in *Brookside* have been portrayed over the last few years, three of them have just walked out and left their children at the drop of a hat ... You see I don't know women like this, that's what irritates me. I don't believe that the programme is really indicative of the way women really are and the pressures that women really face and the fantastic jobs that mothers and women really do ... When you have this very downtrodden image of women where if they can't cope they just

leave, they leave their husbands, they have affairs, you know, morally very 'tacky' people, you give women nothing to feel good about.

(Ibid.)

She had no doubts as to the true source of these distorted portrayals:

Why are there no single women on *Brookside*? Why can't women achieve on their own? It would have made, to me, a far more interesting storyline to watch Chrissy struggle and survive with three children, if Josie was going to leave the kids. So all of a sudden you've got two men living next door to each other both of them their wives have just said 'right, thanks, I'm off' ... there is a very macho misogynist feel ... the way women are being portrayed by *Brookside* as the deceivers, as the leavers, and all these 'poor' men are left behind ... It must be marvellous to have a Close full of such snow-white men! ... I think that comes from an ignorance upstairs and an unwillingness to admit women to the 'winning forum'.

(Ibid.)

This is reflected in the day-to-day working relationships on the set at *Brookside*:

There was a great deal of sexism against female directors. There was one comment from an actor [to] a black female director – 'It's bad enough having to work with a woman, but a *black* woman!'

Also you would find that when people were being viewed by the directors and the editors upstairs in the box, comments about various parts of their body were not uncommon. So you're still not viewed as an equal individual, as a person who works with them, you're just somebody with big bosoms or a person that they would like to explore further given the chance. That just goes to show that there is so much more to be done so that a woman could walk across 'Brookside Close' and you wouldn't notice her bosoms ... and they could be viewed as another individual and not as a sexual object.

(Ibid.)

Following on from this, it was important to establish whether women scriptwriters' experiences of the storyline conferences at *Brookside* had changed. Surprisingly, they were at pains to point out that what they had said before, 'applied under a very different set of circumstances, with different people, which were probably more "true to the world" circumstances'. One of the women continued:

> What we have now at *Brookside* is an enormously happy team under an awfully good producer who has made it possible for me personally to feel totally brave and quite able to hold my own, to speak, to say whatever I want to say, at any time, without ever thinking about whether I sound aggressive and indeed, to be quite pleasantly at ease.
>
> (Interview, 13 April 1992)

Her colleague agreed, saying that she felt this had much to do with the creation of a 'new culture':

> Now the culture of the writing and producing team is a much more 'feminine' culture ... and this used not to be the case ... it's safe, accepting and non-critical.
>
> (Interview, 13 April 1992)

Reasons for this were cited as the 'moderating influence' of a new writer, an ex-nurse with a 'warm, sympathetic personality' and 'enormous sensitivity', but 'there's no way he's a wimp'! Yet when the writers were pressed on decision-taking and power relations within the team little seemed to have changed:

> There's something about him [the producer], who in the end always gets his own way, interestingly enough, but the style whereby he does it is actually quite different.
>
> (Interview, 13 April 1992)

While the 'culture' of the group might have changed, with women in the team feeling 'more comfortable', there had been no real change in the power relations. As one of the women stated:

> There is always a certain amount that we have no control over, which is partly to do with logistics or partly to do with one of Phil's [Redmond] decisions and we know that ...
>
> One of the things that I think perhaps he [the producer] did make a decision over, management-wise, is that he would never try to pretend that the word from God wasn't the word from God. 'Phil says this is going to happen' he says, and we know it's going to

happen, so we don't waste our time.

(Interview, 13 April 1992)

Eithne Browne was no less blunt:

I think that while you've got a male at the top making those decisions and the greater number of male writers, then I can see women can't help but be coerced in some way by the majority.

(Interview, 31 March 1992)

Illusions of empowerment can be very damaging for women and this was confirmed by one of the women scriptwriters:

But you see it's fooled me because I've got rather comfortable and I've fooled myself that because I can function here rather well I kind of thought I could carry this out into the outer world, and although it's given me a lot of confidence, I have actually been in meetings again where that sudden sinking feeling has come over me and I can't say anything – I daren't open my mouth – I don't know the dynamic of this room – I don't know where I am.

(Interview, 13 April 1992)

She concluded:

I don't think it has changed It's just that we happen to be in a very lucky situation where we arc working with some very nice men.

Whether at the level of day to day working relationships of actors, writers, technicians, producers, directors, administrators, or in the portrayal of female characters that ultimately appear on the screen, it is evident that *Brookside* has conveyed clear messages about acceptable and unacceptable roles for women. The tensions and conflicts that surround the process of characterisation and representation are mirror images of the real-life struggles experienced by women who work at *Brookside*. In the same way as Chrissy Rogers, Sue Sullivan, Sheila Grant, and Doreen Corkhill were trapped by characterisations that rendered them subordinate to their respective partners, so too are the real women at *Brookside* debilitated by the individual and collective power of hegemonic masculinity. The women scriptwriters have pointed to a 'more "feminine" culture' in the storyline conferences, implying that their agendas are at last being listened to and discussed. Certainly newer storylines have focused on issues pertinent to women. These included the rape of Diana Corkhill; the physical and sexual violence endured by Mandy Jordache and her two daughters; and the development of Beth Jordache's lesbian identity. Although potentially this signals a process of change, it has already been established that these storylines are not without criticism and remain problematic. The women continue to be portrayed voyeuristically as victims and the storylines are not truly woman-centred. So versatile is the power of hegemony in accommodating resistance, that an apparently more progressive 'culture' has been created at *Brookside*, while fundamentally, at the structural level, there is no change in relationships of dominance and subordination. The illusions remain intact.

Conclusion

Widespread media attention has been given to the popular notion that contemporary women should be reaping the benefits of a 'post-feminist' era, when equal opportunities policies and legislation have supposedly transformed their lives. Indeed, as discussed earlier, much has been made of progressive equal opportunities campaigns within the media itself, designed to redress the traditional male dominance of the industry. However, the experiences of women currently employed at a variety of levels within the media, reveal that relatively little has changed. Discrimination and inequality persist both at the functional level of employment practices and conditions of working and at the ideological level of attitudes, behaviour and representation. Some women, be they creators, producers or conveyers of representations, occupy relatively privileged positions within the media, most being successful, white, and middle-class. Nevertheless, the experiences of those women discussed in this chapter demonstrate that they continue to be oppressed in their professional relationships with male colleagues. Although most of the women made these observations independently of one another, and from within their own unique experiences, they share important reservations about the extent to which they consider themselves to be 'liberated'. Indeed, their comments suggest that beneath the veneer of equal opportunities women continue to feel constrained and controlled at the ideological level, through the power of hegemony.

Struggles which centre on oppressive imagery inform, and are in turn informed by, real life struggles around relationships of dominance and subordination. Indeed, contradictory arguments exist concerning the popular media's commitment to realism. It is possible to argue that a total commitment to representing the harsh realities of oppression could reinforce and perpetuate assumptions that oppression is 'a fact of life' – an inevitable reality. Conversely, not to acknowledge the existence of such oppression is to deny the reality of many people's experiences of oppression. The reason it is inherently problematic to address the issue of the reality of oppression in the media is that the images and representations are constructed and mediated through the hegemonic code of discourse bearing the legacy and hallmarks of imperialism and patriarchy. This hegemony is so pervasive that alternative, positive representations of women created within 'oppositional' codes seldom surface within popular media forms, but remain marginalised within 'fringe' productions (such as those of the Liverpool Black Women's Media Group and Kirkby Response Theatre). Moreover, the process of what is deemed to be 'entertaining' remains caught up with social constructions of visual pleasure. Thus, consumers of stereotyped representations of women have an active role to play in decoding those representations. The consistent popularity of the stereotyped representations identified above suggests that they are indeed being decoded within the context of dominant ideologies.

This critique of representations of working-class Liverpool women in popular television, film and theatre productions reveals consistent assumptions about those women in terms of what Tillie Olsen (1980) has called 'common female realities'. The study has identified a universality about the way in which stereotyped definitions of women – in terms of motherhood, sexuality and emphasised femininity – are constructed within patriarchy. In this sense, Liverpool women receive much the same media treatment as all women: imagery which reinforces the desirability and acceptability of women's roles as servicers to men and children and imagery which reinforces the undesirability and unacceptability of independent, strong and self-willed women. This is borne out in the real-life experiences of the women related in the previous chapters.

The contribution of critical theory has enabled important connections to be made with the structural relations of class and 'race', demonstrating how the oppression of women through the media is inextricably linked to and mediated by other oppressions. The media is doubly prejudicial to working-class women, lesbian women, black women and women from different cultural backgrounds. Critical media analysis and discourse analysis provide an understanding of how stereotyped definitions of women are constructed, legitimated and perpetuated. The textual images and representations identified in the material are related directly to the cultural contexts of spectatorship and the institutional and social/historical contexts of production and consumption, where such images reside. Further, an analysis of subtextual discourse demonstrates the subtleties of the way in which oppressive ideas underpin the manifest content of the text.

The aegis of 'post-feminism' resounds throughout popular discourse and has been no less influential in the realm of media criticism. 'Post-feminist' critics now agonise over the theoretical heritage of 1970s and 1980s 'confrontational', 'evangelical', 'recruitist', feminism which desired 'to transform "ordinary women" into feminists' (Brunsdon, 1991 pp. 380–381). Such ideas are considered *passé* by the 'new generation' of female media critics, whose attention now focuses on introverted debates about where second-wave feminism 'went wrong'. While feminists are embroiled in the angst of such debates, the voices of what 'post-feminists' call 'ordinary women' go unheard. The old oppressive images and representations are reworked and through the power of hegemony maintain the illusion of progress and change. The stronger the communication between women across structural boundaries, researching their own history and experiences, increasing the wealth and diversity of their own images, the more the lie of media neglect, stereotyping and misrepresentation will be exposed and challenged.

Chapter 6

Behind Closed Doors: The Myth of Personal Liberation

Introduction

Out of the struggles and campaigns in the late 1960s and 1970s over women's rights, in relation to social security, housing, health care, child-care, education, training and work opportunities, there emerged a wealth of feminist literature. This focused on the relationship between the state and the family, and on financial, emotional and physical relationships within and outside the family. Much of this work offered new perspectives on key questions within social policy analysis, as well as theoretical questions about the relationship between patriarchy, capitalism and the state. Feminist critiques represented a challenge to the mainstream discipline of social policy in the 1970s: first, by exposing how the main institutions of existing welfare provision fail to meet the specific needs of women, and second, by showing how these institutions reinforce and perpetuate the material and ideological aspects of women's oppression. The main concern of this chapter is to identify and examine the web of assumptions, both explicit and implicit, that are intertwined with developments in social policy and how these, in turn, impact on the personal lives of women.

Elizabeth Wilson's (1977 p. 33) critique of state policy and welfare provision was one of the earliest to challenge the idea that welfare provision is a benign attempt to help solve problems. She argued instead that it has an ideological function, '. . . a set of structures created by men to shape the lives of women'. One of the most important contributions feminism has made to the understanding of women's oppression is its structural analysis of the ways in which the state, and society, regulate women's lives by supporting and perpetuating the idea that the nuclear family is the 'natural' unit for living (Loney *et al.* 1991). Welfare policies assume a particular form of social arrangement – two adults, one of whom is a male wage earner or 'breadwinner' and the other a female home organiser, accompanied by dependent children. This pattern is considered the norm and is the primary referent for the formulation of social policy. Other arrangements – cohabitation, lone parenthood, 'absent' parenthood, gay and lesbian parenthood – are, by implication, deviant. Alternative forms of care, such as nurseries or residential homes, are considered second best.

There are a number of taken-for-granted assumptions about women and women's roles within the home and family which have been and remain fundamental in the construction of social policy. Jalna Hanmer and Daphne Statham (1988 p. 26) point out that:

> irrespective of the *actual* lives of women there are commonly accepted organising principles governing our views about the social correctness of women's lives. These are:
> – whether or not women are living with men,
> – whether or not women have children, and
> – whether or not women take appropriate responsibilities for dependent relatives.

Ruth Levitas (1986) states that women's lives increasingly are deviating from the cultural 'ideal' as people choose different patterns of living. Figures from the General Household Survey (OPCS, September 1991) reveal significant diversity in the pattern of household composition. What has emerged is a considerable gulf between the 'ideal' or 'normal' family, on which the state bases its social policy and welfare provision, and the reality of many people's lives. Clearly, if social policy and welfare provision is constructed using a specific model of the 'traditional' family, it structurally neglects those people whose pattern of living fails to fit the model, whether by comparison or by choice.

Hanmer and Statham (1988 p. 27) suggest that 'ideological responses to and demands on women can be experienced as devastatingly oppressive and restrictive'. Even for those women who attempt to conform and to meet these demands, however, the struggle to achieve and maintain the 'ideal' is hindered by the social and economic context in which they live. The life patterns to which women are expected to conform create, and are created by, women's financial dependency on men and the state, a fact not addressed by two decades of sex equality legislation. Feminist writers have developed analytical frameworks which focus on gendered processes in the labour market, welfare systems and domestic household. Each of these interact to create and maintain women's oppression. These analyses have 'highlighted the social construction of gender divisions and roles which have been passed off as the "natural" assumptions on which social policy rests' (Loney *et al.*, 1991 p. 137).

The economically dependent woman is available as the carer of dependent children and adults in the family while providing a vital resource for contemporary 'community care' policies. Her employment outside the home reduces her availability within it, even though that employment may well keep the family out of poverty. As illustrated in Chapter 4, paid employment has always been central to most women's lives. Yet women's paid work has been socially constructed as subsidiary to their private, domestic role – secondary or supplementary to that of their male partner. Employment policies for young people assume that women will continue to be secondary earners. In government schemes, girls are concentrated overwhelmingly in the traditional, and traditionally low-paid, female sectors of employment – clerical work, catering and caring. This mirrors and maintains the horizontal and vertical segregation of women in the labour market.

The public sphere/private sphere divide has encouraged men into beliefs and practices which place them as the primary breadwinners and determinants of how the 'family wage' is allocated. At a functional level, the sexual division of labour is presented as complementary – a relationship of mutual support and reliance. In practice, however, work in the public sphere retains status and prestige and it brings direct financial rewards while work in the private sphere is secondary, marginalised and taken-for-granted. For most women the distinction between spheres is artificial as they have participated in the labour market and, consequently, have endured the burden of a double workload. By contrast, whatever their job, men's primary responsibilities remain in the public domain.

Adherence to the notion of a 'family wage' and the male breadwinner, on the part of both employers and trade unions, has been used to justify women's low pay and the perpetuation of the myth that women only work for 'pin money'. During economic recession, and encouraged by monetarism, there has been a revival of ideas which suggest that women do not have a right to paid employment. It is reasserted that a 'woman's place' is in the home, caring for 'the family'. Ironically, as highlighted by Rosemary Crompton (1990), a 1988 Government Report predicted considerable reduction in the numbers of young people entering the labour market during the 1990s, which may be offset, in part, by an increase in the recruitment of women. This prediction directly contradicts other aspects of 1980s Government policy in which a dominant belief in women's 'natural' roles as wives and mothers, contained and restricted within the private sphere, was clearly reaffirmed.

The 1986 Wages Act, the abolition of the Fair Wages Resolution and the enforced contracting-out of services in the private sector have hit women particularly hard. In addition, Maternity Allowance was cut by 5 per cent in

1980, the earnings related supplement to maternity grant was abolished in 1982, and in October 1986 part payments of the maternity allowance (paid to women with interrupted employment histories) were abolished. From 1987, Maternity Allowance was replaced by statutory maternity pay, shifting responsibility for payment to the employer and making it taxable. These, and other Government policies such as cuts in public services and the inclusion of work-based nursery provision as a taxable 'perk', have combined to limit women's ability to return to work after the birth of a child. Ultimately these policies are aimed at directing women back into the home at a time when women are increasingly becoming involved in the paid workforce.

The structure of the welfare state has traditionally assumed that women are the dependants of men. Jane Lewis (1983), in her analysis of Beveridge's 1942 plan, suggests that assumptions about married women's dependency were based, in part, on evidence from the inter-war years about the actual numbers of dependent married women. However, she also states that, to some extent, Beveridge projected his own bias in terms of morality, marriage and the family.

Gillian Pascall (1986) points out that many women have no eligibility at all for benefits in their own right, but only as dependants of a male partner. Income maintenance benefits are based on assumptions about typically male patterns of full-time, uninterrupted employment. Women in paid employment which is broken by a period of childbearing and/or other caring responsibilities, women who work part-time and women who are low-paid frequently find themselves ineligible for any benefits other than a means-tested statutory minimum. Where women do qualify for non-means-tested benefits, their lower earnings inevitably attract lower rates of benefit than their male counterparts. Carol Glendinning and Jane Millar (1992, 1989) reported that in 1984, 2.75 million part-time female employees earned weekly wages below the threshold at which they become liable for national insurance contributions, hence making them ineligible for many benefits. Even so moral panics have developed and consolidated around 'welfare mothers': young, single women who, in the face of mass unemployment, apparently sought a social identity through motherhood, supported by state benefits (Campbell, 1984).

Throughout the 1980s and into the 1990s such discourses resounded in the rhetoric of Government ministers and New Right social commentators alike (Abbott and Wallace, 1992; Durham, 1991). David Green, Head of the Health and Welfare Unit at the Institute of Economic Affairs, writing in *Social Work Today* (2 August 1990), had no doubts over Government priorities:

> ... public policy should certainly not encourage single parenthood.

But it does just that by making available additional benefits which are payable to single mums, including one parent benefit ... Two parent families are better for children than one parent families and the benefits system should recognise this ... Removing the special benefits will mean that there will be less children whose lives are blighted by single parenthood and this overrides the *minor hardship* which will flow from removing one parent benefit. In any event, a private remedy is available to lone parents, to get married. [our emphasis]

The Conservative Government's 1986 social security reforms contained many proposals geared towards the redistribution of economic power to male heads of household and the redirection of women to their 'rightful place', the home. The payment of family credit (replacing Family Income Supplement) through the wage packet of the head of household, rather than through the post office where it was invariably collected by female partners, clearly represented one policy decision aimed at unbalancing power relations within the family in favour of men (Lister, 1987). Women's potential for independent living has been severely undermined by measures such as the removal of the right to claim help with furniture, bedding, household goods, fuel bills and other items; legislation forcing single mothers to try to extract maintenance for their children from ex-husbands or 'errant fathers' (Child Support Act, 1991); and the changes in benefit entitlement for 16 to 17-year-olds, which have effectively extended the period of dependency of young people on families. Women's freedom to 'choose' paid employment has been circumscribed by the joint operation of social and economic policies which impose moral obligations of care. Patrick Jenkin, Secretary of State for Social Services, 1979 (cited in David, 1986 p. 158) stated: 'Quite frankly, I don't think that mothers have the same right to work as fathers do. If the Good Lord had intended us to have equal rights to go out to work, he wouldn't have created man and woman. These are biological facts'. The resolve of the New Right to make individuals less dependent on state welfare, and more dependent on their relatives, has made the family the main welfare agency of the 1980s and 1990s. For the 'family', read women.

In 1991 a British Social Attitudes Report showed that, within 75 per cent of families, women still perform most of the unpaid, domestic work of household management as well as caring for children and other dependants and working outside the home (Jowell *et al.*, 1991). Lorna McKee and Colin Bell (1985) emphasise that this inequality in the distribution of unpaid work in the home persists even when the man is unemployed. Although women have been encouraged to remain at home and take responsibility for maintaining the home, and caring for dependants, the idea that housework is 'real' work has never been fully recognised, other than by those who have to do it! Feminist critiques highlight how, for many women, the family represents a private world where the enormous and demanding responsibilities of running a home, doing the housework, caring for dependent children and/or elderly relatives and servicing the needs of a partner go unpaid and unrecognised. Ann Oakley's (1984) research suggests that housework is trivialised and considered insignificant, largely because of its 'invisibility'.

The other main focus of women's unpaid labour in the home is the task of caring. The notion of caring as a 'natural' role for women overlooks a deep-rooted, gendered construction of the caring activity. It is invariably restricted to specific social relations involving women as wives, mothers, daughters, neighbours, friends. Janet Finch and Dulcie Groves (1983 p. 229) state that, 'there is an important sense in which cultural pressures to provide care apply to all women, but those who are married or co-habiting are particularly vulnerable to such pressures'. A Family Policy Studies Institute Report (January 1989) estimated that the state saves about £24 billion on care costs each year, largely because women take on such responsibilities. Developments in social policy invariably have presupposed that caring could, and should, be provided by women in the private sphere – free.

Similarly, the inadequacy of alternative child-care provision clearly reflects an assumption that the care of children is women's responsibility in the private sphere. This has been underwritten by the influential theorising that a child's healthy development depends on the continuous care of its mother (Bowlby, 1953). Such ideology has been enshrined in all child-care legislation since the war. The 1989 Children's Act, for example, proclaimed as a 'children's charter', gives no commitment to the general care and well-being of children. It is assumed that this is 'naturally' provided within a 'normal' family. Hence, state intervention and welfare provision is reserved for a presumed minority of 'dangerous' and/or 'deviant' families (Parton, 1991). Those who seek alternative child-care arrangements in any other circumstances are left to the vagaries of 'the market', where it is assumed private enterprise will respond to demand. In reality this means that those women in privileged economic positions are able to purchase child-care, while most are forced to rely on the long-established practice of depending on the unpaid help and support of women friends or female members of their extended family.

Outside the family it is women who do most of the caring work under the umbrella of the 'welfare state'. Teaching, nursing, social work, are each areas of heavy female employment. Yet it is men who dominate in the senior positions within these professions (Hugman, 1991). Thus, the traditional caring tasks of women have also been organised and defined outside the family by men through the professionalisation of caring.

Clearly a web of assumptions about 'the family', and about gender relations, informs and is, in turn, informed by social policies. The women interviewed for the studies were a broad cross-section, aged between 25 to 75 years, from diverse class backgrounds, educational and employment histories. Their accounts reveal the inherent tensions and contradictions arising from their interpersonal relationships. The three main, interconnected, areas covered by social policies included those relating to the labour market, the welfare benefit system and arrangements for the unpaid domestic labour in the home and many related how these policies directly affect their lives. Women's paid employment is often determined by their ability to fulfil what are perceived to be their duties in the private sphere. They highlighted the fact that men's involvement in the private arena was negligible. As women their 'freedom of choice' was dependent on their success at negotiating such 'choices' with their partners. None of the women considered that this process was satisfactory. Further, their needs and desires were rarely acknowledged or accommodated. For some women maintaining a relationship involved constant compromise, for others the only viable alternative was complete independence. The importance of female friendships, which provide emotional and practical support, were emphasised throughout the women's accounts. From their responses it can be seen that the hegemonic power of 'familism', which inevitably shapes the personal life experiences and relationships of women, remains a key determining context.

Women's Involvement in Paid Employment

Despite the fact that women's contribution to the so-called 'family wage' is substantial, there are inherent contradictions in their position as significant wage earners. These can become an issue which causes stress between partners. Some women felt pressured to continue work because of financial commitments, thus limiting their choices about work and children:

> I suppose I worry that if I ever wanted to stop working it would be quite difficult for us, or if we had other commitments like a mortgage it would be difficult if I stopped working. So it worries me because I feel it puts pressure on me to carry on working.

Stereotyped images of the 'male breadwinner' impact on women's perceptions of their partner's self-image:

> I think he'd find it difficult to handle if I earned a lot more than him because of the old idea of the man being the breadwinner and

> worrying about if I decided to have a child how he would be able to
> support me . . . I think he might feel a failure.

> It was a problem because he was out of work for a large part of the
> time I was working. I think he felt that he wasn't contributing in
> some way and that he felt in some way inferior.

Although some women felt that in theory their career was valued and given
status, in practice this was often not the case:

> . . . It's like studying. I felt distinctly that I had to just carry on, plus
> study, as I always had done. Whereas when he's been working
> towards an essay or something it's been a case of dropping
> everything. And I mean literally just drop everything. It's almost as
> if there's no order left at all, right down to spilling things and leaving
> them.

Some women's careers definitely took second place to those of their partners.
For example, one woman stated that if her partner had to return to work she
had to 'put up with it' but if she stayed late at school or wanted to work at
home he 'got annoyed, sulked and made life difficult' because he saw her as
being there for him. Another commented on how her partner felt totally
threatened by her career:

> I had to watch everything I said and did, who I worked with. I could
> never discuss any highlights or achievements or interests in men I'd
> worked with. And he would get drunk all the time if I went to a study
> group with men. He was jealous if ever I went to an MA tutorial, or
> ever worked with new men who joined the department. He would
> become irrational and aggressive and drink. . . . He would make me
> late for work because he couldn't bear to be in the house when I was
> at work and he'd start packing windsurfers on top of the car and
> would ring me at work and harass me to bring the car home so he
> could go and play squash . . . In terms of career, he was livid when
> he heard I was going to do a PhD, or even interested in doing it. He
> said 'I suppose that cuts out children' because he can't handle my
> relationship academically with any men – academic and sexual
> jealousy.

For women with children the dilemma over whether to participate in paid
work or not is compounded:

Society puts expectations on women with children. If that mother doesn't feel they meet these expectations they begin to devalue themselves which then creates problems.

Often this was exacerbated by feelings of guilt:

At times I feel very guilty because I work. I think the guilt comes from inside me. But I think society is probably responsible for promoting attitudes which make women feel guilty.

However, as one woman stated:

The majority of women now with young children are working too because they've got to – to pay the mortgage.

Sometimes these contradictions are insurmountable:

I think a lot of women stay at home because they feel guilty. They often get pressured by family members to stay at home and look after the children. I think all women with children feel a certain amount of guilt, but husbands or partners don't.

Women are constrained in their choices concerning employment by family commitments, which are based on the social construction of women as primary carers. This is translated into particular forms of family arrangement where women are expected to carry out domestic work and care for dependent children and adults, with little or no help from partners or the state. Many of the women interviewed highlighted the impact on employment prospects. One woman stated:

When I first started back it was a case of doing something I didn't really want to do, but I did it just to get back into the swing again. Now I think it's alright, although I'm at a lower level than when I finished to have my child. At the moment it's a case of taking on work which is convenient. There's no overtime and I'm not expected to stay behind for meetings after organised work.

Another found that her paid work conflicted with the needs of her children:

I considered that I needed to save a little bit of me for my sons, because they had no father.

These issues are summarised in the following quotations:

> Having a family and doing all this [drama group] is very, very hard!

> Marriage changes attitudes towards work; women have something else in their lives apart from work. Even more so when you have children. You become reluctant to do things that you don't have to do in your job like giving up off-duty time.

> The vast majority of women find work that will fit in with the children's needs. Husbands rarely get involved. It is women who take on the responsibility of arranging child-care, and also all the guilt.

Men's Role in the Home

Constructions of masculinity and femininity operate in the home, where family arrangements are often based on dominant gender-based ideologies. Traditionally, it is expected that men will be the providers for dependent women and children with women's role defined as homemaker, childbearer and nurturer of both men and children. Tensions arising from this frequently come into sharp focus with the birth of a first child:

> He downed tools. When I asked why he said that it was my job because I was at home all day. I said, 'But I've got an extra thing to do now. I don't know how to look after a baby'. In the end though I had to accept it.

> People think that, because you are a woman, you're supposed to know about child-care and you don't need help. But you don't – you learn as you go along.

When men are involved in child-care, their contributions are often clearly circumscribed:

> I think that another thing is [that women have got to be careful of] I see lots of young men now taking a much more active part in child-care, but when I sit back and analyse this I see that what they are doing is taking all the nice bits, and all the nasty bits of child-care, all the unpleasant bits, are being left with the women. I think women have got to watch this.

Further, the arrival of 'New' or 'reconstructed' men is to be treated with scepticism:

> They say 'I'll take the kids to the park' or 'I'll play ball with them while you get the washing done, and you get the dinner on and you tidy the bedrooms' and that's not right at all.

Even when men do 'help out', as one woman pointed out: 'You're still only talking about a minority because a lot of men won't accept it'. One woman proposed that this was because 'there's terrible pressure on young men who are really keen to take equal shares in bringing up their children because they are under pressure from other men not to'.

In addition to child-care, women are responsible for domestic work in the home yet the necessity for such work does not register in the consciousness of some men. This reinforces the trivialisation and invisibility of women's unpaid work in the private sphere:

> One bloke's parents came round one evening to drop some stuff off and we must have been in the house about three or four months. We were having a drink and his dad looked round and said 'You can tell there's a woman in this house' to which Tim responded 'Why?' He said 'Well there's no dust anywhere'. Tim said 'Yeah, you know this house never gets dusty' and he really thought he'd found this miraculous house that just didn't acquire house dust. It just never occurred to him that somebody was doing the dusting.

For many women 'help' is only forthcoming when requested: 'I've got complete responsibility for all domestic work, and it would be up to me to ask for help'. Men's contributions were criticised as being less than satisfactory and often carrying an air of martyrdom:

> I think it's just accepted that women can do all those sorts of things. For a lot of men who help with the housework you feel that they're almost martyring themselves. I think it's just accepted that women can cook and clean and that it's no great shakes really. I don't think all men are like that but a lot are. If they do it, they've learned it, and aren't they good and liberated!

One woman's statement was more blunt:

> I feel that men just have absolutely no idea of what's involved in running a house. They think if they pick up something off the floor

or run the hoover round very quickly then they've done the week's chores. They've got no idea. They would never dream of putting the washing in the washing machine, ironing, definitely not. They might dust and hoover but it's only very superficial. They never look beyond – they never see that paint needs washing or curtains need taking down and washing. They would rarely think of cooking. They would go shopping but would only get the bare essentials – they wouldn't get the little bits you need. And as for cleaning the bath or the toilet, my God, that's unheard of.

As two other women pointed out, this issue leads to disagreement and arguments in relationships. These are, more often than not, 'resolved' by the woman conceding to an unsatisfactory level of tidiness or doing the housework herself to avoid confrontation:

I've always had rows about equality with any men that I've lived with. It might be that you come to a compromise but you don't really come to a compromise it's just that I accept a lower standard of cleanliness.

It may change for a while but it soon lapses back to how it always is, with the woman doing the majority of things. I think you just do it because you know if you didn't it just wouldn't get done. And sometimes it's just easier than arguing.

Women's unpaid domestic labour enables men to work long hours, regardless of their class, take on overtime, and become involved in work-related activities in the evenings and at weekends. These include meetings, conferences, courses and social events. Men also often claim the need to work undisturbed at home. Although it is widely accepted that men have a 'right' to regular, planned leisure time away from the home and family women can claim no such 'right'.

'Women's Roles'

For most women interviewed, the expectations of a relationship were similar. They revolved around sharing, understanding, honesty and respect. Most of the women identified a need for mutual independence. Where expectations differed there were difficulties, occasionally insurmountable. For these women disagreement hinged on the perception of *her* role, best summarised by this woman's experience:

After the first year of living together, there were subtle changes at the level of domestic things, at the level of my interests, the things I wanted to do. When we moved and bought the house it was very different ... He would be known as 'the vet' and I would be known as the 'vet's wife' ... Although we thought we would eventually marry we certainly weren't and there were no immediate plans to do so. Again, he didn't think it was quite the done thing and he didn't quite know how his public would relate to that. So very subtle changes moved in then. There was this 'I ought to join the Round Table' sort of thing and then 'You'll have to join the – whatever the hell it is – ladies circle'! I said 'You've got to be kidding'. 'Oh no, it's important for my career.' 'Well it isn't for mine. My credibility will be totally shot at if I join something like that!'

Romantic or stereotyped notions of 'wives' and 'mothers' often cause disagreement and upset, particularly when not shared:

I think I've got fairly realistic ideas about things. I think my partner hasn't. He expects a lot more and is very 'traditional' in many respects ... I suppose it's this idea of romance. It's not something I deny can exist but it's something I think tends to dissipate as time goes on. He doesn't think that's right, which I find quite extraordinary. I would expect that to be the other way round really. Having said that, the bastard forgot my birthday! ...

Judgements on the part of family and friends also tend to be concerned with expectations regarding relationships and children. Women who have not followed 'traditional' paths received comments or judgements from those close to them which emphasised their 'deviation' from 'the norm':

My mother's appalled that I'm 27 and I'm not married, absolutely appalled. If I have a male friend or if I do something for somebody who is male, my mother automatically thinks 'This is it!' – I'm going to get married!

Family members also commented on the nature of relationships, especially if these too were not traditional. For example, the parents of three of the women passed judgement when they or their partners went away alone on conferences or to work temporarily. Two women felt that their parents' judgements were based on concern for their daughters' happiness. Most of the women felt that close friends are supportive and not judgemental of their relationships. If concern is expressed it is, again, out of concern for the women's happiness. However, the women believed that acquaintances, and those not so close, do make judgements about their relationships with male friends. These often focus on the sort of behaviour deemed appropriate. One of the women illustrated this point:

> It's been assumed that I have an immoral attitude to sex and I find that really patronising, especially when it comes from women because they're not only making assumptions about the way I relate to men, they're also assuming that I'm being dishonest. Other men that I've been out with, when they've been jealous, have thrown all sorts of muck at me. I tend to get criticised for spending too much time with other people and giving too much to relationships and putting other people before me. I get criticised about that as though people think they've got a right to tell me I should be more selfish or more individualistic. I feel offended by that because I think it's not for them to tell me how to live my life ... I defend my right to be who I am and not live to other people's standards as long as I'm not hurting other people or making them unhappy wilfully.

Some of the older women in the studies expressed their differential experiences relating to the roles and expectations of women:

> Ten years ago you wouldn't have had us all sitting here doing plays, having a baby as well as doing so many different roles. It was either you were a mother or you were a housewife or you went to college – but you didn't dabble in all of them.

Although they made distinctions between their own lives and those of their daughters, they also inferred a continuity of shared gendered experience:

> My experience was of always having to have their tea on the table on time and I used to say I was a very good wife because I managed this. But I swore my girl was not going to be their slave [her sons] and because of that I made them take part.
>
> In spite of all this I bumped into Glen and Rosie [son and daughter-in-law] late one evening with a shopping bag each, so I stopped and had a chat and as they went away I said to myself, 'Good Lord, his dinner's not ready!' and I was horrified with myself because *hers* wasn't ready either!
>
> My daughter's very liberated, but I can still see him get cups of tea made for him and get waited on.

Many women believed these expectations to be reflected in, and perpetuated by, societal influences, particularly the media, which confuse and limit women. As one woman pointed out, these include 'conditioning and expectations placed on women'. Another woman reinforced this belief when she commented:

> I still think that society makes such demands on women in general in terms of things like the way they look, the way they speak, their attitudes, that women don't have a totally free choice in sexual relationships.

Another woman also raised the issue of 'culturally determined' inhibitions which stop women from doing what they want. She pointed out that, because of social restrictions, lesbian relations are rejected and women have to remain in heterosexual relationships where they experience abuse and violence. Further, the messages presented by the media and other institutions are confusing and conflicting, especially for young women:

> One magazine is telling you it's alright to say 'yes' another's telling you you should say 'no' and you don't even know what you're saying 'yes' and 'no' to at the time that you're reading them, and you've got to pretend that you understand it. It's all forced on young women and young women are really exploited . . . and men, but the effect is much worse on women.

Some of the main expectations imposed on women are those attached to femininity and sexuality. Within this, 'emphasised femininity' is perceived as the norm. Thus, women are expected to look and behave in certain, prescribed ways. Women's sexuality is defined primarily within the context of heterosexual, monogamous relationships and, ultimately, reproduction.

Many women felt they had knowledge and control over their bodies in terms of general health, fitness and well-being. However, there was common recognition of the external influences and pressures to conform to a particular feminine ideal:

> I like to exercise and keep fit. I think I'm probably obsessed with my weight. I think because there's so much emphasis put on how you look these days. I don't think it's a conscious thing that I'm bothered about how I look to other people. I always think I'm doing it for myself. But when I really think about it I suppose it's because I'm bothered about what other people think I look like. And I suspect it's because of images of women in the media and catalogues that come

> through your door. The trouble is, I know I can't do anything to make
> my legs any longer!

Women's physical and mental health can be severely affected by dominant
ideologies and images of 'femininity'. Bulimia nervosa and anorexia nervosa
are manifestations of this pressure to conform. However, it is important to
recognise that under- or over-eating is also a means of resistance for women,
through which they establish some form of control (even if harmful) over
their bodies:

> I do have perfect control over my body but I sometimes don't look
> after it in the way that I should. Once my relationship with John fell
> through I just started to eat and I haven't stopped until now and a part
> of that is, to be honest, to make myself unattractive to men. I don't
> think it was conscious at the time but I know what I've done. It's not
> something I'd admit to a lot of people that I've done but I've
> definitely done it.

Women are encouraged to believe that this pursuit of the feminine ideal is for
themselves. Many of the women acknowledged, however, that this is rarely
the case:

> From time to time I think about my image and may feel that I want
> to change it, but this preoccupation has lessened as I've got older.
> I'm aware of appearance, shape, clothes, but it's hard to know
> whether I'm being truthful in saying this – I feel it's important for
> myself to do this, although it is affected by other people's point of
> view.

When asked if they present themselves the way they wish to be seen the
majority responded that they do not know how they wish to be seen! The
perceptions of others is an influential factor: 'I think you do tend to dress for
other people a lot of the time'.

Women are made acutely aware when they have stepped outside the
parameters of feminine appearance and behaviour, through adverse comments and jokes. Whilst women may decide they will ignore such incidents,
invariably their self-esteem and confidence is undermined:

> One night I remember I went to a ball and a guy said 'You look a
> bit of a hard woman'. That kind of upset me. I thought 'Oh god,
> maybe I do look a bit'. I mean you read in magazines that men like
> women to be more timid and I'm not any more. I probably was a few

years ago but by the very nature of my job I've had to open up a lot more. A girl at work, when she first started, said she thought I was quite unapproachable. But that's in work where I'm quite different because I'm busy running around all over the place. People have said outside work I'm different. It does upset me a bit when people say things like that.

Women's identity is also determined by their 'attachment' to a man. Unattached women are seen to be 'a problem':

> For a woman who is divorced, there's a stigma about being on your own in public. When I divorced my ex-husband I had to 'disappear' completely. You're seen as a threat to other women's husbands!

This stigma is felt by widowed, divorced and single women, particularly when in mixed company, and is reinforced by the promotion of 'couples' as the only acceptable form of grouping at social events.

Motherhood is deemed to be women's 'natural' role. It is expected that women want to have children and assumed that all women have 'maternal instincts' which will automatically enable them to understand and fulfil the needs of an infant. Women who cannot, or choose not to, have children are made to feel 'unnatural' and alienated from their true destiny:

> There's distinct pressure from my mother over children, which is applied to both me and my partner, and that really is the main area ... 'Why don't you give up work and have a family?'

> We have no family and I think that's quite hard. I don't think that's really a joint decision ... I think that's quite an important issue because I do know he has expressed the idea that he would like children. Not to me though, to other people. I think he feels that he shouldn't put me under pressure – I've expressed my opinions. I think he sometimes feels he doesn't know what the purpose of the relationship is if there is no family.

From puberty, women's reproductive potential dominates much of their lives. Part of this relates to how women are expected to deal silently with 'women's problems'. A further dimension is that of decisions about contraception. Some women doubt their knowledge of this vital area and its sources. As one woman remarked: 'I don't think there is any effective form of contraception. It's a constant concern and stress for women'. Another of the women mentioned the dilemma of being anti-pill but remaining unsure about other methods of contraception. A third woman commented:

I've been on the pill in the past and I've had a coil and I don't know what effect they had on me. I think that now I probably wouldn't have used either of those methods ... I think there's a lot of big issues about the way research is being done and about abortion and reproductive technology and the way it's used on women. I think I'm as aware as any woman could be. But I also know that we don't get all the information ...

Autonomy

Women invariably accommodate the perceived needs and desires of those around them, whether children or partners. While it appears that autonomy exists in the daily organisation of home and family, this is related to women's role as wife and mother, where the responsibility is imposed on women out of duty rather than choice. As one woman asked 'the real moral dilemma for women is to what extent do you sacrifice yourself for other people?' For many women, work is the only escape from the isolation and oppression they experience in the private domain. Although it is an economic necessity for women to participate in paid employment, most felt that it is also crucial in the construction of an identity other than that of 'wife' and/or 'mother':

I couldn't stand the idea of being at home as mother and wife seven days a week. I needed to work to be treated as an individual.

For some men, women's participation in paid work is unacceptable:

My husband was very old-fashioned. Once we got married and had our first child there was no way on this earth that he would let me go out to work. He said 'I'm the breadwinner'.

The public sphere is clearly defined as a male sphere, with women's paid work circumscribed by their domestic commitments. Women have to ensure that it does not affect the smooth running of the home or impinge in any way on the lives of their partners. Some of the older women interviewed for the studies were actually prohibited from entering the labour market:

I was desperate to go out to work, I needed to go out to work, but my husband wouldn't let me. And don't think I could have just taken no notice of him and gone out to work because in those days *you couldn't*!

Many believe that these restrictions no longer apply to their daughters and other younger women or that job choice is wider and more fulfilling now:

> These days you're allowed to do an awful lot more than we were. I always said I didn't want my daughter ending up with jobs like I've had to do. It's not that I'm not happy with jobs I've done, but I want her to be able to pick and choose.

Although professional women do have more choice in terms of 'career' options than other women seeking paid employment, their work does have negative consequences within their relationships:

> The bone of contention comes when you work nights and then you want to have your own leisure time because then that doesn't leave much time for being together.

When not at work, the professional women interviewed were expected to spend their leisure time with their partners, but this was not reciprocated:

> He resented me going to dance classes when he was there and expected me not to go ... If he wanted to play golf or go out in the evenings he thought nothing of it. I wouldn't have felt so resentful if he hadn't made such a fuss about my classes.

> Any leisure time I have I save for him, not just because that's what he wants, partly because it's necessary for the relationship. But it can be a problem because I'm not doing some of the things I want to do. From now on I'm planning more what I want to do and this could cause problems.

Living with another person invariably places constraints on women and can threaten their independence:

> It's very difficult to be in a relationship with another person and not feel constrained to some extent ... I felt threatened because all of a sudden here I was living with somebody who was starting to tell me whether I could put up these curtains or not and that was a really big shock to me – to suddenly feel that somebody else could have a say in what I did. I'm quite independent and I don't like being told what to do by anybody else and that's quite difficult when you're living with somebody.

When it comes to decision-making, negotiation and compromise are essential features. For example, one woman had to rationalise everything for her partner because he would not face decisions. He made decisions, including financial ones, to suit himself. He decided to go abroad for three months on a trip paid for by her earnings. Another woman and her partner generally supported each other's independent decisions. However, where there was disagreement she usually gave in after a row. One woman claimed that in the past she had depended on men to make decisions but felt she had become more independent and would not let anyone make decisions for her, whereas another stated she was always decisive and rarely compromised. Still another pointed out that as the nature of decisions changed, the influences on decision-making changed. Had she lived with her partner the decisions taken would be strongly based on being in the relationship and, while her choice would not be taken away from her, for different reasons she might have lost her autonomy in decision-making.

Sometimes the contradictions experienced by women in their relationships were unbearable, and separation or divorce were the ultimate solution. Some of the older women felt that divorce had become a more acceptable and viable option:

> Do you know what they said when they made the divorce easier? They said, 'Oh, men are going to be changing their wives for a newer model'. But they were wrong. It was the women who were going for all the divorces!

I was recognised that this is a difficult decision, accompanied by what can be a long period of adjustment. As one woman pointed out 'Don't forget, when I got divorced I sat there for nearly six years and I did exactly the same as I did when I was married!' Yet when women realised their potential for independence, the experience could be empowering:

> Until I got divorced I didn't see my contribution to the home as being as important as my husband's. When he let me down I suddenly decided I was the breadwinner and I could survive.

One woman suggested that within the 'younger generation' of women, there has developed an expectation of being able to survive independently without embarking on constraining long-term relationships:

> In some ways though it's come full circle because you'll find now that girls are back to 'I want a baby', 'I want a flat', 'I want a Social book', but the difference is they don't want a man, they don't need a man. They'll do it on their own.

The Nature of Relationships

The nature of their relationships with partners is obviously an intrinsic element in the personal lives of women. Heterosexual relationships are encouraged, indeed positively promoted, by all institutions in society. Popular assumptions have led to an expectation of notable differences between the 'traditional' relationships of older women, and the 'enlightened' relationships of younger women. In reality the experiences of the women interviewed highlighted the fact that oppression in the private realm is consistent for women of all ages. The myth of 'New' men was exploded as women described the continuation of 'old' values and attitudes, and as they questioned the practical application of the 'liberated' position espoused by supposedly 'right on' partners. The need for a balance of 'give and take' was repeatedly proposed, but in practice the scales remained heavily weighted against women in a number of ways.

Most of the women discussed the evolving nature of relationships and the value of learning from experiences:

> Relationships can change dramatically over time ... And you do accommodate people and make adjustments.

One of the women commented 'My expectations of a relationship have changed as I've got older. I'm much more prepared to accept people's faults and flaws than I was'. Where relationships, on the whole, were good they were based on discussion and shared values. This was quoted as a vital prerequisite to present or future relationships:

> It's important that there's an understanding of goals or aims or ideas.

> I think you have to have ground rules from the start ... Unless you both want the same things then the relationship isn't going to work.

Although most of the women felt 'give and take' was an important part of a relationship, some felt that they were expected to give too much:

> I did withdraw from an awful lot of things for a peaceful life. And you begin to wonder how far would you have gone for a peaceful life. I think had we gone the whole hog and got married or started a family I probably would have put up with a lot more things to keep the peace. I feel a radically different person now to what I felt a year ago, eighteen months ago, because I was rapidly becoming the

shadow of somebody else. But it's not until you step out of that that you begin to think 'God, was I really like that?'

One woman's experience of her relationship drastically affected how she felt about herself and her future involvement with men. Her feelings reflect the doubts experienced by many women at the end of a relationship, when women seriously consider whether heterosexual relationships can ever be non-exploitative. Additionally, women doubt themselves, their judgements and wonder whether they are to blame:

> I wouldn't assume anything and I wouldn't assume I could influence or change anybody. In fact, I can't imagine having a relationship at the moment, at all, with any man. I just feel I couldn't trust any man ever again. I'm also cynical about how I view relationships. I see someone who looks happy and I say 'I bet they're not. I bet he's a right swine'. That's the sort of attitude I'm going through at the moment. I've had such close contact with my husband and my father-in-law, who treat women in a particular way, that I can't believe that anyone else doesn't do that in private. I don't know if that'll change. I hope so ... You feel 'Well, am I really a hard career woman who doesn't want children?' You start thinking like him. You really start to think 'Well, have I got it all wrong? Perhaps I am like that'. You have self doubts because of all the battles and things you have to go through.

As one woman realistically stated:

> You can't offer simple and easy answers to people – you can't say, 'Here you are girl, if you stand up and tell him to sling his hook all will be well' because it *won't*! You can't offer easy answers to people.

Another woman outlined the dilemmas when she said:

> In a personal situation it's difficult because your emotions are involved as well as your feelings for another person. And then you come back down to all this 'Well, how important is what I want? Is there a compromise or is it all or nothing?'

When they asked themselves these questions, some women felt that ending the relationship was the only solution for them ...

Because there's so much work and effort and trauma gone into it that it really isn't worth it when you get there.

Although painful at the time, two of the women expressed the positive aspects of learning from previous relationships:

I think I had to make a lot of mistakes first and go through one long relationship where perhaps I did a lot of things that I didn't really want to do and perhaps did things because I was frightened that if I didn't then I might lose that person. But now I think I've realised that it's not worth it and you must do what you want to do.

Now I realise that much of what I do I can control and I am responsible for if I want to do it. What I want now is to be myself, and that is central to everything else.

When asked whether it was a good thing for women to be confronted with the reality of their oppression, one woman responded:

When you're a certain age, sometimes it's very bad because you are too old to do something about it, so, is it a good thing for a woman to learn? It can be a very painful experience. It's not just 'God I'm free, break the chains off and let's run around and enjoy it!' – it isn't like that.

Another stated that:

What really came home to me was the fact that so much has changed so that in one way things have improved tremendously for women in that it is easier for them financially. At least now they have the opportunity to rent somewhere to live, whereas years ago nobody would rent accommodation to a woman – only to a man. All these things have improved, but emotionally nothing has changed.

The dilemmas facing women remain the same:

Although there are an awful lot of men around who say they're supportive there are an awful lot of men who aren't and who want to go back to the traditional stereotype. It's very difficult for women to fight that and still create whatever it is they want for themselves.

One woman pointed out, 'being yourself' can carry penalties:

You often don't know what you want but are aware of what you don't want in relationships and it's difficult to say so after a long time because the relationship's gone on for so long that if you say something it means you are questioning other areas of the relationship.

The following comment exemplifies others:

Even if you do know what you want, for me what stops me is having enough energy to be continually battling on my own ... for what I think ought to be everyday respects and rights.

The message of 'post-feminism' is that things have changed dramatically for women, particularly young women. However, as one woman concluded:

For some of the younger generation it's quite different because they've been brought up with different assumptions *and then* they suddenly discover that the 'real world' traps that have been there since the beginning of the world are lying there for them as well. It's very difficult for them to find their way out when they have been brought up to believe that they were kind of free, equal individuals.

Resistance, Coping Strategies and the Way Forward

Far from submissively accepting the oppressive situations women experience in the private sphere, the majority of women find ways of coping with and positively resisting them. In this, women turn to other women for emotional support. Women develop tight networks of female friends because, as one woman suggested:

... we come from a background of being continuously put down, so you learn to keep your thoughts to yourself. It's only when you come together with a number of like-minded women that you allow these thoughts to come out.

For men, 'New' and 'Old', women are the source of emotional succour. The women inferred that this placed a strain on the relationship with their partner because emotional and practical support was rarely reciprocated:

One of the pressures I feel is that I'm my husband's emotional resource and I find that really oppressive. I wish he'd find a nice man to talk to, I really do! And he's not very much my emotional resource. Essentially, about most of the things I need help and support, I turn to women. So it often feels to me that my relationship with him is one in which I support him but I have women who support me. You know, I'm talking about quite a sensitive and caring guy, but it's definitely one-sided. Little does he know that other women are the substructure of our marriage!

Although women depend on other women, their conversations and meetings are often surreptitiously conducted. This was partly to avoid accusations of betrayal and partly to maintain relationships independent of their partner:

Women friends are very important. I have women friends who know things about me that I wouldn't dream of telling my husband and I know I can tell them in absolute confidence. Once my husband heard me talking to her [a close friend] on the 'phone and was absolutely furious and said 'How could you be so disloyal?' It brought home to me the fact that I actually *needed* women friends with whom to explore my experience . . . Now I make sure he doesn't hear me!

Women have always tried to make sense of their experiences and assess the progress made in the struggles for equality. It seems that now more than ever before, women's and men's roles are scrutinised and questioned in all areas of life. As far as personal relationships are concerned, most of the women suggested that:

To improve women's situation, women need to adopt a better attitude about themselves and be more confident in their approach . . . We need to make more demands and say what we want rather than wait for other people to do it for us!

The issue of identifying needs specific to women was seen as vital. Women feel that out of necessity they turn to other women to fulfil this. Many women expressed the optimistic hope that this would change:

I think frequently women's expectations or needs or wants can't be understood by men, let alone accommodated by them. Partly because, for a lot of them, it would be a radical culture shock. I think you can probably get there in the long term in a one to one situation, with a lot of patience and mutual working towards that point.

Men have to be willing participants in the process of achieving equality. The private domain of the home and family is a primary site of oppression. However, many women are actively working for change:

> I think our generation of women have made tremendous strides towards equality. We certainly aren't there yet and your generation have made even better strides. But it's always in my mind that this must never be allowed to slip back, because you've only got to take your mind off it for one minute and those men will be in there! I find myself brainwashing the younger members of my family by sending them birthday cards with 'It's great to be a girl' on them and telling them all the time, (and it's up to us to do that), consistently telling them that there's nothing in this world that you can't do! And I'm continuously telling my sons that these girls are not just a pretty face – they're not just there to wait on you at all – they're people in their own right.

Conclusion

Many of the issues fundamental to liberation, raised and discussed by feminists throughout the century are now claimed to be 'on the agenda'. As the women interviewed illustrate, however, questions about who does the housework, or works a double day, or supports the men and children of the family, have not been addressed. In the public realm, struggles for equality between women and men have focused on policy reform to enable equality of opportunity. Most institutions now claim to have, and to implement, some form of equal opportunities policy. As the previous chapters have shown, these tend to be vague and ineffective. Legislative change, introduced to ensure their application, is minimal and frequently too expensive, complicated and time-consuming to instigate. In the private sphere however, there is little or no legislation to remove or outlaw gender inequality. It is seen to be every individual woman's responsibility to negotiate the organisation and carrying out of domestic and child-care activities. For the majority of women, there is limited or no 'choice' involved in decisions about whether or not to work, have children, or combine the two.

As far as relations within a partnership are concerned, intervention from any outside agencies, when there is a breakdown of communications or when one partner feels aggrieved by the behaviour or actions of the other, is deemed inappropriate. Relations in the private sphere are perceived as strictly private business. This is reinforced by legislation affecting women. However, it is not only the legal system which discriminates against women. There tends to be minimal recognition of the difficulties involved in achieving personal change in societies and institutions dominated by the cultural and stereotypical expectations which define and regulate feminine and masculine sexuality. An emphasis on liberal reform and legislative change, focusing on provision of equal opportunities, in institutions such as education, work and the media, fails to question the origin of such expectations. It also fails to ask who benefits from them. Such commentators, including a few 'former feminists', are now claiming that women should accept their biology as their destiny. In a return to pre-feminist ideology, the 'feminine' virtues of caring, sharing and maternal domesticity are being promoted. It is suggested that women have lost sight of themselves and their abilities in their bid to achieve equality. The consequence has been 'masculine', 'aggressive', 'competitive' females who attain power by becoming 'one of the lads' and rejecting their femininity. Not only does this leave women confused about their identities, it also blows the minds (and hearts) of men, who just do not know what women want any more. If women, and some men, would stop trying to work against traditionally accepted roles, attitudes and values, their dissatisfaction with life would disappear and everyone would know where they stood . . . or so the argument goes.

'Expert' theories abound to 'prove' that female and male roles are based on biological make-up. Whether because of women's reproductive capacity or hormonal composition, it is claimed that their true vocation in life is to find a partner, bear children and live in contented bliss – producing and nurturing offspring, providing and maintaining a clean, comfortable home, fulfilling the material and emotional needs of their partners and families. Divisions between men and women have been forged, and are being exacerbated, by discussion in newspapers, magazines and on television about 'working women' and those who advocate 'family life'. Within the 'working women' classification divisions exist between 'career' women, who have few commitments other than work, and women who combine domestic and working responsibilities. In the latter group, further disagreement is based on differences between women who have to find paid employment, as well as carry out all the domestic and child-care work at home, and those who choose to work while someone else assists or takes responsibility for the children and house.

In all the debates, the term 'post-feminism' is used to describe or explain women's dissatisfaction or disillusionment with life at home and work. There is minimal recognition that such dissatisfaction existed before 'our' so-called 'post-feminist' era, and little analysis of the reasons for it. The answers lie in much of the feminist analysis of women's situation and experience. Women's, and men's, biologies have been socially and politically constructed to enforce and maintain women's oppression. Within patriarchy, female sexuality has been constructed to serve men's needs, interests and desires. In capitalist societies women's labour, in both the home and paid workforce, has been exploited to bolster and preserve capitalist economies and social institutions which are essentially patriarchal. Biological differences between the sexes mean that only women can give birth to children. Once that has occurred, however, the nurturance and rearing of children is seen to remain dependent on the mother or females. There is no acknowledgement, let alone advocacy, of the fact that fathers, or males, are just as capable of feeding and caring for children. Thus, reproductive roles are socially and politically imposed to establish and perpetuate the division of labour, and to support the promotion of the biological family as the only 'proper' economic and social unit.

While many women, including those in the research, refuse to accept patriarchal ideology, they have to struggle in their personal relationships, as well as in the public arena, to resist expectations and assumptions regarding their femininity and their pre-supposed roles. Women often turn to other women for support and assurance that their feelings of anger, frustration or dissatisfaction are not based on selfishness or an inability to relate with others. However, equality will not be achieved until women, and men, question the acceptance and maintenance of female sexuality, and assumptions about femininity, which determine what are deemed as appropriate appearance, behaviour, and roles for females in both the public and private spheres. 'Masculine' and 'feminine' traits and responsibilities should not be polarised. When men and women, regardless of their sexuality, can be assertive, confident, active, expressive, supportive, and can share responsibility for paid and unpaid work and child-care, equality will be a possibility. Until then, 'post-feminism' will continue to be a myth as far as the personal and public lives of women are concerned.

Nevertheless, women continue to explore their own identities, the way they organise their lives and their interpersonal relationships. They are accommodating the conflicting and complementary aspects of partnerships, while defining their needs and desires. As well as having to struggle with these issues on their own, or alongside other women, they are now having to combat pressure on a wider scale. The backlash against feminism, or individual women who do not conform with expected roles or behaviour, has been a major cause of dissent among women. Additionally, it has set up women and men as opposites, with distinctive characteristics, needs and abilities. Although the attack has been fierce, and the consequences suffered by some women have been severe, it is ironic that this anti-feminist propaganda has, in fact, strengthened the resolve of many women to continue their personal and political struggle against patriarchal, capitalist relations which oppress them.

Chapter 7

Conclusion: Beyond the Illusions

In Europe this is the Decade of Women. In Britain it is the era of Opportunity 2000. On 28th October 1991 Opportunity 2000 was launched in a blaze of publicity. The campaign, a *Business in the Community* initiative, was committed to increasing 'the quality and quantity of women's participation in the workforce' by the year 2000 (*Opportunity 2000 Mission Statement*, 1991). The launch had Prime Ministerial support with John Major delivering a keynote address to some 200 business people and politicians representing over 150 organisations. He spoke of a 'social revolution' which was 'happening frankly whether men like it or not'. The rhetoric was powerful and impressive:

> Why should half of our population go through life like a hobbled-horse in a steeplechase? The answer, of course, is that they shouldn't and increasingly, they won't.
>
> (John Major, *BBC News*, 28.10.91)

Just a year later was a different reality as Opportunity 2000 stumbled at the first fence. At the time of its launch 61 employers joined the campaign – each pledging their commitment to equal opportunities for women at work and to the removal of sexist barriers which inhibit equality of opportunity. The organisations paid £1,000 joining fee and undertook to set *achievable* goals based on their own unique circumstances.

In this it was envisaged that programmes would be 'tailor-made' since some members were considered to be further along the equal opportunities road than others. Finally, each organisation was required to publicise its progress at 'agreed intervals'. The first progress reports were due to be published in April 1992. The second progress reports were due to be published in October 1992. Neither sets of reports were published until well into 1993. A somewhat disillusioned Campaign Director at Opportunity 2000 suggested that the lack of response may indicate that members' commitment to Opportunity 2000 possibly represents little more than lip service. Indeed, by May 1994, a survey by the Institute of Management revealed that the number of women managers in British companies had actually decreased (*Remuneration Economics and the Institute of Management*, 1994). The survey showed that while companies continued to join the campaign, any changes were cosmetic. Familiar barriers to women's advancement – sexist attitudes and practices – persist, largely unchecked.

Similarly, the sincerity of John Major's public support for the Campaign did not stand up to scrutiny. It was totally irreconcilable with the cold fact that, since 1979, successive Conservative Governments have created some of the harshest, most hostile conditions for equal opportunities initiatives. Through a continuous stream of repressive social policies existing sexist, racist and classist practices have been reinforced.

Far from promoting equality of opportunity, a 'consumer culture' has been created. The language of 'the market' and the dominance of individualism has spread like a cancer to every corner of social policy-making. The Great Education Reform Bill (GERBIL) of 1987 and subsequent Education Reform Act (1988) have ensured that educational institutions carry the hallmarks of business organisations or 'educational supermarkets' (Hall, 1983 cited in McCarthy, 1989 p. 160). 'Parental choice' and increased control through governing bodies have been heralded as proof of a Government committed to the advancement of individual 'freedom', while hierarchies, competitiveness, and an emphasis on differences have combined to reinforce social, sexual and racial differentiation.

Catastrophic economic policies have created mass unemployment and the pauperisation of millions. Those who have sought to defend their jobs through the legitimate processes of trades union struggles have found themselves criminalised and brutalised by repressive anti-trade union legislation and the unprecedented extension of police powers (Criminal Justice Bill, 1994; Public Order Act, 1986; Police and Criminal Evidence Act 1984; Trades Unions Act, 1984; Employment Acts, 1982; 1980). For those fortunate to remain in employment, decent levels of pay and working conditions are not assured. Britain remains the only Member State of the European Community (EC) to oppose the Charter of Fundamental Social Rights (Social Charter) which would guarantee certain minimum legal rights including: the freedom of movement of workers, social benefits, fair wages and equal treatment for men and women. The abolition of Wages Councils has effectively made Britain the only EC country with no minimum wage protection (Trades Union and Reform of Employment Rights Act, 1992). Sixty-five per cent of UK workers earning less than the Council of Europe's decency threshold are women. Eighty-six per cent of all part-time workers in the UK are women (Faludi, 1992).

The massive increase in deregulated work, that is part-time, contracted-out employment, has particularly affected those jobs traditionally considered to be the preserve of women (e.g. cleaning and catering). Companies have been forced into competitive tendering for contracts and so look to the advantages of employing women on short-term and part-time contracts, to cut hours, wages and therefore costs. The average hourly rate for a part-time worker in 1990 was little more than half that of male full-time earnings (Labour Party, 1991). Despite an increase in women's employment, their hourly earnings were just 78.8 per cent of men's earnings in 1992 (*Employment Gazette*, 1992). The UK has the lowest provision of paid maternity leave in Europe and the poorest child-care provision (Faludi, 1992). Applications to the Equal Opportunities Commission for funding to pursue sex discrimination cases rose by nearly 60 per cent during the Thatcher administration (Collins, 1992).

While mass unemployment has forced unprecedented numbers into dependency on state benefits, these people have also had to endure the double humiliation of being labelled 'work-shy scroungers'. As the 'burden' on social security budgets has grown, through its commitment to minimising public expenditure, central government has sought to 'justify' benefit cuts. In the context of rhetoric around a 'dependency culture' the 1980, 1986 and 1988 Social Security Acts introduced widespread financial cut-backs and regulation reforms reminiscent of the Victorian Poor Laws. Ruth Lister (1989) has noted how the notion of 'obligation' has increasingly replaced that of 'rights'. More than ever before social welfare has been consolidated as conditional; targeted towards the 'deserving' and away from the 'undeserving'. Enforced economic dependency on men and/or the state has traditionally left women, children and young people materially vulnerable. Ninety per cent of lone parents are women (Haskey, cited in Bradshaw, 1989 p. 9). In its research into Household Budgets and Living Standards, the Family Budget Unit (1992) found that only approximately 30 per cent of lone mothers achieved the 'modest but adequate' standard of living. Over half of lone mothers, however, failed to reach even the 'low-cost' standard. Further, for those women in this second category only 77 per cent of their 'low-cost' budget was met via Income Support, thus condemning them to a standard of living well below the breadline. The succession of changes in income maintenance and social security legislation has directly and indirectly resulted in the increased economic dependency of women on men (Child Support Act, 1991; Social Security Act, 1986) and of young people, elders, the disabled and the mentally ill on 'the family' (National Health Service and Community Care Act, 1990; Social Security Act, 1988). A mixed economy of welfare, whereby the state is rolled back in favour of private, voluntary and informal care arrangements, lies at the heart of health and social welfare reforms and policy recommendations throughout the last decade. This 'wider' conception of welfare is predicated on an assumption of 'the family' as *the* 'natural' site for the provision of care and the meeting of all needs.

British social policy has consistently assumed, reinforced and perpetuated a particular ideological notion of sexual relationships and 'the family' – a heterosexual, married couple with naturally conceived children. However in the late 1970s, in response to what had been identified as the failure of liberal welfarism, the newly elected Thatcher government embarked on a series of social and economic policies built on powerful notions of family morality. So-called 'permissive' liberal ideologies of the 1960s and early 1970s, 'pandering' to the interests of single-issue groups such as feminists, gays and lesbians, were proclaimed to be the cause of social, and particularly familial, disintegration. It has been suggested that marital breakdown, single parents, working mothers, delinquency, homosexuality, under-age sex, illegitimacy, easy abortion, AIDS and neglected and abused children are together the result of the breakdown of the traditional patriarchal family (Davies *et al.*, 1993; Dennis, 1993; Dennis and Erdos, 1992). The hidden agenda is that central government, in the face of economic crises, has attempted to escape its financial responsibilities imposed by liberal welfare ideologies, policies and practices. To this end, it has been imperative to recall the 'traditional family' to take up the burden and to mediate the consequences of mass impoverishment and imiseration. Beyond this, a sequence of homophobic policies emerged which focused on the centrality of 'the family' to the economic and moral well-being of the nation (Human Fertilisation and Embryology Act, 1990; Paragraph 16 of the draft family placement guidance to the 1989 Children Act; Section 28 of the Local Government Act, 1988, formerly Section 2A Local Government Act, 1986; Warnock Report, 1984).

The pro-family crusade of both neo-conservative and New Right politicians has been allowed free rein by the lack of any coherent alternative stance on 'the family' from the Left. In its 1991 paper *The Family Way* it was difficult to distinguish the Labour Party's approach from that of the Tories. The Conservative Government's homophobic and anti-feminist attacks were ignored by Labour as Neil Kinnock was advised that gay rights was a vote-loser. The absence of any critique of the 'traditional family' as an oppressive institution suggests that it remains conceptualised as being unproblematic. At best the paper drew on the 'trusted' and established welfarist principle of 'children come first', while neglecting the fundamental issues. Nor was it reassuring to learn that some of the Labour Party's women supported Bryan Gould for the Party leadership contest in 1992 because 'he is the least macho among the men' (Margaret Hodge, cited in Herbert, 1992). This is all the more demoralising given that the prime contender, (and eventual winner), the late John Smith, supported Enoch Powell's Unborn Children (Protection Bill) in 1985 and voted for the second reading of David Alton's 1988 abortion-curbing Bill. As Bea Campbell (*The Guardian*, 28 May 1992) states, 'Left-of-centre parties are not only frightened of women's radicalism but of radicalism itself. The progressive space is not one the two major opposition parties dare to inhabit'. In this, the Labour Party has over-whelmingly justified Zillah Eisenstein's (1982 p. 569) scepticism concerning the faith many women have placed in the use of liberal ideology to improve their situation. She suggests that 'feminist demands uncover the truth that capitalist patriarchal society cannot deliver on its "liberal" promises of equality or even equal rights for women without destabilising itself'.

Since the late 1970s the most progressive developments in equality legislation have come from the European Community (EC). Since 1973 the European Commission has made a powerful contribution to developing equality of opportunity through successive directives, awareness campaigns and action programmes. Throughout the 1980s successive Thatcher Govern-ments found themselves at odds with Community directives on equal treatment, equal pay and social protection. Some changes in UK law resulted directly from European Court judgments (i.e. Employment Act, 1989; Sex Discrimination Act, 1986; and Equal Pay (Amendment) Act, 1983). How-ever, the EC itself remains limited in so far as it can only *recommend* what must happen in a directive. It is left to each individual member state to develop national law complying with its recommendations. Significantly, more complaints have gone to the European Court of Justice in Luxembourg from the UK than from any other country and a large proportion of these complaints relate to employment. This provides a clear indication that the increase in the number of sex discrimination cases taken by women has not been matched by the *effective* implementation of equal opportunities policies and legislation. It is a damning track record which flies in the face of claims about progressive equality policy and practice.

Although the legal foundations for change have been laid, it has become evident that laws and directives intended to abolish inequality have failed. While equal opportunities initiatives are in vogue and the issue is superficially on the agenda, campaigns such as Opportunity 2000 and liberal sentiments of good intent do nothing to address the problem of *de facto* discrimination. Even in countries considered 'progressive' and 'advanced' in terms of equal opportunities, women work more hours than their male counterparts for less pay, live in fear of sexual violence and are denied full control over reproduction (Ericson and Jacobsson, 1985). In theory the legislative means to secure equality are available to women. Yet the full dimensions and structural causes of gender inequality go unrecognised and denied by liberal democratic government. Consequently the theory is not borne out in practice.

The preceding chapters on education, work, media and interpersonal relationships comprehensively illustrate women's continued subordination both personally and collectively. A review of education policy since the 1970s, coupled with a feminist analysis of girls' experiences at school, revealed that legislation has had little effect on the hidden curriculum in schools. This means that opportunities available for girls and young women are severely restricted by limited access to subject choice, negative attitudes and stereotyped expectations of teachers, and sexual harassment by male peers and teachers. The in-depth analysis of women's paid work experiences revealed that they experienced discrimination at a number of levels. Their access to training and their promotion opportunities were limited. Even when employed in the same job as men, the actual, or expected, duties of the women were different. Invariably these focused on servicing roles. Women's unpaid domestic responsibilities were the focus of attention in job interviews and were linked to expectations about women's ability to realise their occupational duties successfully. Many of the women interviewed had experienced sexual harassment in the workplace at a range of levels. Women working in the media also experienced discrimination in employment practices and conditions of work. At a personal level they experienced the negative effects of stereotyped assumptions about appropriate and inappropriate behaviour and appearance for women. The research demonstrated how such assumptions, relating to motherhood, sexuality and emphasised femininity, underpin dominant representations of women.

All the women interviewed related the tensions, dilemmas and contradictions they experienced in interpersonal relationships. They described how clearly-defined expectations about their roles as wives, partners and/or mothers impact on domestic responsibilities and other social arrangements. They also described how idealised representations of women affect their self-image and personal identity, placing limitations on their lives. While the research interviews did not focus directly on male violence within personal relationships, the incontrovertible broader evidence remains that women's subjugation is underpinned by men's persistent use of physical power. The use of violence extends from harassment through to acts of brutality, from the street to the home, from girl children to elderly women. Patriarchies establish 'father-right' based on phallocentrism within heterosexual relations and, historically, the rule of law protects and sustains these relations of power and exploitation, reflected in the constant fear of violence under which women live (Stoltenberg, 1991). It is a fear daily born out by individual cases and through a cursory glance at the statistics. Child sexual abuse is predominantly the action of men directed against girl children. Violence in relationships is dominated by men's physical, psychological and sexual brutalisation of their partners. The 'safe haven' of the home is the very place where women are most at risk from those with whom they have established relationships. Rape and the fear of rape remains the primary control through which men collectively exert power over women. Without doubt this has the consequence of setting real limits on women's access to social space, leisure facilities and the streets.

There has been some effort within criminal justice policy to take seriously crimes of violence against women, with a range of police forces offering rape counselling and 'domestic violence' suites. However, established rape crisis centres and women's aid refuges continue to be run on a shoestring with many initiatives closing or offering restricted services because of underfunding. At the very time when women need increased facilities offered by women for women, the provision of local government funding has diminished. Within statutory agencies social workers consistently argue that necessary interventions are abandoned or reduced as they compete with other important initiatives for effective and appropriate budgets. The pervasiveness of men's violence against women has meant that men have benefited from physical domination, as one important expression of male power, even if they are not predatory in their own actions. Much of this debate has been conducted around the statements that 'all men are rapists' or 'all men are potential rapists'. The real significance of the debate, however, is that rape and other acts of male terrorism compound and maintain male power at a range of levels and on many sites: work, home, streets, clubs, pubs . . . It reveals a fear which instils terror, inhibits movement and destroys women's lives. It is precisely the unpredictability of men's violence, from lovers, friends, acquaintances or strangers, which often reveals to women the 'stranger' in the men they thought they knew. Any claims for women's advancement have to be measured in this context of women's fear and men's physical control.

Other limitations on women's lives are revealed in contemporary studies which illustrate that although women prioritise their careers, institutionalised sexism prohibits their advancement. The National Council of Women of Great Britain commissioned a survey which found that for nearly 80 per cent of women aged under 35, having children was secondary to a successful career. Although 76 per cent of working mothers in the survey sought paid employment, or promotion within existing employment, 40 per cent expressed dissatisfaction with career prospects and doubted whether they would achieve their career goals. Many felt undervalued and one third of those aged 35-44 years stated that their skills were not being used to their full potential (*The Guardian*, 25.11.92). These findings were reinforced by an independent survey commissioned by the Lord Chancellor's Department and the Bar Council. This study revealed the institutional discrimination faced by women in the male-dominated legal profession. Men, particularly those in positions of power, refused to acknowledge this situation. Yet one out of 27 Court of Appeal Judges, four out of 83 High Court Judges, and 24 out of 480 Circuit Judges, were women. At interview women continue to be asked discriminatory questions about marriage and having children. They earned less than men and were less likely to be able to work in their choice of specialism, often relegated to the less prestigious and poorer paid sectors of the profession (family and criminal law). Such discrimination is compounded by the persistence of the 'old-boy' network, as patronage plays a key part in the judicial appointments system (Institute of Management, 1992).

Given this statistical evidence, and coupling it to the accounts of the women within the research, it is clear that the claims of 'post-feminism' cannot be sustained. This is not to say that nothing has changed for women and some aspects of women's daily experiences can be defined as 'progressive'. Women have rights to suffrage, education, employment, to own property. Women, theoretically, have more choice than their predecessors regarding work, relationships and reproduction. However, what ostensibly are considered to be gains may, essentially, represent the broadening out of oppressive relations from the predominantly narrow confines of the private sphere to the more diffuse, less concrete, public arena. Thus, while things may be *different* for women, this does not guarantee, nor translate into, equality or liberation. Within each of the areas cited as gains for women, progress has been remarkably fragile and uneven. Gender inequality persists.

At best 'post-feminism' is a concept appropriate to professional women. It is only these women who are in a position to make 'choices' about whether or not to follow a career and combine it with motherhood. They are the women whose occupations provide the financial resources to 'buy-in' high quality child-care and domestic support. Alternatively they are the women who are in a position to reject the opportunities open to them, favouring a return to traditional roles. Either way, the options available to them are *not* available to most women. The majority of women do not experience the opportunities open to white, heterosexual, middle-class women. As Nancy K Miller (cited in Modleski, 1992 p. 22) states 'only those who have it can play with not having it'.

Moreover, the appealing images of caring, sharing New Men, so abhorred by Robert Bly (1990) and others, not surprisingly, are hard to find in real life. Undoubtedly, there are real attempts by some men to change their politics and practice. These men should, as Kimberley Leston (1990) suggests, be given the right to 'attempt to re-invent themselves'. Otherwise they are denied the rights for which so many women have struggled and been denied. It is only when men change that the oppression of women can cease.

But the alteration of a tiny minority cannot mask the continued dominance by the majority of men. Judging from the lived experiences of the women in the studies it is questionable whether much has changed for women in the private realm, including professional women. The 'New Man' is a mythical, media figure. There has been minimal and superficial redistribution of domestic labour in the home. In addition, child-care has been delegated to 'nannies' or child-minders for those who can afford to exploit their poorer 'sisters', or is organised and carried out by women in addition to their paid employment.

Another serious flaw in the 'post-feminist' discourse, concerning the creation and consolidation of opportunities for women, is that this 'liberation' remains within male-defined parameters. Women can succeed but only on men's terms in a man's world. Women can compete equally at work if they adopt 'assertive' (i.e. aggressive) strategies, are single-minded, and are prepared to work fifteen hours a day. Women can combine a career with motherhood if they organise child-care and domestic arrangements which do not impinge on their partner's work or leisure time. Women can wear make-up and dress in stilettos, short skirts, shoulder-padded jackets or silk business suits because these are feminine and promote acceptable images of appearance which emphasise femininity. It is claimed that the liberated women of this 'enlightened age' can achieve all these things *for themselves*.

Admittedly, some women have tried to determine their own needs and desires. Those women with high popular profiles, such as Annie Lennox, Madonna, Sinead O'Connor and Tina Turner, have expressed, both in personal interviews and through their own representation, the need for women to explore and establish their own sexuality. Although many young women see these women as role-models, and from their example develop their own styles of dress and behaviour, this tends to take one of two forms. The first is 'alternative' dressing, in which women's bodies are largely concealed by baggy, unobtrusive, de-sexing clothes. The second is overtly 'feminine' or 'erotic' dress which emphasises the shape and form of women's bodies. Both are claimed to be positive expressions of women's sexuality or identity. However, the former almost denies a woman's sex while the latter tends to conform with patriarchal expectations or fantasies about women, whether the woman chooses to present that image or not. Additionally, what is perceived as 'acceptable' or 'fashionable' appearance is determined by availability of styles in shops or catalogues. Thus, 'the market' plays a major role in the ability of women to decide what they want and whether they can acquire it.

Chris Pegg (1990, p. 159) wryly points out that '"Women's culture" has become institutionalised within the capitalist system'. She suggests that many publishing companies have made vast profits from the publication of books by and for women. The relatively recent interest in, and celebration of, women's writing, and the concern with 'gender issues', is also reflected in popular magazines such as *Cosmopolitan*. Articles and features on health, fitness, beauty, 'how to find and keep a man', etc. are intermingled with the latest statistics about women's position in the public or private spheres and reviews of feminist literature. More radical magazines also participate in the sale of 'women's culture'. For example, 'everything from trekking in Nepal to writing weekends in Wiltshire exclusively in the company of one's sisters is on offer on the back pages of *Spare Rib*' (Pegg, 1990). The availability of literature written by women, and of direct interest to them, is significant but it is hardly a revolutionary advance. Women have always been authors. Women have always documented their thoughts, feelings and ideas. Women have always wanted to find out about 'herstory' and been interested in the experiences of other women. The fact that only recently have they been able to make some in-road into the mainstream does not imply that material, and demand for it, did not exist before. It merely serves as an illustration of the primacy allocated to men, men's experience/knowledge/view of the world, and the domination of the literary world at every level by men.

Frigga Haug (1989) suggests that in most European countries there has been a 'nationalisation' of the woman question. In this, women's problems have been moderately institutionalised. Official posts concerned with women's affairs have been created and filled by a few women who are expected to identify women's problems, make their grievances public and suggest remedies. The result has been a handful of professorships for women, a few ameliorating laws, increased 'talk' about women and a small number of focused demands which have allowed one woman to 'rise and enjoy the fruits of the struggles of many' (ibid., p. 112). This has occurred at the level of state and within political parties.

In Britain, the legacy of Thatcherism, manifested in the four major themes of the 1992 Conservative Party Election Manifesto – opportunity, choice, ownership and responsibility – theoretically applies to all men and all women. Chris Pegg (1990, p. 159) argues that Thatcherite ideology encompassed the notion that special provision for women was not necessary since equality had been achieved: 'The notion of "post-feminism" is bandied about – surely British women are emancipated and liberated by now, and there's a condom machine in every pub loo to prove it!'

Through the creation of an illusion of progress, male dominance and female subordination continues. The language and politics of social democracies remain dominated by liberal notions of equality. The assumptions of liberal pluralism, upon which 'post-feminist' discourse rests, have structured the 'equality' agenda. Contemporary policies have been based on the promotion of personal achievement. Individual autonomy, independence, freedom of choice, equality of opportunity and equality before the law are the liberal ideals which have been successfully hijacked by right-wing governments. By co-opting the language of 'choice' and 'opportunity' the British Government has politically and ideologically managed to sustain a *symbolic* attachment to the principle of equality. A reality gap exists. The rhetoric of equal opportunities creates an illusion of advancement towards equality while policies and practices which reaffirm and reinforce inequality are implemented. In this the manipulation of 'ideas' is central. Patriarchal discourses are *institutionalised* at *all* levels of British society, functioning as relations of power and domination. Hegemony, and the social relations which ensue, has the capacity for change, adaptation and transformation. Its ability to neutralise opposition was forcefully illustrated throughout the early 1980s in the treatment of seemingly radical, 'positive action' oriented, local governments, such as the Greater London Council. Their efforts were eventually undermined by right-wing political and ideological smear campaigns targeting what became popularised as 'loony-left' Labour authorities. Subsequently, many other local authorities were compelled to disown anti-racist and anti-sexist policies in favour of more 'acceptable' liberal equal opportunities policies.

Hegemony also accommodates contradiction. It is precisely the *illusion* of 'freedom', 'choice' and 'opportunity' which remains fundamental to the political management of conflict and resistance. Notions of 'liberation', co-opted from the political struggles of the women's movement in the 1970s, have been taken up and reworked in a different context over time. Thus while 'equality', ostensibly, has been incorporated within the political agenda and 'concessions' have been won, fundamental structural relations have *not* changed. The political ideology of freedom is incongruous with the reality of a social order characterised by domination and subordination. This is not to infer a uni-directional conspiracy organised by groups of men or by individual men. The process is far more diffuse and less tangible. Hegemonic discourse is effective because of its widespread appeal to 'common-sense' assumptions. Clearly there exists a dialectical relationship between dominant, historically developed, social forces and the politics of resistance which has arisen through such historical development. It is important to stress that social movements regularly emerge in opposition to the power relations embodied in the policies and practices of political, economic and social institutions. It has been the strength of 'established order' politics, however, that they have been able to accommodate, even incorporate, such opposition, and through what appears to be a more progressive discourse, maintain intact its centres of power. What this demonstrates is that hegemony services and reproduces a form of state power that is not static nor absolute, but it enables and provides the structures of dominance through the illusion of negotiation.

There are potential tensions and contradictions in applying a term such as 'backlash' to women's struggles in contemporary Britain. Is the oppression that women experience *now* fundamentally any more intense than previously and, if so, has this intensification been in direct response to a female challenge to male privilege? Sheila Rowbotham (*Everywoman*, July/August 1992b) suggests that anti-women 'backlashes' are not new but that they are a recurring feature. She cites numerous examples over the last 200 years when 'backlash rhetoric' rose up after 'radical attempts to change society'. In this it is important to recognise the convergence of the interests of capitalism and patriarchy at specific historical moments. Historical analysis reveals that women's 'advances' invariably coincide with junctures when it has been in the material interests of capital and patriarchy for women to work outside the home. Similarly, at times of economic crisis, capitalist and patriarchal interests join forces to exclude women from the workplace, along with other marginalised groups. At such times there have been heightened *material* and *ideological* pressures placed on women, particularly from the Right. In this sense the 'backlash phenomenon' has always existed, albeit having something of a temporal identity. Germaine Greer (*The Guardian*, 23 September 1992b) emphasises, however, that 'male hostility to women is a constant' and that 'men have always found feminism provoking'. Nevertheless, she is hesitant to concur with the view that 'women have invaded the male preserve to the extent that they have begun to oppress men' and that this, in turn, has provoked men into a backlash. The danger of such a view is that it gives men a justification for their unrelenting tyrannical behaviour. While the sex war can be identified as constant, it is clear that the potential always exists for the mobilisation of a latent, shared, male response. In this, men react strongly towards women over a shorter sustained period of time. Discourses proclaiming the advent of 'post-feminism' are in danger of yet again putting *men* 'centre stage' and diverting the attention of feminism from more pressing matters (Modleski, 1992; Roberts, 1992).

Indeed, rather than achieving 'equality' only to have it snatched away by avenging men, most women have actually, as Lynne Segal states, remained 'as removed as ever from the centres of men's economic, political and social power' (*Everywoman*, May 1992). With this in mind, what relevance does a concept like 'backlash' have to the majority of women? Is it realistic to infer that black women, lesbian women, disabled women, working-class women and women elders have had the same 'taste of equality' as young, white, middle-class, heterosexual, able-bodied women? While a 'backlash' of political, social, economic and ideological repression is felt by all women, the current 'backlash' is not against all women. It is focused, primarily, on those who have been privileged enough to benefit from the liberal reforms of the 1970s – white, middle-class professional women. In addition, it appears to be taking the form of exclusive, introverted, intellectual debates, in which a small number of women, typically established 'feminist experts', battle it out with Lyndon, Bly, Thomas, Farrell, Paglia and company in the pages of the 'quality' newspapers, magazines and feminist journals. In all this the views of black and white working-class women on 'backlash' and 'post-feminism' have not been heard. Their struggles to resist and survive, not only in the face of personal and institutionalised sexism, but personal and institutionalised racism and extreme poverty have remained marginal. In this respect, feminism stands accused of speaking only to an elite. Despite centuries of global oppression and resistance, women do not readily identify with the label of feminism. Rebecca West, as long ago as 1913, specified the problem:

> I myself have never been able to find out precisely what feminism is: I only know that people call me a feminist whenever I express sentiments that differentiate me from a doormat.
> (Cited in Faludi, 1992 p. 17)

This is not exclusively the fault of elitist, academic tendencies within feminist theory and politics. The part played by the media in perpetuating negative stereotyped images of feminism, with which the majority of women feel unable or unwilling to identify, has long been acknowledged. Most of the women in the research made powerful statements which undeniably identified them with a feminist politics. Yet they invariably qualified these statements with comments such as, 'I'm not a feminist, but ...'. Clearly, while women's consciousness has been raised by public exposure to feminist debates, the feminist *agenda* has had more success than the feminist label.

The Women's Liberation Movement of the 1960s demanded social transformation at all levels. It developed during a decade which celebrated British affluence and the 'consumer dream'. The politics formulated then provided a basis for discussion and development of feminist theory and practice. Although the movement of the 1960s now appears parochial and ethnocentric, the current feminist movement is grounded on the objectives formulated then and builds on the limitations as well as advances made by previous movements. At present 'feminism is learning to reconstitute itself as a social force that takes account of women's differences rooted in experiential identities', i.e. the politics of identity (Editorial, *Feminist Review* 1989). The danger is that in the context of a preoccupation with female anti-essentialism there is a risk that all become pluralised beyond their own resistances. What becomes obvious is that the two dimensions of women's struggle, equality and difference, need to be reunited. For the *Spare Rib* Collective (1990, pp. 187–8) it is out of fragmentation that the Women's

Movement 'has the potential to develop a new political union, with alternative frameworks and strategies'. This can be achieved through 'greater flexibility, openness and sensitivity to issues and methods as defined by different groups of women for themselves'. Women and feminists have always maintained a resistance to oppression through action, politics and theory which have not necessarily occurred under the label of feminism. It is the contention here that the way forward is based on an acknowledgement and acceptance of diversity while recognising that there are connections between women which can be embraced and embodied within feminism as an international social force. In this, the dimensions of autonomy/alliance, and reform/revolution should be united. As Yvonne Roberts (1992, p. xii) states 'feminism is about nothing if it is not about social justice: for women and men; in the First World and the Third'.

Women's struggle is international. Its end depends on the diminution of patriarchies and the breakdown of compulsory heterosexuality. Thus women, and men, will be free to define and pursue their sexualities and women's, and men's, behaviour and choice of role will not be regulated or constrained by the institutions of marriage and family or the promotion of these by other institutions in society. Within feminist theory and practice there must be a recognition of the problems involved when a compromise with patriarchal forces is accepted on the basis of religion, culture or belief. The threat posed by the marginalisation of feminist politics by the New Right and Left Realists needs to be acknowledged. By taking account of the complexities involved in women's lives, and the personal and structural relations affecting them, feminist theories and politics will provide the basis for the advancement and achievement of real equality for individual and collective women.

Bibliography

ABBOTT, P. and WALLACE, C. (1992) *The Family and the New Right*, London: Pluto Press.

ACKER, S. (1986) 'What Feminists Want From Education' in Hartnett, A. and Naish, M. (eds) *Education and Society Today*, London: Falmer.

ACKER, S. (1987) *Feminist Theory and the Study of Gender and Education*, University of Bristol, School of Education.

ACKER, S. and WARREN PIPER, D. (1984) *Is Higher Education Fair to Women?*, London: Nelson.

ALBERTI, J. (1989) *Beyond Suffrage*, Houndmills: Macmillan.

ALEXANDER, S. (1976) 'Women's Work in 19th Century London: A Study of the Years 1820–50' in Mitchell, J. and Oakley, A. (eds) *The Rights and Wrongs of Women*, Harmondsworth: Penguin.

ALLEN, S. *et al.* (1986) *The Experience of Unemployment*, London: Macmillan.

ALTHUSSER, L. (1971) 'Ideology and Ideological State Apparatuses' in Althusser, L. *Lenin and Philosophy and other Essays*, London: NLB.

ALTHUSSER, L. (1984) *Essays on Ideology*, London: Verso.

AMMA (1987) *Multi-Cultural and Anti-Racist Education Today*, London: Falmer Press.

AMOS, V. and PARMAR, P. (1984) 'Challenging Imperial Feminism' *Feminist Review*, No 17.

AMOS, V. and PARMAR, P. (1987) 'Resistances and Responses: The Experiences of Black Girls in Britain' in Arnot, M. and Weiner, G. (eds) *Gender and the Politics of Schooling*, London: Hutchinson.

ANDERSON, B.S. and ZINSSER, J.P. (1988) *A History of Their Own: Women in Europe from Prehistory to the Present. Vol. 2*, Harmondsworth: Penguin.

ANTHIAS, F. and YUVAL-DAVIES, N. (1993) *Racialized Boundaries*, London: Routledge.

ARCANA, J. (1979) *Our Mother's Daughters*, Berkeley, CA: Shameless Hussy Press.

ARDITTI, R., DUELLI-KLEIN, R., and MINDEN, S. (1984) *Test Tube Women: What Future for Motherhood*, Pandora Press: London.

ARENDS, J. and VOLMAN, M. (1992) 'A Comparison of Different Policies: Equal Opportunities in Education in the Netherlands and the Policy of the ILEA', *Gender and Education*, 4, 112, pp. 57–66.

ARNOT, M. (1987) 'Political Lip-service or Radical Reform? Central Government Responses to Sex Equality as a Policy Issue' in Arnot, M. and Weiner, G. (eds) *Gender and the Politics of Schooling*, London: Hutchinson.

ARNOT, M. and WEINER, G. (eds) (1987) *Gender and the Politics of Schooling*, London: Hutchinson.

ARNOT, M. and WEINER, G. (eds) (1992) 'Special Double Issue: Women's Education in Europe', *Gender and Education*, **4**, 112.

ASKEW, S.and Ross, C. (1988) *Boys Don't Cry: Boys and Sexism in Education*, Milton Keynes: Open University Press.

ATKINS, S. (1986) 'The Sex Discrimination Act 1975: The End of a Decade', *Feminist Review*, No. 24.

ATKINSON, D. and HORNSBY, P. (eds) (1993) *The Suffragettes*, Elm Publications.

ATTAR, D. (1990) *Wasting Girls' Time. The History and Politics of Home Economics*, London: Virago.

BAEHR, H. and DYER, G. (1987) *Boxed In: Women and Television*. London: Pandora.

BALLASTER, R. (1991) *Women's Worlds: Ideology, Femininity and Women's Magazines*, Houndmills: Macmillan.

BANKS, O. (1986) *Faces of Feminism*, Oxford: Basil Blackwell.

BANKS, O. (1993) *The Politics of British Feminism*.

BARON, P.A. and SWEEZY, P.M. (1966) *Monopoly Capital: An Essay on the American Economic and Social Order*, Harmondsworth: Penguin.

BARRET-DUCROCQ, F. (1991) *Love in the time of Victoria*, London: Verso.

BARRETT, M. (1980) *Women's Oppression Today*, London: Verso.

BARRETT, M. and MCINTOSH, M. (1982) *The Anti-Social Family*, London: Verso.

BARRETT, M. and PHILLIPS, A. (eds) (1992) *Destabilising Theory, Contemporary Feminist Debates*, London: Polity Press.

BARRON, J. (1990) *Nor Worth the Paper . . . ? Effectiveness of Legal Protection for Women and Children Experiencing Domestic Violence*, England: Women's Aid Federation.

BART, P.B. (ed.) (1993) *Violence Against Women*, London: Sage.

BARTHES, R. (1967) *Elements of Semiology*, London: Jonathan Cape.

BARTHES, R. (1973) *Mythologies*, London: Paladin.

BARTKY, S.L. (1990) *Femininity and Domination. Studies in the Phenomenology of Oppression*, London: Routledge.

BASSIN, D. (ed.) (1994) *Representations of Motherhood*, New Haven, CT: Yale University Press.

BBC (14.3.91) *Spot the Difference*, BBC.

BECTU (25.8.91) *Grievous Bodily Harm?*, BECTU.

BEDELL, G. (1992) 'Who's Who in the Sex War' in *Independent on Sunday*, 27.9.92.

BEECHEY, V. (1987) *Unequal Work*, London: Verso.

BEECHEY, V. and PERKINS, T. (1987) *A Matter of Hours. Women Part-time Work and the Labour Market*, Cambridge: Polity Press.

BELL, V. (1993) *Interrogating Incest: Feminism, Foucault and the Law*, London: Routledge.

BENSTON, M. (1969) 'The Political Economy of Women's Liberation' in Malos, E. (ed.) (1980) *The Politics of Housework*, London: Allison and Busby Ltd.

BERER, M. (1986) 'Breeding Conspiracies: Feminism and the New Reproductive Technologies', *Trouble and Strife*, 9, Summer.

BERGER, J. (1972) *Ways of Seeing*, Harmondsworth: BBC Penguin.

BETTERTON, R. (1987) *Looking On: Images of Femininity in the Visual Arts and Media*, London: Pandora.

BEVERIDGE, W. (1942) *Social Insurance and Allied Services*, (The Beveridge Report) London: HMSO.

BINNEY, V., HARKELL, G. and NIXON, J. (1981) *Leaving Violent Men: A Study of Refuges and Housing for Battered Women*, London: Women's Aid Federation.

BIRKE, L. (1986) *Women, Feminism and Biology*, Brighton: Wheatsheaf.

BLACK, C. (ed.) (1983) *Married Women's Work*, London: Virago.

BLEASDALE, A. (1985) *Boys from the Blackstuff*, London: Hutchinson.

BLOS, P. (1969) 'Three typical constellations in female delinquency' in Pollack, O. and Friedman, A. (eds) *Family Dynamics and Female Sexual Delinquency*, Palo Alto, CA: Science and Behaviour Books.

BLY, R. (1990) *Iron John*, Dorset: Element.

BOLOTIN, S. (1982) 'Voices from the Post-Feminist Generation', *The New York Times Magazine*, 17.10.82.

BOLT, C. (1993) *The Women's Movement in the US and Britain from 1790s–1920s*, London: Harvester Wheatsheaf.

BONNER, F., GOODMAN, L., ALLEN, R., JONES, L. and KING, C. (eds) (1992) *Imagining Women*, Cambridge: Polity Press/OUP.

BORZELLO, F. *et al.* (1985) 'Living Dolls and "Real Women"' in Kuhn, A. *The Power of the Image: Essays on Representation and Sexuality*, London: Routledge and Kegan Paul.

BOSTON WOMEN'S HEALTH COLLECTIVE (1978) *Our Bodies, Ourselves*, Harmondsworth: Penguin.

BOURLET, A. (1990) *Police Intervention in Marital Violence*, Milton Keynes: Open University Press.

BOURNE, J. (1983) 'Towards an Anti-racist Feminism', *Race and Class*, XXV.

BOWLBY, J. (1953) *Child Care and the Growth of Love*, Harmondsworth: Penguin.

BOWLBY, R. (1987) '"The Problem With No Name": Rereading Friedan's The Feminine Mystique', *Feminist Review*, No. 27.

BOWLES, S. and GINTIS, H. (1976) *Schooling in Capitalist America*, London: RKP.

BOYLAN, E. (1991) *Women and Disability*, London: Zed Books.

BRADLEY, H. (1989) *Men's Work, Women's Work*, Cambridge: Polity Press.

BRADSHAW, J. (1989) *Lone Parents: Policy in the Doldrums*, London: Family Policy Studies Centre.

BRAH, A. and MINHAS, R. (1985) 'Structural Racism or Cultural Difference: Schooling for Asian Girls' in Weiner, G. (ed.) *Just a Bunch of Girls*, Milton Keynes: Open University Press.

BRAVERMAN, H. (1974) *Labour and Monopoly Capital: The Degradation of Work In the Twentieth Century*, New York: Monthly Review Press.

BRAYDON, G. and SUMMERFIELD. P. (1987) *Out of The Cage: Women's Experiences in Two World Wars*, London: Pandora Press.

BRISCOE, J. (1992) 'Is There a War Against Women?' *Company*, March.

BROOKSIDE PRODUCTIONS (1988) *Brookside*, Brookside Productions Ltd.

BROWN, S. and RIDDELL, S. (eds) (1992) *Class, Race and Gender in Schools: New Agenda for Policy and Practice in Scottish Education*, Scottish Council for Research in Education.

BROWNE, N. and FRANCE, P. (1985) '"Only Cissies Wear Dresses": A Look at Sexist Talk in the Nursery' in Weiner, G. (ed.) *Just a Bunch of Girls*, Milton Keynes: Open University Press.

BROWNMILLER, S. (1976) *Against Our Will. Men, Women and Rape*, Harmondsworth: Penguin.

BRUEGEL, I. (1979) 'Women as a Reserve Army of Labour: A Note on Recent British Experience', *Feminist Review*, No. 3.

BRUNSDON, C. (1991) 'Pedagogies of the Feminine: Feminist Teaching and Women's Genres', *Screen*, No. 4, Winter.

BRYAN, B., DADZIE, S. and SCAFE, S. (1985) *The Heart of the Race: Black Women's Writing in Britain*, London: Virago.

BRYSON, L. (1992) *Welfare and the State*, Houndmills: Macmillan.

BUNCH, C. (1986) 'Lesbians in Revolt' in Pearsall, M. (ed.) *Women and Values*, CA: Wadsworth Belmont.

BURCHALL, H., and MILLMAN, V. (eds) (1988) *Changing Perspectives on Gender*, Milton Keynes: Open University Press.

BURGELIN, O. (1972) 'Structural Analysis and Mass Communication' in McQuail, D. *Sociology of Mass Communication*, Harmondsworth: Penguin.

BURGESS, R.C. (1985) *Strategies of Educational Research Qualitative Methods*, London: Falmer Press.

BYRNE, E.M. (1987) 'Education for Equality' in Arnot, M. and Weiner, G. (eds) *Gender and the Politics of Schooling*, London: Hutchinson.

BYRNE, E.M. (ed.) (1990) *Gender in Education*, Multilingual Matters.

CAIN, M. (ed.) (1989) *Growing Up Good: Policing the Behaviour of Girls in Europe*, London: Sage.

CAMPBELL, A. (1981) *Delinquent Girls*, Oxford: Basil Blackwell.

CAMPBELL, B. (1984) *Wigan Pier Revisited: Poverty and Politics in the 80s*, London: Virago.

CAMPBELL, B. (1992) 'Shooting the Messenger', *The Guardian*, 28.5.92.

CAMPLING, J. (1981) *Images of Ourselves. Women with Disabilities Talking*, London: RKP.

CAPUTI, J. (1987) *The Age Of The Sex Crime*, London: The Women's Press.

CARBY, H. (1982) 'White Women Listen! Black Feminism and the Boundaries of Sisterhood' in CCCS, *The Empire Strikes Back*, London: Hutchinson.

CARBY, H. (1987) 'Black Feminism and the Boundaries of Sisterhood' in Arnot, M. and Weiner, G. (eds) *Gender and the Politics of Schooling*, London: Hutchinson.

CARTER, E. (1984) 'Alice in the Consumer Wonderland: West German Case Studies in Gender and Consumer Culture' in McRobbie, A. and Nava, M. (eds) *Gender and Generation*, London: Macmillan.

CASSELL, J. (1977) *A Group Called Women: Sisterhood and Symbolism in the Feminist Movement*, New York: David McKay.

CCCS (1977) *On Ideology*, London: Hutchinson.

CCCS (eds) (1978) *Women Take Issue*, London: Hutchinson.

CHADWICK, W. (1991) *Women, Art and Society*, London: Thames and Hudson.

CHANANA, K. (ed.) (1988) *Socialization, Education and Women: Exploration in Gender Identity*, Sangam Books.

CHAPKIS, W. (1988) *Beauty Secrets. Women and the Politics of Appearance*, London: The Women's Press.

CHARLES, N. (1993) *Gender Divisions and Social Change*, Hemel Hempstead: Harvester Wheatsheaf.

CHESLER, P. (1986) *Mothers on Trial: The Battle for Children and Custody*, New York: McGraw Hill.

CHESLER, P. (1988) *Sacred Bond, Motherhood Under Siege. Surrogacy, Adoption and Custody*, London: Virago.

CHESLER, P. (1991) 'Mothers on Trial: The Custodial Vulnerability of Women', *Feminism and Psychology*, **1**, 3.

CHETWYND, J. and HARTNETT, O. (eds) (1978) *The Sex Role System: Psychological and Sociological Perspectives*, London: RKP.

CHIGWADA, R. (1991) 'Policing Black Women' in Cashmore, E. and McLaughlin, E. (eds) *Out of Order? Policing Black People*, London: Routledge.

CHIVERS, T.S. (ed.) (1987) *Race and Culture in Education. Issues arising from the Swann Committee Report*, Berkshire: NFER-Nelson.

CHODOROW, N. (1978) *The Reproduction of Mothering: Psychoanalysis the Sociology of Gender*, Berkeley, CA: University of California Press.

CHODOROW, N. and CONTRATTO, S. (1982) 'The Fantasy of the Perfect Mother' in Thorne,

B. and Yallom, M. (eds) *Rethinking the Family: Some Feminist Questions*, Harlow: Longman.

CIXOUS, H. (1981) 'The Laugh of Medusa' in Marks, E. and de Courtivron, I. (eds) *New French Feminisms*, New York: Schocken Books.

CLARK, L. and LEWIS, D. (1977) *Rape: The Price of Coercive Sexuality*, Toronto: The Women's Press.

CLARRICOATES, K. (1987) 'Dinosuars in the Classroom – The "Hidden" Curriculum in Primary Schools' in Arnot, M. and Weiner, G. (eds) *Gender and the Politics of Schooling*, London: Hutchinson.

CLINE, S. (1990) *Just Desserts. Women and Food*, London: Andre Deutsch.

CLINE, S. and SPENDER, D. (1987) *Reflecting Men at Twice Their Natural Size. Why Women Work at Making Men Feel Good*, Fontana (Collins).

COCKBURN, C. (1981) 'The Material of Male Power', *Feminist Review*, No. 9.

COCKBURN, C. (1985) *Machinery of Dominance. Women, Men and Technical Know-how*, London: Pluto Press.

COCKS, J. (1984) 'Wordless Emotions: Some Critical Reflections on Radical Feminism', *Politics and Society*, **13**, 1.

COLLINS, H. (1992) *The Equal Opportunities Handbook: A Guide to Law and Best Practice in Europe*, Oxford: Blackwell.

CONDELL, D. and LIDDIARD, J. (1987) *Working for Victory?: Images of Women in the First World War 1914–1918*, London: Routledge.

CONNELL, R.W. (1985) 'Theorising Gender', *Sociology*, **19**, 2.

CONNELL, R.W. (1987) *Gender and Power*, Cambridge: Polity Press.

COOLE, D. (1993) *Women in Political Theory. From Ancient Misogyny to Contemporary Feminism*, Hemel Hempstead: Harvester Wheatsheaf.

COONTZ, S. and HENDERSON, P. (1986) *Women's Work, Men's Property: The Origins of Gender and Class*, London: Verso.

COOTE, A. and CAMPBELL, B. (1987) *Sweet Freedom*, 2nd edn, Oxford: Basil Blackwell.

COOTE, A., HARMAN, H. and HEWITT, P. (1991) *The Family Way*, Institute for Public Policy Research.

COOTE, A. and PATTULLO, P. (1990) *Power and Prejudice. Women and Politics*, London: Weidenfeld and Nicholson.

COREA, G. (1985a) *The Mother Machine: Reproductive Technologies from Artificial Insemination to Artificial Wombs*, New York: Harper and Row.

COREA, G. (1985b) *Man-Made Women. How New Reproductive Technologies Affect Women*, London: Hutchinson.

COULSON, M., BRANKA, M. and WAINWRIGHT, H. (1975) 'The Housewife and Her Labour Under Capitalism: A Critique', *New Left Review*, No. 89.

COUNTS, D A. (1992) *Sanctions and Sanctuary: Cross-Cultural Perspectives on Violence Towards Women*, Westview Press.

COVENEY, L., JACKSON, M. and JEFFREYS, S. (1984) *The Sexuality Papers. Male Sexuality and the Social Control of Women*, London: Hutchinson.

COVERDALE, S.A. and TAYLOR, D. (eds) (1992) *Sexual Harassment. Women Speak Out*, Freedom, CA: The Crossing Press.

COWARD, R. (1981) 'Socialising Feminism and Socialist Feminism' in *The Feminist Anthology Collective*, London: The Women's Press.

COWARD, R. (1992a) 'Collusion or Backlash?', *Everywoman*, October.

COWARD, R. (1992b) *Our Treacherous Hearts*, London: Faber and Faber.

COWIE, E. (1977) 'Women, Representation and The Image', *Screen Education*, No. 23, Summer.

COWIE, J., COWIE, V. and SLATER, E. (1968) *Delinquency in Girls*, London: Heinemann.

COYLE, A. and SKINNER, J. (1988) *Women and Work*, London: Macmillan Education.

CRAWFORD, V., ROUSE, J.A. and WOODS, B. (eds) (1993) *Women in the Civil Rights Movement. Trailblazers and Torchbearers 1941–1965*, Bloomington, IN: Indiana University Press.

CROMPTON, R. and SANDERSON, K. (1990) *Gendered Jobs and Social Change*, London: Unwin Hyman.

CROWTHER REPORT (1959) *15–18*, Ministry of Education, London: HMSO.

CURRAN, J. *et al.* (eds) (1986) *Bending Reality: The State of the Media*, London: Pluto Press.

DALE, R. *et al.* (eds) (1981) *Education and the State Volume 1 Politics, Patriarchy and Practice*, London: Falmer.

DALLA COSTA, M. and JAMES, S. (1972) *The Power of Women and the Subversion of the Community*, Bristol: Falling Wall Press.

DALTON, K. (1961) 'Menstruation and Crime', *British Medical Journal*, **II**, Prt. II.

DALTON, K. (1978) *Once a Month*, London: Fontana.

DALTON, K. (1982) 'Legal Implications of PMT' *World Medicine*.

DALY, M. (1973) *Beyond God the Father: Towards a Philosophy of Women's Liberation*, Boston: Beacon Press.

DALY, M. (1978) *Gyn/Ecology. The Metaethics of Radical Feminism*, London: The Women's Press.

DALY, M. (1984) *Pure Lust. Elemental Feminist Philosophy*, London: The Women's Press.

DAVID, M.E. (1984) 'Teaching Motherhood Formally and Informally', paper for Girl Friendly Conference, Manchester Polytechnic.

DAVID, M.E. (1986) 'Moral and Maternal: The Family in the New Right' in Levitas, R. (ed.) *The Ideology of the New Right*, Cambridge: Polity Press.

DAVID, M.E. (1993) *Parents, Gender and Education Reform*, Cambridge: Polity Press.

DAVIES, A.M., HOLLAND, J. and MINHAS, R. (1990) *Equal Opportunities in the New ERA*, London: Tufnell Press.

DAVIES, J. (ed.) (1993) *The Family: Is It Just Another Lifestyle Choice?*, London: IEA Health and Welfare Unit.

DAVIS, A.Y. (1981) *Women, Race and Class*, London: The Women's Press.

DAVIS, A.Y. (1984) *Women, Culture and Politics*, London: The Women's Press.

DAVIS, K., LEIJENAAR, M. and OLDERSMA, J. (1991) *The Gender of Power*, London: Sage.

DAVIS, S.E. (ed.) (1988) *Women Under Attack. Victories, Backlash and the Fight for Reproductive Freedom*, Boston, MA: South End Press.

DE BEAUVOIR, S. (1949/1972) *The Second Sex*, (ed. Parshley, H.M.) Harmondsworth: Penguin.

DEEGAN, M.J. and BROOKS, N. (1985) *Women and Disability. The Double Handicap*, Oxford: Transaction Books.

DEEM, R. (1984) *Co-education Reconsidered*, Milton Keynes: Open University Press.

DELAMONT, S. and DUFFIN, L. (eds) (1978) *The Nineteenth Century Woman: Her Cultural and Physical World*, London: Croom Helm.

DELPHY, C. (1976) *The Main Enemy*, London: WRRC.

DELPHY, C. and LEONARD, D. (1992) *Familiar Exploitation: A New Analysis of Marriage in Contemporary Western Societies*, Cambridge: Polity Press.

DENNIS, N. (1993) *Rising Crime and the Dismembered Family: How Conformist Intellectuals Have Campaigned Against Common Sense*, London: IEA Health and Welfare Unit.

DENNIS, N. and ERDOS, G. (1992) *Families Without Fatherhood*, London: IEA Health and Welfare Unit.

DEPARTMENT OF HEALTH (1990) *The Children Act 1989: Draft Guidance and Regulations*

Vol 3 Family Placements, London: HMSO.

DES (1967) *Children and Their Primary Schools. Report of the Central Advisory Council for Education Vol. 1*, London: HMSO.

DES (1977) *Health Education in Schools*, London: HMSO.

DES (1986) *Geography from 5 to 16. Curriculum Matters 7*, London: HMSO.

DES (1987) *Circular No. 11/87 Sex Education At School*, London: HMSO.

DES (1988) *History from 5 to 16. Curriculum Matters 11*, London: HMSO.

DES (1989) *Design and Technology for Ages 5 to 16. Proposals of the Secretary of State for Education and Science and the Secretary of State for Wales*, London: HMSO.

DES (1990) *Technology and the National Curriculum*, London: HMSO.

DES (1991a) *Physical Education for ages 5 to 16. Proposals of the Secretary of State for Education and Science and the Secretary of State for Wales*, London: HMSO.

DES (1991b) *Geography in the National Curriculum*, London: HMSO.

DES (1991c) *History in the National Curriculum*, London: HMSO.

DICKEY, J. *et al.* (1985) *Women in Focus; Guidelines for Eliminating Media Sexism*, London: CPBF.

DINNERSTEIN, D. (1976) *The Rocking of the Cradle: And the Ruling of the World*, Souvenir Press.

DOBASH, R.E. and DOBASH, R. (1980) *Violence Against Wives: A Case Against the Patriarchy*, London: Open Books.

DOBASH, R.E. and DOBASH, R. (1992) *Women, Violence and Social Change*, London: Routledge.

DONALD, J. and HALL, S. (eds) (1986) *Politics and Ideology*, Milton Keynes: Open University Press.

DUNHILL, C. (1989) *The Boys in Blue*, London: Virago.

DURHAM, M. (1991) *Sex and Politics: The Family and Morality in the Thatcher Years*, London: Macmillan.

DWORKIN, A. (1981) *Pornography: Men Possessing Women*, New York: Perigree Books.

DWORKIN, A. (1982) *Our Blood: Prophecies and Discourses on Sexual Politics*, London: The Women's Press.

DWORKIN, A. (1987) *Intercourse*, London: Secker and Warburg.

DYHOUSE, C. (1989) *Feminism and the Family in England 1880–1939*, Basil Blackwell: Oxford.

EAGLETON, T. (1991) *Ideology: An Introduction*, London: Verso.

EASLEA, B. (1981) *Science and Sexual Oppression. Patriarchy's Confrontation with Women and Nature*, London: Weidenfeld and Nicholson.

ECKER, G. (ed.) (1985) *Feminist Aesthetics*, London: The Women's Press.

EDITORIAL (1989) *Feminist Review*, No. 31.

EDITORIAL (1990) 'TV: The News According to Men?' *G.H.*, July.

EDUCATION MINISTRY OF GREAT BRITAIN (1959) *Fifteen to Eighteen. A Report of the Central Advisory Council for Education (England) Vol. 1. The Crowther Report*, London: HMSO.

EDUCATION MINISTRY OF GREAT BRITAIN (1963) *Half Our Future. The Newsom Report*, London: HMSO.

EDWARDS, A. (1987) 'Male Violence in Feminist Theory: An Analysis of the Changing Conceptions of Sex/gender Violence and Male Dominance' in Hanmer, J. and Maynard, M. (eds) *Women, Violence and Social Control*, London: Macmillan.

EDWARDS, S. (1981) *Female Sexuality and the Law*, Oxford: Martin Robertson.

EDWARDS, S. (1987) '"Provoking Her Own Demise": From Common Assault to Homicide' in Hanmer, J. and Maynard, M. (eds) *Women, Violence and Social Control*, London: Macmillan.

EDWARDS, S. (1988) 'Mad, Bad or Pre-Menstrual?' *New Law Journal*, July.

EDWARDS, S. (1989) *Policing 'Domestic' Violence*, London: Sage.

EHRENREICH, B. and ENGLISH, D. (1979) *For Her Own Good: One Hundred and Fifty Years of the Experts' Advice to Women*, New York: Anchor Press.

EISENSTEIN, H. (1984) *Contemporary Feminist Thought*, London: Unwin.

EISENSTEIN, Z.R. (1982) 'The Sexual Politics of the New Right: Understanding the "Crisis of Liberalism" for the 1980s' *Signs*, 7, 31.

EMPLOYMENT GAZETTE (1992) November Edition.

ENGELS, F. (1891/1985) *The Origin of the Family, Private Property and the State*, (ed. Barrett, M.) Hardmondsworth: Penguin.

EOC (1990a) *Women and Men in Britain 1990*, London: HMSO.

EOC (1990b) *Some Facts About Women*, London: EOC Statistics Unit.

EOC (1992a) *New Earnings Survey*, London: HMSO.

EOC (1992b) *Equal Opportunities Commission Annual Report 1992: The Equality Challenge*, Manchester: EOC.

EOC (1994) *Guidance on Legal Implications of House of Lords Judgement in R v Secretary of State Employment . . .*, ex parte EOC.

EPSTEIN, D. (ed.) (1994) *Challenging Lesbian and Gender Inequalities in Education*, Buckingham: Open University Press.

EQUITY (1992) *Equal Opportunities in the Mechanical Media*, Equity, March.

ERICSON, Y. and JACOBSSON, R. (eds) (1985) *Side by Side: A Report on Equality between Women and Men in Sweden*, Sweden: Gotab.

EVANS, S. (1980) *Personal Politics. The Roots of Women's Liberation in the Civil Rights Movement and the New Left*, New York: Vintage Books.

EVANS, T.D. (1988) *Gender Agenda*, London: Unwin Hyman.

EVERINGHAM, C. (1994) *Motherhood and Modernity: An Investigation into the Rational Dimension of Mothering*, Buckingham: Open University Press.

EVERYWOMAN (1988) *Pornography and Sexual Violence: Evidence of the Links*, London: Everywoman.

FALUDI, S. (1992) *Backlash*, London: Chatto and Windus.

FAMILY BUDGET UNIT (1992) 'Household Budgets and Living Standards', *Social Policy Research Findings*, No. 31, November, York.

FAULKNER, W. and ARNOLD, E. (1985) *Smothered by Invention*, London: Pluto Press.

FEDERICI, N., OPPENHEIM MASON, K. and SOGNER, S. (1993) *Women's Position and Demographic Change*, Oxford: Clarendon Press.

FERGUSON, A. (1989) *Blood at the Root: Motherhood, Sexuality and Male Dominance*, London: Pandora Press.

FEVERSHAM COMMITTEE (1960) 'Report of the Departmental Committee on Human Artificial Insemination', CMND 1105, London: HMSO.

FIELD, M.A. (1990) *Surrogate Motherhood: The Legal and Human Issues*, Cambridge, MA: Harvard University Press.

FIGUEIRA-McDONOUGH, J. and SARRI, R. (eds) (1987) *The Trapped Woman. Catch-22 in Deviance and Control*, London: Sage.

FINCH, J. and GROVES, D. (1983) *A Labour of Love: Women, Work and Caring*, London: RKP.

FINCH, J. and MASON, J. (1992) *Negotiating Family Responsibilities*, London: Routledge.

FIRESTONE, S. (1972) *The Dialectic of Sex*, London: Paladin.

FLANAGAN, M. (1985) 'In Whose Image?' in Steiner-Scott, L. (ed.) *Personally Speaking . . .*, Dublin: Attic Press.

FOLBRE, N. (1994) *Who Pays for the Kids?: Gender and the Structure of Constraint*, London: Routledge.

FOSTER, M. (1985) 'A Curriculum for all?. The Relationship between Racism, Feminism and Schooling: A Personal View' in Weiner, G. (ed.) *Just a Bunch of Girls*, Milton Keynes: Open University Press.

FOSTER, P. (1990) *Policy and Practice in Multicultural and Anti-racist Education. A Case Study of a Multi-ethnic Comprehensive School*, London: Routledge.

FOUCAULT, M. (1977) *Discipline and Punish: The Birth of the Prison*, London: Allen Lane.

FOX, B. (ed.) (1980) *Hidden in the Household. Women's Domestic Labour under Capitalism*, Toronto: Women's Educational Press.

FRANKENBERG, R. (1993) *White Women, Race Matters: The Social Construction of Whiteness*, London: Routledge.

FRANKLIN, A. and FRANKLIN, B. (1990) 'Age and Power' in Jeffs, T. and Smith, M. (eds) *Young People, Inequality and Youth Work*, London: Macmillan.

FREEDMAN, R. (1988) *Beauty Bound: Why Women Strive for Physical Perfection*, London: Columbus.

FRENCH, M. (1985) *Beyond Power: On Women, Men and Morals*, New York: Summit Books.

FRENCH, M. (1992) *The War Against Women*, London: Hamish Hamilton.

FRIDAY, N. (1977) *My Mother/My Self*, New York: Delacorte.

FRIEDAN, B. (1963) *The Feminine Mystique*, Harmondsworth: Pelican.

GALLAGHER, M. (1979) *The Portrayal and Participation of Women in the Media*, Paris: UNESCO.

GALLAGHER, M. (1990) *Women and Men in Broadcasting: Prospects for Equality in the 90's*, Commission of the European Communities Steering Committee for Equal Opportunities in Broadcasting.

GARDINER, J. (1975) 'Women's Domestic Labour', *New Left Review*, No. 89, Jan–Feb.

GARNER, D.M. and GARFINKEL, P.E. (1980) 'Socio-Cultural Factors in the Development of Anorexia Nervosa', *Psychological Medicine*, No. 10.

GARNER, L. (1984) *Stepping Stones to Women's Liberty. Feminist Ideas in the Women's Suffrage Movement 1900–1918*, London: Heinemann.

GASKELL, J. (1991) *Gender Matters from School to Work*, Milton Keynes: Open University Press.

GELLES, R.J. and CORNELL, C.P. (1990) *Intimate Violence in Families*, 2nd edn, London: Sage.

GH (1990) 'TV: The News According to Men?' *GH*, July.

GIFFORD, LORD QC., BROWN, W. and BUNDEY, R. (1989) *Loosen the Shackles: First Report of the Liverpool 8 Inquiry into Race Relations in Liverpool*, London: KARIA Press.

GILL, D., MAYOR, B. and BLAIR, M. (eds) (1992) *Racism and Education. Structures and Strategies*, London: OUP/Sage.

GITTENS, D. (1985) *The Family in Question: Challenging Households and Familiar Ideologies*, London: Macmillan.

GLENDINNING, C. and MILLAR, J. (1989) 'New Directions for Research on Women and Poverty: Challenges to our Thinking and Practice' in Graham, H. and Popay, J. (eds) *Women and Poverty: Exploring the Research and Policy Agenda*, London: Thomas Coram Research Unit.

GLENDINNING, C. and MILLAR, J. (eds) (1992) *Women and Poverty in Britain. The 1990s*, Hemel Hempstead: Harvester Wheatsheaf.

GLENN, E.N. (1994) *Mothering, Ideology, Experience and Agency*, London: Routledge.

GLUCKSMANN, M. (1990) *Women Assemble. Women Workers and the New Industries in Inter-war Britain*, London: Routledge.

GOLDBERG, S. (1974) *The Inevitability of Patriarchy*, London: Temple Smith.

GORDON, L. (1982) 'Why Nineteenth-Century Feminists Did Not Support "Birth

Control" and Twentieth-Century Feminists Do: Feminism, Reproduction and the Family' in Thorne, B. and Yalom, M. (eds) *Rethinking the Family: Some Feminist Questions*, Essex: Longman.

GORDON, L. (1989) *Heroes of Their Own Lives: The Politics and History of Family Violence*, London: Virago.

GORDON, P. (1981) *Passport Raids and Checks*, London: Runnymead Trust.

GORHAM, D. (1982) *The Victorian Girl and the Feminine Ideal*, London: Croom Helm.

GRAFTON, T., MILLER, H., SMITH. L., VEGODA, M. and WHITFIELD, R. (1987) 'Gender and Curriculum Choice' in Arnot, M. and Weiner, G. (eds) *Gender and the Politics of Schooling*, London: Hutchinson.

GRAHAM, H. (1993) *Hardship and Health in Women's Lives*, Hemel Hempstead: Harvester Wheatsheaf.

GRAHAM, H. and POPAY, J. (eds) (1989) *Women and Poverty: Exploring the Research and Policy Agenda*, London: Thomas Coram Research Unit.

GRAMSCI, A. (1971) *Selections from the Prison Notebooks*, London: Lawrence and Wishart.

GRANT, J. (1993) *Public Policy and the New Right. The Impact of Ideology*, Pinter.

GREEN, D. (1990) 'Family Fortunes' *Social Work Today*, 2.8.90.

GREER, G. (1970) *The Female Eunuch*, London: Granada Publishing.

GREER, G. (1992a) *The Change: Women, Ageing and the Menopause*, Hamish Hamilton.

GREER, G. (1992b) 'Two Fingers to the Bullying', *The Guardian*, 23.9.92.

GREGORY, J. (1982) 'Equal Pay and Sex Discrimination: Why Women Are Giving Up the Fight', *Feminist Review*, No. 10.

GRIFFIN, C. (1985) *Typical Girls? Young Women from School to the Job Market*, London: RKP.

GRIFFIN, C. (1993) *Representations of Youth*, Cambridge: Polity Press.

GRIFFIN, S. (1971) 'Rape: The All American Crime', *Ramparts*, 26.9.71.

GRIFFIN, S. (1978) *Woman and Nature: The Roaring Inside Her*, New York: Harper and Row.

GRIFFIN, S. (1981) *Pornography and Silence: Culture's Revenge Against Nature*, New York: Harper and Row.

GUARDIAN, THE (1992a) 'Women "aspire first to getting on in their job"', *The Guardian*, 25.11.92.

GUARDIAN, THE (1992b) 'Legal rules "favour men"', *The Guardian*, 25.11.92.

GUNEW, S. (ed.) (1991) *A Reader in Feminist Knowledge*, London: Routledge.

GUNEW, S. (ed.) (1992) *Feminist Knowledge. Critique and Construct*, 2nd edn, London: Routledge.

HACKER, S. (1989) *Pleasure, Power and Technology. Some Tales of Gender, Engineering and the Cooperative Workplace*, London: Unwin Hyman.

HACKER, S. (1990) *'Doing it the Hard Way'. Investigations of Gender and Technology*, London: Unwin Hyman.

HADJIFOTIOU, N. (1983) *Women and Harassment at Work*, London: Pluto Press.

HAKIM, C. (1979) *Occupational Segregation: Research Paper No. 9*, London: Department of Employment.

HALEH, A. (ed.) (1990) *Women, Poverty and Ideology*, London: Macmillan.

HALL, C. (1992) *White, Male and Middle Class: Explorations in Feminism and History*, Cambridge: Polity Press.

HALL, S. (1973)*Encoding and Decoding in the Television Discourse*, Birmingham: Birmingham Centre for Cultural Studies.

HALL, S. (1982) *Managing Conflict, Producing Consent*, D102 Social Sciences Course Block 5, Unit 21. Milton Keynes: Open University.

HALL, S. (1986) 'Media Power and Class Power' in Curran, J. *et al.* (eds) *Bending*

Reality: The State of the Media, London: Pluto Press.

HANCOCK, E. (1990) *The Girl Within: A Radical New Approach to Female Identity*, London: Pandora Press.

HANEFIN, J. and NICHARTHAIGH, D. (1993) *Co-education and Attainment*, University of Limerick, Centre for Studies in Gender and Education.

HANMER, J. (1981) 'Sex Pre-determination, Artificial Insemination and the Maintenance of Male Dominated Culture' in Roberts, H. (ed.) *Women Health and Reproduction*, London: RKP.

HANMER, J. and MAYNARD, M. (1987) *Women, Violence and Social Control*, Houndmills: Macmillan.

HANMER, J., RADFORD, J. and STANKO, E.A. (1989) *Women, Policing and Male Violence. International Perspectives*, London: Routledge.

HANMER, J. and SAUNDERS, S. (1984) *Well-Founded Fear*, London: Hutchinson.

HANMER, J. and STATHAM, D. (1988) *Women and Social Work*, Houndmills: Macmillan.

HARAN, M. (1992) *Having It All*, London: Signet.

HARDEY, M. and CROW, G. (eds) (1991) *Lone Parenthood: Coping with Constraints and Making Opportunities*, Hemel Hempstead: Harvester Wheatsheaf.

HARDING, S. (1987) 'Is There a Feminist Method?' in *The Science Question in Feminism*, Milton Keynes: Open University Press.

HARDING, S. (1991) *Whose Science? Whose Knowledge?: Thinking from Women's Lives*, Milton Keynes: Open University Press.

HARDY, M.T. (1989) *Girls, Science and Gender Bias in Institutional Materials*, University of Nottingham, School of Education.

HARRIS, J. (1993) *Private Lives, Public Spirit. A Social History of Britain 1870–1914*, Oxford: Oxford University Press.

HARRISS, K. (1989) 'New Alliances: Socialist Feminism in the Eighties', *Feminist Review*, No. 31, Spring.

HARTMANN, H. (1979) 'The Unhappy Marriage of Marxism and Feminism: Towards a More Progressive Union' in Sargent, L. (ed.) *Women and Revolution: A Discussion of the Unhappy Marriage of Marxism and Feminism*, London: Pluto Press.

HARTNET, A. and NAISH, M. (eds) (1986) *Education and Society Today*, London: Falmer Press.

HATHAWAY, M. (1993) *Motherhood*, Lion Publishing.

HAUG, F. (1987) *Female Sexualisation*, London: Verso.

HAUG, F. (1989) 'Lessons from the Women's Movement in Europe', *Feminist Review*, No. 31, Spring.

HAUG, F. (1992) *Beyond Female Masochism. Memory Work and Politics*, London: Verso.

HEARN, J. and PARKIN, W. (1987) *'Sex' at 'Work'. The Power and Paradox of Organisation Sexuality*, Brighton: Wheatsheaf.

HEKMAN, S. (1990) *Gender and Knowledge: Elements of a Postmodern Feminism*, Cambridge: Polity Press.

HELLER, Z. (1992) 'Don't Look Back', *The Independent on Sunday*, 22.3.92.

HERBERT, C. (1992) 'War of the Red Roses', *The Guardian*, 10.6.92.

HEREK, G. and BERRILL, K. (eds) (1992) *Hate Crimes: Confronting Violence Against Lesbians and Gay Men*, London: Sage.

HEWITT, M. (1992) *Welfare, Ideology and Need. Developing Perspectives on the Welfare State*, Hemel Hempstead: Harvester Wheatsheaf.

HEWITT, P. (1993) *About Time. The Revolution in Work and Family Life*, London: Rivers Oram Press.

HILL COLLINS, P. (1991) *Black Feminist Thought: Knowledge, Consciousness and the Politics of Empowerment*, London: Routledge.

HM GOVERNMENT (1987) *Education Reform Bill*, London: HMSO.

HM GOVERNMENT (1990) *Human Fertilization and Embryology Bill*, London: HMSO.

HOBSBAWM, E.J. (1969) *Industry and Empire*, Harmondsworth: Penguin.

HOLLIS, P. (1979) *Women in Public: The Women's Movement 1850–1900*, London: Allen and Unwin.

HOOKS, B. (1984) *Feminist Theory: From Margin to Center*, Boston, MA: Southend Press.

HOOKS, B. (1986) 'Sisterhood: Political Solidarity Between Women', *Feminist Review*, No. 23.

HORLEY, S. (1985) 'Fall out in the Refuges', *New Society*, 28.6.85.

HORSFALL, J. (1991) *The Presence of the Past*, Sydney: Allen & Unwin.

HUDSON, A. (1983) 'The Welfare State and Adolescent Femininity', *Youth and Policy*, **2**, 1.

HUGHES, P. (1991) *Gender Issues in the Primary Classroom*, Lemington Spa: Scholastic.

HUGMAN, R. (1991) *Power in Caring Professions*, London: Macmillan.

HUMM, M. (1992) *Feminisms: A Reader*, Hemel Hempstead: Harvester Wheatsheaf.

HUNT, A. (1975) *Management Attitudes and Practices Towards Women at Work*, London: HMSO.

HYNES, P. (ed.) (1989) *Reconstructing Babylon: Women and Technology*, London: Earthscan.

IBA (1991) *Final Report and Accounts*, IBA.

ILEA (1985) *Race, Sex and Class 6: A Policy for Equality: Sex*, London: ILEA.

INSTITUTE OF MANAGEMENT (1992) *The Key to the Men's Club: Opening the Doors to Women in Management*, London: Institute of Management.

IRELAND, M.S. (1993) *Reconceiving Motherhood: Separating Motherhood from Female Identity*, Guildford Press.

IRIGARAY, L. (1981) 'This Sex Which Is Not One' in Marks, E. and de Courtivron, I. (eds) *New French Feminisms*, New York: Shocken Books.

ITZIN, C. (1993) *Pornography: Women, Violence and Civil Liberties – A Radical View*, Oxford: Oxford University Press.

JACKSON, S. (ed.) (1993) *Women's Studies: A Reader*, Hemel Hempstead: Harvester Wheatsheaf.

JAGGAR, A. (1983) *Feminist Politics and Human Nature*, Hemel Hempstead: Harvester Wheatsheaf.

JAMES, S.M. and BUSIA, A.P.A. (eds) (1993) *Theorizing Black Feminisms. The Visionary Pragmatism of Black Women*, London: Routledge.

JEFFREYS, S. (1985) *The Spinster and her Enemies. Feminism and Sexuality 1830–1930*, London: Pandora.

JENKINS, T. (1988) 'As I am', *Trouble and Strife*, No. 13, Spring.

JOHNSON-ODIM, C. and STROBEL, M. (1992) *Expanding the Boundaries of Women's History: Essays on Women in the Third World*, Bloomington, IN: Indiana University Press.

JOHNSON, L. (1993) *The Modern Girl. Girlhood and Growing Up*, Buckingham: Open University Press.

JOHNSTON, J. (1974) *Lesbian Nation: The Feminist Solution*, New York: Simon and Schuster.

JONES, C. (1985) 'Sexual Tyranny: Male Violence in a Mixed Secondary School' in Weiner, G. (ed.) *Just a Bunch of Girls*, Milton Keynes: Open University Press.

JONES, C. and MAHONY, P. (1989) *Learning Our Lines. Sexuality and Social Control in Education*, London: The Women's Press.

JOSEPH, G. (1981) 'The Incomplete Ménage à Trois: Marxism, Feminism and Racism' in Sargent, L. (ed.) *The Unhappy Marriage of Marxism and Feminism: A Debate on*

Class and Patriarchy, London: Pluto Press.

JOWELL, R. *et al.* (1991) *British Social Attitudes – The 8th Report*, SCPR.

KAPLAN, M.M. (1992) *Mothers' Images of Motherhood: Case Studies of Twelve Mothers*, London: Routledge.

KAPPELER, S. (1986) *The Pornography of Representation*, Cambridge: Polity Press.

KELLY, A. (1987) 'The Construction of Masculine Science' in Arnot, M. and Weiner, G. (eds) *Gender and the Politics of Schooling*, London: Hutchinson.

KELLY, L. (1988) *Surviving Sexual Violence*, Cambridge: Polity Press.

KELLY, L. and RADFORD, J. (1987) 'The Problem of Men: Feminist Perspectives on Sexual Violence' in Scraton, P. (ed.) *Law, Order and the Authoritarian State*, Milton Keynes: Open University Press.

KENWAY, J. and BLACKMORE, J. (eds) (1993) *Gender Matters in Educational Administration and Policy: A Feminist Policy*, London: Falmer Press.

KENWAY, J. and WILLIS, S. (eds) (1990) *Hearts and Minds: Self-esteem and the Schooling of Girls*, London: Falmer Press.

KHAYATT, M.D. (1992) *Lesbian Teachers: An Invisible Presence*, New York: University of New York Press.

KINGSLEY KENT, S. (1990) *Sex and Suffrage in Britain 1860–1914*, London: Routledge.

KITZINGER, S. (1992) *Ourselves as Mothers: Universal Experience of Motherhood*, Doubleday.

KLEIN, R.D. *et al.* (1985) 'Talking Down the Technodocs', *Spare Rib*, No. 161, December.

KNOWLES, J.P. (1991a) *Women Defined Motherhood*, Harrington Park Press.

KNOWLES, J.P. (1991b) *Motherhood: A Feminist Perspective*, Haworth Press.

KOEDT, A. (1973) 'The Myth of the Vaginal Orgasm' in *Radical Feminism*, New York.

KRAMARAE, C. and SPENDER, D. (eds) (1993) *The Knowledge Explosion: Generations of Feminist Scholarship*, Hemel Hempstead: Harvester Wheatsheaf.

KRISTEVA, J. (1981) 'Women Can Never Be Defined' in Marks, E. and de Courtivron, I. (eds) *New French Feminisms*, New York: Schocken Books.

KUHN, A. (1984) 'Women Genres', *Screen*, **25**, 1.

KUHN, A. (1985) *The Power of the Image: Essays on Representation and Sexuality*, London: RKP.

LABOUR PARTY (1991a) *A New Future for Women*, Labour Party.

LABOUR PARTY (1991b) *Putting Equality into Practice*, A Shadow Ministry of Women Consultation Document. Labour Party.

LACOMBE, D. (1988) *Ideology and Public Policy: The Case Against Pornography*, Garamond Press.

LAFRANCE, M. (1991) 'School for Scandal: Different Educational Experiences for Females and Males', *Gender and Education*, **3**, 1.

LANDESMAN, C. (1990) 'Machismo turned Masochismo', *The Guardian*, 20. 6. 90.

LANE, C. and CHAPMAN, J. (1975) 'The Liver Birds', English Theatre Guild Ltd.

LAWS, S. (1985) *Seeing Red: The Politics of PMT*, London: Hutchinson.

LEES, S. (1986) *Losing Out. Sexuality and Adolescent Girls*, London: Hutchinson.

LEES, S. (1987) 'The Structure of Sexual Relations in School', in Arnot, M. and Weiner, G. (eds) *Gender and the Politics of Schooling*, London: Hutchinson.

LEES, S. (1993) *Sugar and Spice: Sexuality and Adolescent Girls*, Harmondsworth: Penguin.

LEICESTER, M. (1991) *Equal Opportunities in School: Sexuality, Race, Gender and Special Needs*, Harlow: Longman.

LENEMAN, L. and WHATLEY, C.A. (eds) (1993) *Martyrs in our Midst: Dundee, Perth and the Forcible Feeding of Suffragettes*, Abertay: History Society.

LENSKYJI, H. (1986) *Out of Bounds: Women, Sport and Sexuality*, Toronto: Women's Press.

LESTON, K. (1990) 'Love, Lust and Phoney Baloney', *The Guardian*, 21.6.90.

LEVINE, P. (1987) *Victorian Feminism. 1850–1900*, London: Hutchinson.

LEVI-STRAUSS, C. (1966) *The Savage Mind*, London: George Weidenfeld and Nicholson.

LEVITAS, R. (ed.) (1986) *The Ideology of the New Right*, Cambridge: Polity Press.

LEVY, B. (ed.) (1991) *Dating Violence: Young Women in Danger*, Seattle: The Seal Press.

LEWIS, J. (1983) *Women's Welfare, Women's Rights*, London: Croom Helm.

LEWIS, J. (1986a) 'Anxieties About the Family and the Relationships Between Parents, Children and the State in 20th Century England' in Richards, M. and Light, P. (eds) *Children of Social Worlds*, Cambridge: Polity Press.

LEWIS, J. (1986b) *Labour and Love. Women's Experience of Home and Family*, Oxford: Blackwell.

LICHT, B.G. and DWECK, C.S. (1987) 'Sex differences in achievement orientations' in Arnot, M. and Weiner, G. (eds) *Gender and the Politics of Schooling*, London: Hutchinson.

LIDDINGTON, J. (1984) *The Life and Times of a Respectable Rebel: Selina Cooper 1864–1946*, London: Virago.

LIDDINGTON, J. (1989) *The Long Road to Greenham: Feminism and Anti-Militarism in Britain since 1820*, London: Virago.

LIDDINGTON, J. and NORRIS, J. (1979) *One Hand Tied Behind Us: The Rise of the Women's Suffrage Movement*, London: Virago.

LISTER, R. (1987) 'Future Insecure: Women and Income Maintenance under a Third Tory term', *Feminist Review*, No. 27.

LISTER, R. (1989) 'Social Security' in McCarthy, M. (ed.) *The New Politics of Welfare: An Agenda for the 1990's*, London: Macmillan.

LLEWELYN, S. and OSBORNE, K. (1990) *Women's Lives*, London: Routledge.

LLEWELYN-DAVIES, N. (ed.) (1931/1990) *Life As We Have Known It. By Co-operative Working Women*, London: Virago.

LLOYD, B.B. and DUVEEN, G. (1992) *Gender Identities and Education: The Impact of Schooling*, Hemel Hempstead: Harvester Wheatsheaf.

LOBBAN, G. (1978) 'The Influence of the School in Sex Role Stereotyping' in Chetwynd, J. and Hartnett, D. (eds) *The Sex Role System: Psychological and Sociological Perspectives*, London: RKP.

LOMBROSO, C. and FERRERO, W. (1895) *The Female Offender*, London: Fisher Unwin.

LONDON FEMINIST HISTORY GROUP (1983) *The Sexual Dynamics of History. Men's Power, Women's Resistance*, London: Pluto Press.

LONEY, M. *et al.* (1991) *The State of the Market*, London: Sage.

LONSDALE, S. (1990) *Women and Disability*, London: Macmillan.

LORBER, J. and FARRELL, S.A. (eds) (1991) *The Social Construction of Gender*, London: Sage.

LOVELL, T. (ed.) (1990) *British Feminist Thought*, Oxford: Basil Blackwell.

LYNDON, N. (1992a) 'Feminism's Fundamental Flaws', *The Independent*, 29.3.92.

LYNDON, N. (1992b) *No More Sex War: The Failures of Feminism*, London: Sinclair Stevenson.

MacCANNELL, J. (1991) *The Regime of the Brother: After the Patriarchy*, London: Routledge.

MacDONALD, B. and RICH, C. (1984) *Look Me in the Eye: Old Women and Ageism*, London: The Women's Press.

MacDONELL, D. (1986) *Theories of Discourse: An Introduction*, Oxford: Basil Blackwell.

MacKINNON, C. (1982) 'Feminism, Marxism, Method and State: An Agenda for Theory' in Keohane, N.O. *et al.* (eds) *Feminist Theory*, Brighton: Harvester Press.

MacKINNON, C. (1987) *Feminism Unmodified: Disclosures on Life and Law*, Cambridge,

MA: Harvard University Press.

MACKINNON, C. (1994) *Only Words*, London: Harper Collins.

MACLEOD, S. (1981) *The Art of Starvation*, London: Virago.

MCCARTHY, M. (ed.) (1989) *The New Politics of Welfare: An Agenda for the 1990s?*, London: Macmillan.

MCFARLAND, B. (1991) *Shame and Body Image: Culture and the Compulsive Eater*, Health Communications.

MCKEE, L. and BELL, C. (1985) 'His Unemployment, Her Problem: The Domestic and Marital Consequences of Male Unemployment' in Allen, S., Purcell, K., Waton, A., and Wood, S. (eds) *The Experience of Unemployment*, London: Macmillan.

MCLELLAN, D. (1986) *Ideology*, Milton Keynes: Open University Press.

MCNAY, L. (1992) *Foucault and Feminism*, Cambridge: Polity Press.

MCNEIL, M. (1990) *New Reproductive Technologies*, London: Macmillan.

MCQUAIL, D. (1972) *Sociology of Mass Communication*, Harmondsworth: Penguin.

MCQUAIL, D. (1987) *Mass Communication Theory: An Introduction*, London: Sage.

MCRAE, S. (1993) *Cohabiting Mothers: Changing Marriage and Motherhood*, London: Policy Studies Institute.

MCROBBIE, A. (1978) 'Working Class Girls and the Culture of Femininity' in CCCS (ed.) *Women Take Issue*, London: Hutchinson.

MCROBBIE, A. (1982) 'Jackie: An Ideology of Adolescent Femininity' in Wales, B. *et al.* (eds) *Popular Culture: Past and Present*, Milton Keynes: Croom Helm/Open University Press.

MCROBBIE, A. (1991) *Feminism and Youth Culture*, Houndmills: Macmillan.

MCROBBIE, A. and NAVA, M. (1984) *Gender and Generation*, London: Macmillan.

MAHONY, P. (1985) *Schools for the Boys. Co-Education Re-assessed*, London: Hutchinson.

MAHONY, P. (1989) 'Sexual Violence in Mixed Schools' in Jones, C. and Mahony, P. (eds) *Learning Our Lines. Sexuality Control in Education*, London: The Women's Press.

MAMA, A. (1989) *The Hidden Struggle: Statutory and Voluntary Sector Responses to Violence Against Black Women in the Home*, London: London Race and Housing Research Unit.

MARKS, E. and DECOURTIVRON, I. (eds) (1981) *New French Feminisms*, New York: Shocken Books.

MARSH, L.R. (1990) *Gender and Education: An Introduction to the Problem*, Scottish Consultative Council on the Curriculum.

MARSHALL, C. (ed.) (1992) *New Politics of Race and Gender: The 1992 Yearbook of the Politics of Education Association*, London: Falmer Press.

MARTIN, E. (1989) *The Woman in the Body. A Cultural Analysis of Reproduction*, 2nd edn, Milton Keynes: Open University Press.

MASSEY, I. (1991) *More Than Skin Deep. Developing Anti-racist Multicultural Education in Schools*, London: Hodder and Stoughton.

MAYNARD, M. AND PURVIS, J. (ed.) (1994) *Researching Women's Lives from a Feminist Perspective*, London: Taylor and Francis.

MEASOR, L. and SIKES, P.J. (1992) *Gender and Schools*, London: Cassell.

MEEHAN, E.M. (1985) *Women's Rights At Work. Campaigns and Policy in Britain and the United States*, London: Macmillan.

MENDUS, S. and RENDALL, J. (eds) (1989) *Sexuality and Subordination*, London: Routledge.

MILES, M. (1986) *Patriarchy and Accumulation on a World Scale: Women and the International Division of Labour*, London: Zed Books.

MILL, J.S. (1869/1983) *The Subjection of Women. Enfranchisement of Women*, London: Virago.

MILLETT, K. (1970/1989) *Sexual Politics*, London: Virago.

MILLETT, K. (1991) *The Loony Bin Trip*, London: Virago.

MITCHELL, J. (1971) *Woman's Estate*, Harmondsworth: Penguin.

MITCHELL, J. (1974) *Psychoanalysis and Feminism*, Penguin: Harmondsworth

MITCHELL, J. and OAKLEY, A. (1976) *The Rights and Wrongs of Women*, Penguin: Harmondsworth.

MITSCH-BUSH, D. (1987) 'The Impact of Family and School on Girls' Aspirations and Expectations: The Public/Private Split and the Reproduction of Gender and Inequality' in Figueira-McDonough, J. and Sarri, R. (eds) *The Trapped Woman. Catch 22 in Deviance and Control*, London: Sage.

MITTER, S. (1986) *Common Fate. Common Bond*, London: Pluto Press.

MODLESKI, T. (1992) *Feminism Without Women*, London: Routledge.

MOIR, A. and JESSEL, D. (1991) *Brain Sex. The Real Difference Between Men and Women*, 2nd edn, London: Mandarin.

MOLYNEUX, M. (1979) 'Beyond the Domestic Labour Debate', *New Left Review*, No. 116, July–August.

MOORE, S. (1992) 'The Gender Agenda', *The Weekend Guardian*, 30.5.92.

MOORE, W. (1992) 'Sick and Tired', *The Guardian*, 31.3.92.

MORGAN, R. (ed.) (1970) *Sisterhood is Powerful: An Anthology of Writings from the Women's Liberation Movement*, New York: Vintage.

MORGAN, R. (1990) *The Demon Lover: On the Sexuality of Terrorism*, London: Mandarin.

MORPHY, L. (1984) *Sexuality: Pictures of Women. A Guide*, Channel Four Television.

MORRELL, C. (1981) '*Black Friday'. Violence Against Women in the Suffragette Movement*, London: Women's Research Resources Centre.

MORRIS, A. and NOTT, S. (1991) *Working Women and the Law. Equality and Discrimination in Theory and Practice*, London: Routledge.

MORRIS, A. and WILKINSON, C. (1983) 'Secure Care: Just an Easy Answer', *Community Care*, No. 22.

MORRIS, J. (1989) *Able Lives. Women's Experience of Paralysis*, London: The Women's Press.

MORRIS, J. (1991) *Pride Against Prejudice*, London: The Women's Press.

MORRIS, L. (1990) *The Workings of the Household*, Cambridge: Polity.

MORT, F. (1987) *Dangerous Sexualities: Medico-Moral Politics in England Since 1830*, London: RKP.

MOUNT, F. (1982) *The Subversive Family*, London: Jonathan Cape.

NATIONAL CURRICULUM COUNCIL (1989) *A Framework for the Primary Curriculum*, York: NCC.

NATIONAL CURRICULUM COUNCIL (1990) *The Whole Curriculum*, York: NCC.

NATIONAL UNION OF EQUAL CITIZENSHIP (1929) *Manifesto to the Women Voters Of Great Britain*, Labour History Museum Exhibition, Liverpool, July 1990.

NAVA, M. (1992) *Changing Cultures: Feminism, Youth and Consumerism*, London: Sage.

NEAD, L. (1986) 'Feminism's Influence on Art History' in Rees, A.L. and Borzello, F. (eds) *The New Art History*, London: Campden Press.

NEAD, L. (1988) *Myths of Sexuality: Representations of Women in Victorian Britain*, Oxford: Basil Blackwell.

NEWSOM REPORT (1963) *Half Our Future: A Report of the Central Council for Education (England)*, Ministry of Education, London: HMSO.

NEUSTATTER, A. (1990a) 'Velvet Chains of the Old New Age', *The Guardian*, 7.2.90.

NEUSTATTER, A. (1990b) *Hyenas in Petticoats. A Look at Twenty Years of Feminism*, Harmondsworth: Penguin.

Notman, M.T. and Nadelson, C. (eds) (1991) *Women and Men. New Perspectives on Gender Differences*, London: American Psychiatric Press.

Oakley, A. (1974) *Housewife*, Harmondsworth: Penguin.

Oakley, A. (1979) *From Here to Maternity: Becoming a Mother*, Harmondsworth: Penguin.

Oakley, A. (1981) 'Interviewing Women: A Contradiction in Terms' in Roberts, H. (ed.) *Doing Feminist Research*, London: RKP.

Oakley, A. (1984) *The Captured Womb: A History of the Medical Care of Pregnant Women*, Oxford: Basil Blackwell.

Oakley, A. (1992) *Social Support and Motherhood*, Oxford: Blackwell.

O'Brien, E.M. (1989) *Developing an Equal Opportunities Policy on Gender*, Houndmills: Macmillan.

O'Brien, M. (1981) *The Politics of Reproduction*, London: RKP.

O'Brien, M. (1986) 'Feminism and the Politics of Education', *Interchange*, **17**, 2.

O'Connor, P. (1991) *Friendship Between Women*, Hemel Hempstead: Harvester Wheatsheaf.

O'Donnell, C. (1984) *The Basis of the Bargain. Gender, Schooling and Jobs*, London: Allen and Unwin.

O'Sullivan, S. (1982) 'PMT', *Spare Rib*, No. 116, March.

O'Sullivan, S. (1987) *Women's Health. A Spare Rib Reader*, London: Pandora.

Oldfield, S. (1994) *This Working-Day World: Women's Lives and Culture in Britain 1914–1945*, London: Taylor and Francis.

Olsen, T. (1980) *Silences*, London: Virago.

Opportunity 2000 (1991) *Opportunity 2000: Towards a Balanced Workforce*, London: Business in the Community.

Orbach, S. (1979) *Fat is a Feminist Issue*, Middlesex: Hamlyn.

Orbach, S. (1993) *Hunger Strike*, 2nd edn, Harmondsworth: Penguin.

Ord, F. and Quigley, J. (1985) 'Anti-sexism as Good Educational Practice: What Can Feminists Realistically Achieve?' in Weiner, G. (ed.) *Just a Bunch of Girls*, Milton Keynes. Open University Press.

Osler, A. (1989) *Speaking Out: Black Girls in Britain*, London: Virago.

Overholser, G. (1986) 'What "Post-Feminism" Really Means', *The New York Times*, 19.9.86.

Paglia, C. (1990) *Sexual Personae*, New Haven, CT: Yale University Press.

Pahl, J. (ed.) (1985) *Private Violence and Public Policy*, London: RKP.

Parton, N. (1991) *Governing the Family. Child Care, Child Protection and the State*, London: Macmillan.

Pascall, G. (1986) *Social Policy: A Feminist Analysis*, London: Tavistock.

Pascall, G. and Cox, R. (1993) 'Education and Domesticity', *Gender and Education*, **5**, 1.

Payne, S. (1991) *Women, Health and Poverty*, Hemel Hempstead: Harvester Wheatsheaf.

Pegg, C. (1990) 'A "Pretended Family"' in Scanton, J. *Surviving the Blues*, London: Virago.

Pfeffer, N. (1993) *The Stork and the Syringe: A Political History of Reproductive Medicine*, London: Polity Press.

Phillips, A. and Taylor, B. (1980) 'Sex and Skill: Notes Towards Feminist Economics', *Feminist Review*, No. 6.

Phizacklea, A. (1990) *Unpackaging the Fashion Industry. Gender, Racism and Class in Production*, London: Routledge.

Pizzey, E. (1974) *Scream Quietly or the Neighbours Will Hear*, Penguin: Harmondsworth.

PIZZEY, E. and SHAPIRO, G. (1992) *Prone to Violence*, Feltham: Hamlyn.

PLOWDEN REPORT (1967) *Children and Their Primary Schools*, London: HMSO.

POLITY READER IN GENDER STUDIES, THE (1994) *The Polity Reader in Gender Studies*, Cambridge: Polity.

POLITY READER IN SOCIAL THEORY, THE (1994) *The Polity Reader in Social Theory*, Cambridge: Polity.

POLLACK-PETCHESKEY, R. (1980) 'Reproductive Freedom: Beyond a Woman's Right to Choose', *Signs*, **5**, 4.

POLLACK-PETCHESKEY, R. (1986) *Abortion, a Woman's Choice*, London: Verso.

POLLOCK, G. (1977) 'What's wrong with images of women?', *Screen Education*, No.24, Autumn.

POLLOCK, S. (1984) 'Refusing to Take Women Seriously: "Side Effects" and the Politics of Contraception' in Arditti, R., Duelli-Klein, R. and Minden, S. (eds) *Test-Tube Women. What Future for Motherhood?*, London: Pandora.

POOVEY, M. (1989) *Uneven Developments. The Ideological Work of Gender in Mid-Victorian England*, London: Virago.

PUGH, M. (1992) *Women and the Women's Movement in Britain 1914–1959*, Houndmills: Macmillan.

QUEST, C. (ed.) (1992) *Equal Opportunities: A Feminist Fallacy*, London: IEA Health and Welfare Unit.

QUEST, C. (ed.) (1994) *Liberating Women from Modern Feminism*, London: IEA Health and Welfare Unit.

RADFORD, J. and RUSSELL, D.E.H. (eds) (1992) *Femicide. The Politics of Women Killing*, Buckingham: Open University Press.

RAEBURN, A. (1976) *The Suffragette View*, Newton Abbot: David and Charles.

RAKOW, L. AND KRAMARAE, C. (eds) (1990) *The Revolution in Words: Righting Women 1868–1871*, London: Routledge.

RAMAZANOGLU, C. (1989) *Feminism and the Contradictions of Oppression*, London: Routledge.

RAMAZANOGLU, C. (ed.) (1993) *Up Against Foucault. Explorations of some Tensions between Foucault and Feminism*, London: Routledge.

RAYMOND, J. (1984) 'Feminist Ethics, Ecology and Vision' in Arditti, R. Duelli-Klein, R. and Minden, S. (eds) *Test-Tube Women. What Future for Motherhood?*, London: Pandora.

REDCLIFT, N. and SINCLAIR, M.T. (eds) (1991) *Working Women. International Perspectives on Labour and Gender Ideology*, London: Routledge.

REID, M. (1843/1988) *A Plea for Women*, Edinburgh: Polygon.

RENUMERATION ECONOMICS AND THE INSTITUTE OF MANAGEMENT (1994) *The National Management Salary Survey 1994*, London: Renumeration Economics and the Institute of Management.

RICH, A. (1977) *Of Woman Born: Motherhood as Experience and Institution*, London: Virago.

RICH, A. (1980) 'Compulsory Heterosexuality and Lesbian Existence', *Signs*, **5**, 4.

RICHARDSON, D. (1993) *Women, Motherhood and Childrearing*, Houndmills: Macmillan.

RIDDELL, S.I. (1992) *Gender and the Politics of the Curriculum*, London: Routledge.

RILEY, D. (1988) *'Am I That Name?' Feminism and the Category of 'Women' in History*, Houndmills: Macmillan.

RIORDAN, C. (1991) *Girls and Boys in School: Together or Separate?*, London: Teachers' College Press.

ROBERTS, H. (1990) *Women's Health Counts*, London: Routledge.

ROBERTS, M. (ed.) (1981) *Women, Health and Reproduction*, London: RKP.

ROBERTS, Y. (1992) *Mad About Women*, London: Virago.

ROBINSON, K.H. (1992) 'Classroom Discipline: Power, Resistance and Gender. A Look at Teacher Perspectives', *Gender and Education*, **4**, 3.

ROBINSON, O. (1988) 'The Changing Labour Market: Growth of Part-time Employment and Labour Market Segmentation in Britain' in Walby, S. (ed.) *Gender Segregation at Work*, Milton Keynes: Open University Press.

RODIN, J. (1991) *Women and New Reproductive Technologies: Medical, Psychological, Legal and Ethical Dilemmas*, Erlbaum.

ROSE, S.O. (1992) *Limited Livelihoods. Gender and Class in Nineteenth-Century England*, Berkeley, CA: University of California Press.

ROSE, S., KAMIN, L.T. and LEWONTIN, R.C. (1984) *Not in Our Genes. Biology, Ideology and Human Nature*, Harmondsworth: Penguin.

ROSEN, A. (1974) *Rise Up, Women! The Militant Campaign of the Women's Social and Political Union 1903-14*, London: RKP.

ROSS, E. (1994) *Love and Toil: Motherhood in Outcast London, 1870–1918*, New York: Oxford University Press.

ROTHSTEIN, S.W. (1991) *Identity and Ideology: Sociocultural Theories of Schooling*, London: Greenwood Press.

ROWBOTHAM, S. (1973) *Woman's Consciousness, Man's World*, Penguin: Harmondsworth.

ROWBOTHAM, S. (1981) 'The trouble with "patriarchy"' in Feminist Anthology Collective (ed.) *No Turning Back*, London: The Women's Press.

ROWBOTHAM, S. (1992a) *Women in Movement*, London: Routledge.

ROWBOTHAM, S. (1992b) 'How Quiet Can You Get?', *Everywoman*, July/August.

ROWBOTHAM, S. (1993) *Homeworkers Worldwide*, London: Merlin Press.

ROWBOTHAM, S., SEGAL, L. and WAINWRIGHT, H. (1979) *Beyond the Fragments. Feminism and the Making of Socialism*, London: Martin Press.

RUDDUCK, J. (1993) *Developing a Gender Policy in Secondary Schools*, Buckingham: Open University Press.

RUSSELL, W. (1986) *Educating Rita, Stags and Hens and Blood Brothers: Two Plays and a Musical*, Methuen.

RUSSELL, W. (1988) *Shirley Valentine and One For The Road*, Methuen.

RYAN, B. (1992) *Feminisms and the Women's Movement. Dynamics of Change in Social Movement Ideology*, London: Routledge.

SALTZMAN CHAFETZ, J. (1990) *Gender Equity. An Integrated Theory of Stability and Change*, London: Sage.

SARGENT, L. (1981) *The Unhappy Marriage of Marxism and Feminism*, London: Pluto Press.

SAVAGE, W. (1988) *A Savage Enquiry: Who Controls Childbirth?*, London: Virago.

SCAA (1994) *Key Stages 1 and 2 Compendium. Draft Proposals*, London: HMSO.

SCANLON, J. (ed.) (1990) *Surviving the Blues: Growing Up in the Thatcher Decade*, London: Virago.

SCOTT, M. (1980) 'Teach Her a Lesson: Sexist Curriculum in Patriarchal Education' in Spender, D. and Sarah, E. (eds) *Learning to Lose. Sexism and Education*, London: The Women's Press.

SCOTT, S. (1985) 'Feminist Research and Qualitative Methods: A Discussion of Some of the Issues' in Burgess, R.G. (ed.) *Issues In Educational Research*, London: Falmer Press.

SCRATON, P. (1981) 'Policing Society, Policing Crime' in Block 2, prt. 5 *Issues in Crime and Society*, Milton Keynes: Open University Press.

SCRATON, P. (1985) 'The State -v- The People: An Introduction' in Scraton, P. and Thomas, P. *The State -v- The People*, Oxford: Blackwell.

SCRATON, P. (ed.) (1987) *Law, Order and the Authoritarian State*, Milton Keynes: Open University Press.

SCRATON, P. (1989) 'Scientific Knowledge or Masculine Discourses?: Challenging Patriarchy in Criminology' CSCSJ, Edge Hill College.

SCRATON, P. (1991) 'Scientific Knowledge or Masculine Discourses?' in Gelsthorpe, L. and Morris, A. (eds) *Feminist Perspectives in Criminology*, Milton Keynes: Open University Press.

SCRATON, S. (1987) '"Boys Muscle in Where Angels Fear to Tread" – Girl's Sub-cultures and Physical Activities" in Horne, J., Jary, D. and Tomlinson, A. (eds) *Sport, Leisure and Social Relations*, Milton Keynes: Open University Press.

SCRATON, S. (1989) 'Shaping Up to Womanhood', unpublished PhD.

SCRATON, S. (1992) *Shaping Up to Womanhood: Gender and Girls' Physical Education*, Milton Keynes: Open University Press.

SCREEN (1992) *The Sexual Subject: A Screen Reader in Sexuality*, London: Routledge.

SCRUTON, R. (1985) 'Ignore the Body: Lose Your Soul' *The Times*, 5.3.85

SCRUTON, R. (1986) *Sexual Desire*, London: Weidenfeld and Nicolson.

SCULLY, D. (1990) *Understanding Sexual Violence*, London: Unwin Hyman.

SCUTT, J. (1990) *Baby Machine. The Commercialisation of Motherhood*, London: Greenprint.

SEAGER, J. (1993) *Earth Follies: Feminism, Politics and the Environment*, London: Earthscan.

SEARS, J.T. (ed.) (1992) *Sexuality and the Curriculum: The Politics and Practices of Sexuality Education*, Teachers' College Press.

SECOMBE, W. (1974) 'The Housewife and Her Labour Under Capitalism', *New Left Review*, No. 83 Jan–Feb.

SEGAL, L. (1992) 'The Empire Strikes Back', *Everywoman*, May.

SEGAL, L. and MCINTOSH, M. (1992) *Sex Exposed: Sexuality and the Pornography Debate*, London: Virago.

SEIDLER, V.J. (1991) *Recreating Sexual Politics. Men, Feminism and Politics*, London: Routledge.

SHANAHAN, K. (1992) *Crimes Worse than Death. An Exposé of How Violence is Terrorising Women*, Dublin: Attic Press.

SHARPE, S. (1984) *Double Identity: The Lives of Working Mothers*, Harmondsworth: Penguin.

SHILLING, C. (1989) *Schooling for Work in Capitalist Britain*, London: Falmer Press.

SHOWALTER, E. (1987) *The Female Malady. Women, Madness and English Culture 1830–1980*, London: Virago.

SHOWSTACK SASSOON, A. (ed.) (1982) *Approaches to Gramsci*, London: Writers and Readers Cooperative.

SINGH, B.R. (ed.) (1994) *Improving Gender and Ethnic Relations for Schools and Further Education*, London: Cassell.

SIRAJ-BLATCHFORD, I. (ed.) (1993) *'Race', Gender and the Education of Teachers*, Milton Keynes: Open University Press.

SIVANANDAN, A. (1990) 'Left, Right and Burnage' in *Communities of Resistance. Writings on Black Struggles for Socialism*, London: Verso.

SKELTON, C. (1994) 'Sex, Male Teachers and Young Children', *Gender and Education*, **6**, 1.

SMART, C. (1984) *The Ties that Bind*, London: RKP.

SMART, C. (1987) '"There Is of Course the Distinction Dictated by Nature": Law and the Problem of Paternity' in Stanworth, M. (ed.) *Reproductive Technologies: Gender, Motherhood and Medicine*, London: Basil Blackwell.

SMART, C. (ed.) (1992) *Regulating Womanhood: Historical Essays on Marriage, Motherhood and Sexuality*, London: Routledge.

SMART, C. and SEVENHUIJSEN, S. (eds) (1989) *Child Custody and the Politics of Gender*, London: Routledge.

SMART, C. and SMART, B. (1978) *Women, Sexuality and Social Control*, London: RKP.

SMEETH, M. (1990) 'Can You Hear Me at the Front?' in Scanlon, J. (ed.) *Surviving the Blues*, London: Virago.

SMITH, D.E. (1973) 'Women's Perspective as a Radical Critique of Sociology', *Sociological Inquiry*, **44**, 1.

SMITH, D.E. (1975) 'An Analysis of Ideological Structures and How Women are Excluded: Considerations for Academic Women', *Canadian Review of Sociology and Anthropology*, **12**, 4.

SMITH, H. (1989) 'Creating a Politics of Appearance', *Trouble and Strife*, No. 16 Summer.

SMITH, R. (1983) 'A Feminist in View' in Paterson, R. (1984) *Boys From The Blackstuff*, BFI Dossier 20, BFI.

SMITHERS, A. and ZIENTEK, P. (1991) *Gender, Primary Schools and the National Curriculum*, NASUWT.

SNELL, M. (1979) 'The Equal Pay and Sex Discrimination Acts: Their Impact on the Workplace', *Feminist Review*, No. 1.

SONTAG, S. (1978) 'The Double Standard of Ageing' in Carver, V. and Liddiard, P. (eds) *An Ageing Population*, Milton Keynes: Open University Press.

SPENCER, A. and PODMORE, D. (eds) (1987) *In a Man's World. Essays on Women in Male-dominated Professions*, London: Tavistock.

SPENDER, D. (1980) *Man Made Language*, London: RKP.

SPENDER, D. (1982) *Invisible Women. The Schooling Scandal*, Writers and Readers Publishing.

SPENDER, D. (1983) *There's Always Been a Women's Movement This Century*, London: Pandora Press.

SPENDER, D. (1987) 'Education, the Patriarchal Paradigm and the Response to Feminism' in Arnot, M. and Weiner, G. (eds) *Gender Under Scrutiny. New Inquiries in Education*, London: Hutchinson.

SPENDER, D. and SARAH, E. (eds) (1980) *Learning to Lose*, London: The Women's Press.

STANKO, E.A. (1985) *Intimate Intrusions. Women's Experiences of Violence*, London: RKP.

STANKO, E.A. (1990) *Everyday Violence: How Women and Men Experience Sexual and Physical Danger*, London: Pandora.

STANLEY, L. (ed.) (1990) *Feminist Praxis: Research Theory and Epistemology in Feminist Sociology*, London: Routledge.

STANLEY, L. and WISE, S. (1983) *Breaking Out: Feminist Consciousness and Feminist Research*, London: RKP.

STANLEY, L. and WISE, S. (1993) *Breaking Out Again*, London: Routledge.

STANWORTH, M. (1981) *Gender and Schooling. A Study of Sexual Divisions in the Classroom*, WRRC.

STANWORTH, M. (ed.) (1987) *Reproductive Technologies*, London: Polity Press.

STOLTENBERG, J. (1991) *Refusing to Be a Man*, London: Fontana.

STORR, A. (1978) *Human Aggression*, Harmondsworth: Penguin.

STRACHEY, R. (1928/1988) *The Cause: A Short History of the Women's Movement in Great Britain*, London: Virago.

STRATHERN, M. (1992) *Representing the Future: Essays on Anthropology, Kinship and the New Reproductive Technology*, Manchester: Manchester University Press.

SULEIMAN, L. and SULEIMAN, S. (1985) '"Mixed Blood – That Explains a Lot of Things". An Education in Racism and Sexism' in Weiner, G. (ed.) *Just a Bunch of Girls*, Milton Keynes: Open University Press.

SUMMERFIELD, P. (1984) *Women Workers in the Second World War*, Beckenham: Croom Helm.

SWANN, LORD (Chair) (1985) *Education for All. The Report of the Committee of Inquiry into the Education of Children from Ethnic Minority Groups*, London: HMSO.

SWERDLOW, A. (1993) *Women Strike for Peace: Traditional Motherhood and Radical Politics in the 1960s*, Chicago, IL: University of Chicago Press.

SZIROM, T. (1988) *Teaching Gender? Sex Education and Sexual Stereotypes*, London: Allen Unwin.

TAYLOR, B. (1983) *Eve and the New Jerusalem. Socialism and Feminism in the Nineteenth Century*, London: Virago.

TAYLOR, D. (1985) *Women: A World Report*, London: Methuen.

TAYLOR, R. (1993) *In Letters of Gold: Story of Sylvia Pankhurst and the East London Federation of the Suffragettes in Bow*, London: Stepney Books.

TAYLOR MILL, H. (1851) 'Enfranchisement of Women' in Rossi, A.S. (ed.) (1970) *Essays on Sex Equality*, Chicago, IL: University of Chicago Press.

THORNE, B. (1993) *Gender Play, Girls and Boys in School*, Buckingham: Open University Press.

THORNE, B. and YALLOM, M. (eds) (1982) *Rethinking the Family: Some Feminist Questions*, Harlow: Longman.

TONG, R. (1989) *Feminist Thought: A Comprehensive Introduction*, London: Unwin Hyman.

TUC (1984) *Images of Inequality: The Portrayal of Women in the Media and Advertising*, TUC Twentieth Century Press Ltd.

USSHER, J.M. (1989) *The Psychology of the Female Body*, London: Routledge.

USSHER, J.M. (1991) *Women's Madness. Misogyny or Mental Illness?*, Hemel Hempstead: Harvester Wheatsheaf.

USZKURAT, C.A. (1990) 'A Classic Mistake', *Trouble and Strife*, No. 18, Spring.

VICINUS, M. (1985) *Independent Women. Work and Community for Single Women 1850–1920*, London: Virago.

WALBY, S. (1988) *Gender Segregation at Work*, Milton Keynes: Open University Press.

WALBY, S. (1992) 'Post Post-Modernism? Theorizing Social Complexity' in Barrett, M. and Phillips, A. (eds) *Destabilizing Theory. Contemporary Feminist Debates*.

WALKER, C.A. (1990) *Family Violence and the Women's Movement: Conceptual Politics of Struggle*, Toronto: University of Toronto Press.

WALKER, D. (1988) *Gender Equality: An Effective Resource for Today's Classroom*, Learning Development Aids.

WALKERDINE, V. and LUCEY, H. (1989) *Democracy in the Kitchen. Regulating Mothers and Socialising Daughters*, London: Virago.

WALTON, I. (1994) *Sexuality and Motherhood*, Books for Midwives.

WARE, V. (1992) *Beyond the Pale*, London: Verso.

WARNOCK, M. (1984) 'Report of the Committee of Inquiry into Human Fertilization and Embryology', CMND 9314, London: HMSO.

WEBB, D. (1984) 'More on Gender and Justice: Girl Offenders on Supervision', *Sociology*, Vol. 18.

WEEKS, J. (1991) *Against Nature. Essays on History, Sexuality and Identity*, London: Rivers Oram Press.

WEINER, G. (1985) 'Equal Opportunities, Feminism and Girls' Education: Introduction' in Weiner, G. (ed.) *Just a Bunch of Girls*, Milton Keynes: Open University Press.

WEINER, G. and ARNOT, M. (1987) *Gender under Scrutiny. New Inquiries in Education*, London: Hutchinson.

WELLDON, E.V. (1992) *Mother, Madonna, Whore: Idealization and Denigration of Motherhood*, Guildford Press.

WENDELL, S. (1987) 'A (Qualified) Defense of Liberal Feminism', *Hypatia*, **2**, 2, Summer.

WETHERELL, M. and POTTER, J. (1992) *Mapping the Language of Racism: Discourse and the Legitimation of Exploitation*, Hemel Hempstead: Harvester Wheatsheaf.

WHEELWRIGHT, J. (1990) *Amazons and Military Maids: Women Who Dressed as Men in Pursuit of Life, Liberty and Happiness*, London: Pandora.

WHYLD, J. (ed.) (1983) *Sexism and the Secondary Curriculum*, London: Harper Row.

WHYLD, J. (1986) *Anti-Sexist Teaching with Boys*, Whyld Publishing Co-operative.

WHYLD, J. (1992) *Countering Objections to Anti-sexist Work*, Whyld Publishing Co-operative.

WHYTE, J., DEEM, R., KANT, L. and CRUICKSHANK, M. (1985) *Girl Friendly Schooling*, London: Methuen.

WIBAUT, M.B. (1973) *Working Women and the Suffrage*, reprinted as ILP Pamphlet *Women in Rebellion 1900*.

WILKINSON, L.G. (1973) *Women's Freedom 1910*, reprinted as ILP Pamphlet *Women in Rebellion 1900*.

WILKINSON, S. and KITZINGER, C. (eds) (1993) *Heterosexuality. A Feminism and Psychology Reader*, London: Sage.

WILLIAMS, F. (1989) *Social Policy. A Critical Introduction*, Cambridge: Polity Press.

WILLIAMS, J. (1987) 'The Construction of Women and Black Students as Educational Problems: Re-evaluating Policy on Gender and Race' in Arnot, M. and Weiner, G. (eds) *Gender and the Politics of Schooling*, London: Hutchinson.

WILLIAMSON, J. (1978) *Decoding Advertisements: Ideology and Meaning in Advertising*, Marion Boyars Publishers Ltd.

WILSON, E. (1977) *Women and the Welfare State*, London: Tavistock Publications.

WILSON, E. (1983) *What Is to Be Done About Violence Against Women?*, Harmondsworth: Penguin.

WILSON, E. (1985) *Adorned in Dreams: Fashion and Modernity*, London: Virago.

WILSON, M. (ed.) (1991) *Girls and Women in Education: A European Perspective*, Oxford: Pergamon.

WISE, S. and STANLEY, L. (1987) *Georgie Porgie: Sexual Harassment in Everyday Life*, London: Pandora Press.

WITZ, A. (1992) *Professions and Patriarchy*, London: Routledge.

WOLF, N. (1990) *The Beauty Myth*, London: Chatto & Windus.

WOLLSTONECRAFT, M. (1792/1985) *Vindication of the Rights of Women*, Harmondsworth: Penguin.

WOLPE, A. (1988) *Within School Walls: Role of Discipline, Sexuality and the Curriculum*, London: Routledge.

WOMEN'S AID FEDERATION (1989) *Unhelpful Myths and Stereotypes About Domestic Violence*, London: Women's Aid Federation.

WOMEN'S NATIONAL COMMISSION (1985) *Violence Against Women: Report of An Ad-Hoc Working Group*, London: Cabinet Office.

WOOD, J. (1987) 'Groping Towards Sexism: Boy's Sex Talk' in Weiner, G. and Arnot, M. (eds) *Gender under Scrutiny*, London: Hutchinson.

WOOLF, V. (1938/1992) *Three Guineas*, Oxford: Oxford University Press.

WRIGHT, E.O. (1978) *Class, Crises and the State*, London: New Left Books.

WRIGLEY, J. (ed.) (1992) *Education and Gender Equality*, London: Falmer Press.

YOUNG, I. (1981) 'Beyond the Unhappy Marriage: A Critique of the Dual Systems Theory' in Sargent, L. *The Unhappy Marriage of Marxism and Feminism*, London: Pluto Press.

Acts of Parliament

ABORTION ACT, THE (1967) London: HMSO.
EQUAL PAY ACT, THE (1970) London: HMSO.
SEX DISCRIMINATION ACT, THE (1975) London: HMSO.
DOMESTIC VIOLENCE AND MATRIMONIAL PROCEEDINGS ACT, THE (1976) London: HMSO.
HOUSING (HOMELESS PERSONS) ACT, THE (1977) London: HMSO.
EMPLOYMENT ACT, THE (1980) London: HMSO.
SOCIAL SECURITY ACT, THE (1980) London: HMSO.
EMPLOYMENT ACT, THE (1982) London: HMSO.
EQUAL PAY (AMENDMENT) ACT, THE (1983) London: HMSO.
POLICE AND CRIMINAL EVIDENCE ACT, THE (1984) London: HMSO.
TRADES UNION ACT, THE (1984) London: HMSO.
EDUCATION ACT, THE (1986) London: HMSO.
PUBLIC ORDER ACT, THE (1986) London: HMSO.
SOCIAL SECURITY ACT, THE (1986) London: HMSO.
SEX DISCRIMINATION ACT, THE (1986) London: HMSO.
WAGES ACT, THE (1986) London: HMSO.
EDUCATION REFORM ACT, THE (1988) London: HMSO.
LOCAL GOVERNMENT ACT, THE (1988) London: HMSO.
SOCIAL SECURITY ACT, THE (1988) London: HMSO.
EMPLOYMENT ACT, THE (1989) London: HMSO.
CHILDRENS ACT, THE (1989) London: HMSO.
NATIONAL HEALTH SERVICE AND COMMUNITY CARE ACT, THE (1990) London: HMSO.
CHILD SUPPORT ACT, THE (1991) London: HMSO.

Notes on Authors

Vicki Coppock is a Senior Lecturer in Social Policy and Social Work and a Research Associate of the Centre for Studies in Crime and Social Justice at Edge Hill College, Ormskirk, Lancashire.

Deena Haydon is a Lecturer in Primary Education and a Research Associate of the Centre for Studies in Crime and Social Justice at Edge Hill College, Ormskirk, Lancashire.

Ingrid Richter is a Lecturer in Sociology and Social Policy at Bradford and Ilkley Community College, Ilkley, West Yorkshire, and a Research Associate of the Centre for Studies in Crime and Social Justice at Edge Hill College, Ormskirk, Lancashire.

Index